Business Skills

Yvonne Locker

M
MACMILLAN

Acknowledgements

The author would like to thank Geoff Kenyon, Carol Hunter and Julie Ward from Adwick School; Anglian Windows; Aston Services Limited; Judith Bourne of Isle College, Wisbech; Alan Brentnall; British Gas; British Telecom; Companies House, Cardiff – J.D.M. Stephens; Data Protection Registrar; Department of Employment; East Midland Regional Examinations Board; Girobank; HMSO; Halifax Building Society; Harford Dictation Systems Ltd, Coventry, particularly J. Richard Sadler; Health and Safety Executive; John Jackman; Lloyds Bank Plc; Macmillan Press, particularly Isobel Munday; Marks & Spencer; Pitney Bowes; Royal Mail, particularly Steve Loxley; Tesco, Enid Simpson; Sally Vince.

Editorial Development John Jackman Publishing

First published 1994 by
THE MACMILLAN PRESS LTD
Houndmills, Basingstoke, Hampshire RG21 2XS
and London
Companies and representatives
throughout the world

ISBN 0–333–59721–4

A catalogue record for this book
is available from the British Library

Printed in Hong Kong

10 9 8 7 6 5 4 3 2 1
03 02 01 00 99 98 97 96 95 94

Contents

Introduction – the office

A working office

Some students study the office and the activities carried out in it without any prior business studies knowledge. This can sometimes make it difficult for them to relate what they learn to the business world, in which the office has a major role to play.

The office, the work carried out in it, the equipment and resources available and the way in which they are arranged and used will be determined by the type and size of the business. Therefore, in order fully to understand the office and the importance of the work carried out in it, it is useful to acquire some background knowledge of the business world. After all, all businesses, small and large, have an office of some kind.

The assumptions students make about offices are often wrong. Write down your answers to the following two questions. Then read the responses some other students have given to the questions and make a note of whether you agree or disagree with each response and why.

Question 1: What is an office?

Students' responses:

1 'An office is a room where communications are exchanged between different businesses.'
2 'Somewhere where people work in a large building.'
3 'A room where a group of people work.'
4 'A place where people sit dealing with paperwork or using typewriters and computers.'
5 'It is a place where there are computers which are used by office workers.'

Each of the students' responses could be correct for any *particular* office, but none gives the whole answer. When you were looking through each statement, did you consider the following:

1 Are communications exchanged only between offices in *different* businesses?
2 Are *all* office buildings large?
3 Is an office one room or can it be more, and do groups of people work in all offices?
4 Do *all* office workers deal with paperwork and use typewriters or computers?
5 Are there *only* typewriters and computers in offices, or is there likely to be other types of equipment, too?

Question 2: Every business will have an office, but who owns the business?

Students' responses:

1 'The manager.'
2 'Don't really know – perhaps the partners.'
3 'The person whose name is on the door.'
4 'A company's shareholders.'
5 'The person who runs the business.'

Again, any of these answers could be correct for a *particular* business, but there is no one right answer. For example, when you were reading through the students' responses to the question, did you think of the following:

1 Many owners of businesses employ one or more managers to run the business or part of it.
2 Do *all* businesses have partners? If not, who owns the ones which don't?

3 When you visit your bank manager you will find his or her name on the door, but you know that does not mean that he or she owns the bank.
4 Do *all* businesses have shareholders? If not, who owns the ones which don't?
5 Does the owner or owners of a business run it as well? See (1) above.

It is probably becoming very clear to you that there is much to learn about the office and its environment. There are very many different offices, employing different people undertaking different roles for different businesses or organisations. However, there are many common factors, and this text provides information and activities to help you build up your knowledge and skills to enable you to address questions such as:

- Who owns and controls different types of organisations?
- Why is a well-organised office so important to any business, large or small?
- How are firms structured and organised internally?
- How are workers protected and affected by employment legislation?
- How is information technology used in business and how does it help firms be more competitive?
- What type of work is carried out by office employees?

As you work through this book read the information carefully, then write down your answers to the questions under the heading 'How much can you remember?' If you can, try out the activities, which ask you to apply your knowledge in a variety of situations including researching, role play, essay writing, preparing displays, and so on. Some of the activities require you to work in groups.

Chapter 1 Business ownership

By the end of this chapter you should be able to explain:

- the difference between primary, secondary and tertiary activities
- the benefits of limited liability
- the principal characteristics of the main forms of business organisation in the public and private sectors, in terms of ownership, sources of funding, control and distribution of profit
- the procedure for setting up a limited company
- the terms 'privatisation' and 'nationalisation'.

Types of enterprise

We read about current business developments in the local and national press and we listen to news broadcasts, but we seldom dwell on the question of who owns a particular business. Ownership and control of a firm vary and are determined by the type and size of the business. For example, you would not expect to find that one person owns and controls a company as large as Marks & Spencer, while common sense will tell you that your local newsagency is not owned and controlled by thousands of shareholders.

UK economy – public/private sectors

The UK economy is divided into two sectors – private and public. A country that has private and public sectors is said to have a mixed economy.

The private sector is the part of the economy which is owned and run by private individuals. They raise the money to set up and run various types of business and as owners make decisions about how it is run.

The public sector, on the other hand, is the part of the economy that is controlled by the government on behalf of the nation. The government uses the money received from taxes to help run the country for the benefit of everyone. Therefore, it belongs to the people, hence the name public sector. The government makes decisions about how much to spend and how public enterprises are run.

We will be looking at public and private sector organisations in more detail in this chapter.

Types of business activity

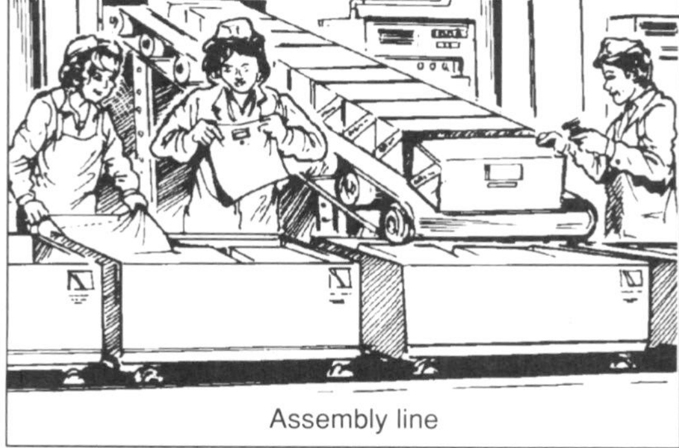

Primary, secondary and tertiary activities

Businesses can be categorised into being involved in either primary, secondary or tertiary activities. These terms are explained below.

Primary Organisations involved in extracting natural resources – for example, mining, fishing and farming – are known as primary industries, as the activities they carry out form the first stage of production.

Secondary Manufacturing firms use the resources extracted at the primary stage to produce different products. Some firms produce parts which need to be put with other parts before they become a finished product. Primary goods which can be consumed often have to be treated or changed in some way before being sold to the consumer; for example, milk may be treated and sold in a container, or used as an ingredient for another product, such as butter. The manufacturing or processing described takes place at the secondary stage of production.

Tertiary Most retailing establishments do not produce their own goods. Retailers who have the capital to buy in large quantities and the space to store goods, buy direct from the manufacturer. Other retailers buy from a wholesaler (middleman). A wholesaler buys in bulk from a manufacturer, then sells to retailers in smaller quantities. Goods are then sold to the consumer. Retailing is a service offered to the public and therefore forms part of the tertiary and final stage of production. There are numerous other services in the tertiary sector and they are not all involved in the production process – for example, banking and insurance, the medical and police services and leisure facilities.

The risks involved in owning a business

Ownership ranges from the small individual trader, such as your local greengrocer, to very large national and international companies, such as Ford and BP. Owning or being a part-owner of a business always carries some risk. However, certain types of business are more risky than others for the individuals involved.

Unlimited liability

Unlimited liability

Unlimited liability means that owners are totally responsible for the payment of all debts. If the business fails, the owner's personal possessions may have to be sold to pay creditors (people to whom money is owed). This is because the law does not separate the business from its owners – the two are recognised legally as one item. Two types of business which have unlimited liability are sole traders and general partnerships (these will be looked at in detail later in this chapter).

Limited liability

Limited companies have limited liability, which means that the company and its owners have separate legal identities. This gives some protection to shareholders because if a company cannot pay its debts, shareholders may lose their share investment but not their personal possessions. As a limited company is a legal entity, different owners can come and go, but the company will continue to exist and function. The company itself can also sue and be sued.

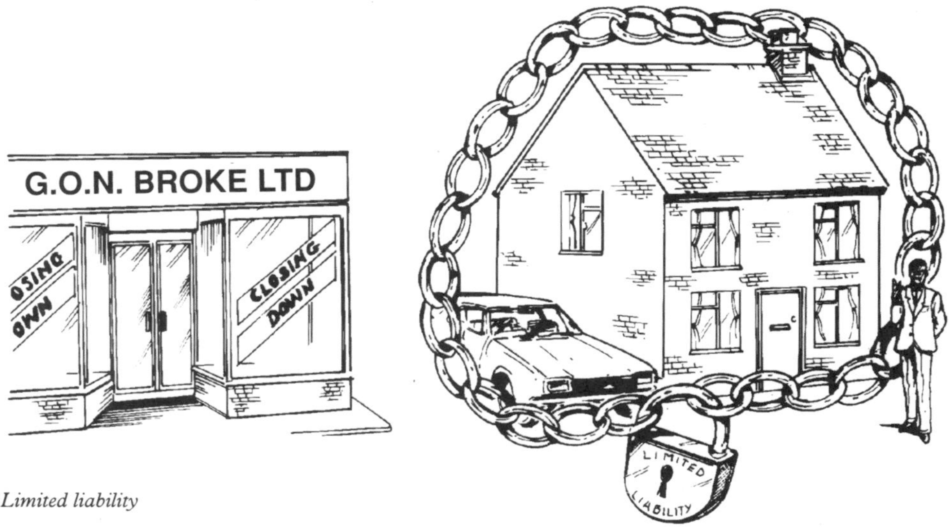

Limited liability

Shares in a company are sold to private individuals and other institutions and the buyers become part owners (shareholders). If a company makes a profit, the shareholders benefit by receiving a dividend (a percentage of the profit) each year. The amount of the dividend received depends on how much profit the company has made, and how many shares are owned. A company will not pay out all its profit to its shareholders, some is retained for future investment. How limited companies are set up and run is explained later in this chapter.

How much can you remember?

1 List the three stages of production and explain the difference between them.
2 What is meant by the private sector and the public sector? Write a simple definition of each.
3 Explain the difference between unlimited and limited liability.
4 The UK has a mixed economy. What does this term mean?

Activity 1.1

Businesses find themselves in the news for various reasons. It may be because a firm has won a large order, is closing down, making workers redundant, moving location or making an important change to its management structure.

task 1

Understanding the theory of business studies is of limited use unless that theory is related to the real world so that current events can be more easily understood. To complete this task you have to bring yourself up to date with what is happening in the business world and to do this you must gather information from television and newspapers. Do this in three stages:

(a) (i) Using radio and TV listings, find out at which times there are news broadcasts and programmes relating to current or past business issues. Produce this information in the form of a table which can be used as a quick reference guide to help you to complete later tasks.

(ii) Read parts (b) and (c) below and then identify on your chart which programmes you intend to watch.

(b) Over a period of seven days try to listen to one radio or TV news broadcast each day and listen to or watch at least one documentary/ interview relating to a business issue past or present. Under the heading 'Business review', prepare an account which gives details of business news involving private and public sector enterprises. You may decide to follow one major news story throughout the week or choose several different ones. There are often documentaries which examine various business situations.

(c) Read newspapers during the same week as you monitor the radio and TV programmes and extract relevant business articles from your daily national and local papers. Some of the stories you select from the national press will be related to the news broadcasts/current documentaries you have already seen and heard, but others, particularly local stories, will not.

task 2

Using your research from task 1, choose a minimum of two storylines, preferably one national and one local, and assuming the role of newsreader, prepare a broadcast for your study group. Your presentation should last no less than five minutes but not exceed 15 minutes. You may use any visual aids available to you.

task 3

(a) Evaluate your own performance. To do this ask yourself the following questions:

- How well did I research and prepare my material?
- How well did I understand the material I chose?
- How well did I project my voice?
- How well did I use the visual aids available to me?
- How interesting did I make my broadcast?
- How could I have made my presentation better and in what way?

(b) Allow the group to evaluate your performance. Ask them the same questions and compare their answers with your own.

The private sector

The main forms of ownership in the private sector are shown in the diagram below. Some types of organisation within the private sector, such as building societies and voluntary organisations, do not fall into any of the divisions shown. For simplicity, only the types referred to in the diagram will be discussed below.

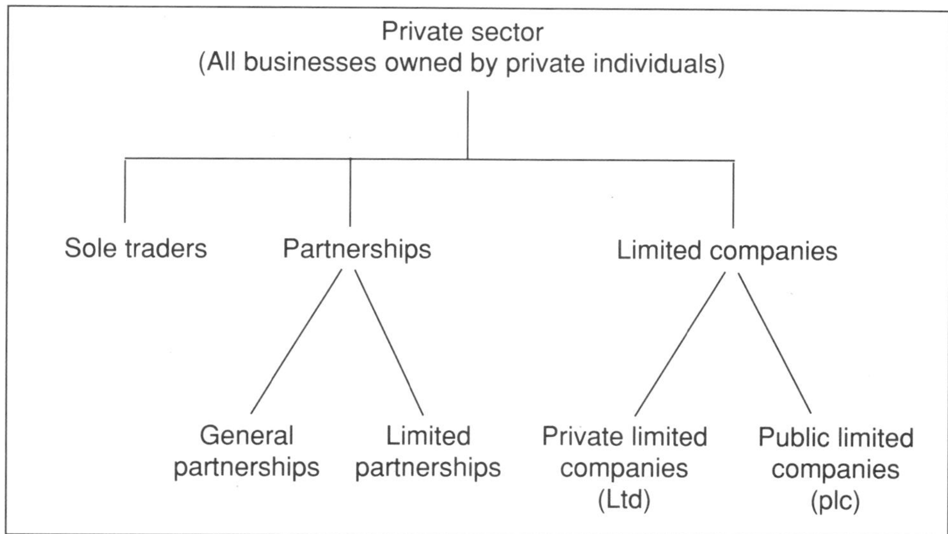

The main forms of ownership in the private sector

Sole trader

This is the term given to a business which is owned by one person, but it does not necessarily mean that there is only one person in the business. A sole trader often employs people to help with the running of the business. Sometimes these are members of the sole trader's family. Examples of this type of business are: butcher, plumber, hairdresser and driving school instructor. Money (capital) is invested into the business by the owner, usually from personal savings, a bank loan or a loan or gift from family and friends. This capital is often too low to enable the business to expand. If capital can be raised, this type of business is easy to set up, but because it has unlimited liability there are risks associated with it too.

Advantages

The owner can:

- Keep any profit which is made.
- Keep all financial affairs private. Except for the owner and the Inland Revenue, no one has to know how much money is being made or spent.
- Choose the working hours.
- Offer a personal and friendly service to the local people.
- Have complete freedom in running the business as decisions can be made without consulting anyone else.

Disadvantages

- The limited amount of capital restricts expansion.
- Competing with large companies can prove difficult as they are able to buy goods in bulk and obtain large discounts, which means they can then sell goods more cheaply to the consumer. The sole trader does not always have the capital to do this nor the space to store goods in bulk, and therefore prices are often higher as a result.
- Many sole traders are forced to work long hours, either to bring in extra business by staying open or working late when the larger concerns are closed, or to do the paperwork once the business has closed for the day.
- Unlimited liability.
- The future of the business may be threatened if the owner is ill and cannot carry on running it.
- Many sole traders have very few holidays as they are not prepared or cannot afford to leave their business in the hands of someone else while they go away. If the sole trader is providing a service, such as a freelance bookkeeper, he or she would not be able to earn any money during holiday periods.

Partnerships

Many problems that sole traders experience can be solved by changing the ownership of the business to a partnership. Legally, this type of business can consist of a group of between 2 and 20 people, but in special circumstances it can exceed this number.

A partnership

The most common arrangement of a partnership is that each partner contributes some capital and shares any profits or losses made. The rules are usually written down in a deed or contract of partnership. This is not enforced by law, but if there is a dispute between the partners and no deed of partnership exists then the Partnership Act of 1890 comes into force and everything is shared out equally. The deed of partnership will specify how such things as work, profits or losses will be shared out and it will also record the initial investment of each partner and the agreed drawings (the amount each person takes from the business for personal use). An example of a deed of partnership is given in the illustration on page 12.

In a general partnership all the partners have unlimited liability and are involved in the running of the business. They are known as general partners.

Advantages

- The work is shared.
- The risks/losses are shared.
- There will be more capital available to spend on things such as larger premises and better equipment.
- Each person will bring his or her own skills into the business and so a greater service can be offered to the public.
- Partners may be able to specialise. Specialisation allows each partner to do the job he or she is best at and so a better quality of work can be offered than from one person doing everything.
- If one partner becomes ill or goes on holiday, the other partners can carry on working, so there is less risk of the business failing.

DEED OF PARTNERSHIP

between

Richard Mosely & Hannah Spencer

NAME OF BUSINESS:	Mosely & Spencer
ADDRESS OF BUSINESS:	33 Main Road, Sometown SM1 2HE
TYPE OF BUSINESS:	Unisex hairdressing
CAPITAL:	Initially each partner will contribute £12,000.
PROFITS:	To be shared equally.
NEW PARTNERS:	No new partner can join the partnership without the full consent of both existing partners.
TERMINATION OF PARTNERSHIP:	This will occur on the death of a partner or when the partners agree to a termination.

RIGHTS, DUTIES & OBLIGATIONS OF EACH PARTNER

(a) All major decisions must have the agreement of both partners.

(b) The partners must not behave in a way which could damage the business.

(c) Partners ...

A deed of partnership

Disadvantages

- Joint decisions have to be made and this slows down the decision-making process.
- Partners may have different views and disagree over some issues.
- If one of the partners dies, retires or wishes to leave, the partnership will cease to exist unless it has been written in the deed of partnership that it should continue. The remaining partners would have to draw up a new deed of partnership.
- All general partners have unlimited liability.

Limited partnerships

If a partnership needs more capital, one option is to have a sleeping or limited partner. This is a person who invests money in a partnership, shares any profit/loss (in a proportion agreed), but does not take part in the running of the business. The limited partner has the benefit of limited liability. When this type of arrangement is set up, the law specifies that there must be at least one general partner in the group who has unlimited liability.

How much can you remember?

1 What is a sole trader?
2 Why is limited capital a disadvantage for the sole trader?
3 What other disadvantages are associated with this type of business?
4 Wherever there are risks there are benefits too. What are the benefits of being a sole trader?
5 Suggest how a sole trader may resolve some of the problems associated with this type of business.
6 How does a limited partnership differ from a general partnership?
7 What is meant by a deed of partnership and what is the major disadvantage of not having one?
8 What are the main advantages and disadvantages of a partnership?

Activity 1.2

Interview a sole trader and write/type/word process an account of the interview. The purpose of the interview is to find out as much as you can about this type of business and relate it to what you have already learned. You may find the following steps useful.

(a) Design a questionnaire. You should set yourself a target of around, say, ten questions, but take care to avoid ones that are too personal as they may offend the interviewee (for example, those relating to finances). When designing your questions, remember the purpose of your interview and do not ask questions you already know the answer to. For example, you already know that all sole traders have unlimited liability so you would not use this as a question. Some examples are given below of the type of question you may wish to ask:

- Does having unlimited liability worry you and did this make you hesitate at all when you were thinking about setting up on your own in business?
- Was it difficult to raise the money to start your business?
- Is setting up as a sole trader as easy as we are led to believe?
- In what way has the recession affected your business?

(b) (i) When you have completed your questionnaire, show it to a friend to see if he or she agrees that the questions are:

- suitable
- not too personal
- worded in such a way that the answers will provide the information required
- relevant and not repetitive
- clear, precise and in a logical order
- presented to allow enough space after them for the responses.

(ii) Make any changes to your questionnaire following your friend's evaluation of it.

(c) When you are satisfied with your questionnaire, make an appointment with an agreeable sole trader and carry out your interview. It may be helpful to send your interviewee a copy of the questionnaire in advance of the interview, to allow the trader to think about the answers beforehand. Try to avoid giving a questionnaire to someone and leaving it to be completed. This method often leads to yes/no answers and limits the amount of information gathered.

(d) Once the interview has taken place, select and extract from your questionnaire the most interesting and relevant material for your account.

alternatively

As a group, invite one or more sole traders into college/school and set up a question time session. Steps (a) to (c) above can be adapted to suit this situation.

Activity 1.3

(a) Using the classified telephone directory (Yellow Pages) to give you ideas, choose a particular type of firm suitable for a partnership – for example, a garage, florist, estate agents – and in groups of no more than six draw up a deed of partnership.

(b) Examine the deeds prepared by the other groups and make a note of any important points they have included but which you have omitted from your document.

(c) Amend your deed where appropriate and prepare a final copy for your file.

Limited companies

The Companies (Single Member Private Limited Companies) Regulation amending the 1985 Companies Act now permits companies with a single shareholder. Previously, both private and public limited companies had to have a minimum of two people to set it up, but there is no maximum restriction. Both types of company raise finance by selling shares and this enables more capital to be raised than by a sole trader or partnership, which makes it easier to expand the business.

As limited companies often have access to and handle such large amounts of money belonging to other people, government legislation ensures that the formation and running of these companies is carefully monitored.

Private limited companies

This type of limited company is usually, but not always, fairly small. Many private limited companies are family businesses. The company name has the letters Ltd (Limited) after it and these letters act as a warning to all its creditors that the owners of the company have limited liability.

Advantages

- It is possible to raise more capital than with a partnership.
- As a limited company is a legal entity separate from its owners, if someone dies or retires, the business continues to operate.
- All shareholders have limited liability.
- There are restrictions which are set out in the articles of association (the document setting out the rules for running the company) regarding the selling of shares. This helps to prevent the founder members losing control of the company and reduces the risk of takeovers by other companies.

Disadvantages

- Shares cannot be advertised or sold on the stock exchange to the public and this limits the amount of capital which can be raised.
- The accounts have to be properly audited each year and sent to the Registrar of Companies. This is a government department which checks up on anyone wishing to set up a limited company and it makes sure that companies, once running, keep their business dealings within the law.
- Finances can no longer be kept private.

Public limited companies

Many very large businesses are public limited companies. The initials plc stand for Public Limited Company and are put at the end of the company name. Public limited companies are so called because the public (the shareholders) invests money in them and not because they are in the public sector.

If a private limited company is very successful and wishes to expand beyond its current capital capability, one solution would be to go public.

Advantages

- Shares can be advertised and sold on the stock exchange to the public. This allows large amounts of capital to be raised and bigger projects to be attempted, sometimes on an international scale.
- The situation with regard to liability is the same as for a private limited company.

Disadvantages

- It is very expensive to set up a plc and there are strict legal procedures.
- You need a minimum of £50,000 to set up.
- The law requires plcs to produce a report each year which must be published, and this involves a great deal of expense.
- Company information is made public and this makes plcs more vulnerable to takeovers.
- Plcs can become very large and impersonal and this can lead to slower decision-making and poor communication.

Multi-national companies

Many larger plcs are multi-nationals. These are companies that have established a base in other countries, in addition to the one in which they originated. One advantage of being a multi-national is that you are closer to your foreign market and this reduces transport costs. It also spreads the risks, because one country's economy might be much stronger than another's.

A multi-national company

Forming a limited company

There are strict legal procedures for setting up and running a limited company. The first step in this process is to engage a solicitor to draw up two documents: a memorandum of association and articles of association.

Memorandum of association

The memorandum of association (see illustration below) describes the company that is to be formed. It is a public document and is held at Companies House where it can be inspected by any member of the public. This is useful for anyone who intends to deal with the company because they can find out relevant information about it before committing themselves. It contains information about the company's external details – for example, the company name, the address of the registered office, the amount of share capital it intends to raise, a statement that all shareholders will have limited liability and the names of one director and the company secretary. It also has to set out the objectives of the company, that is, the business activities in which the company will be involved. This is to make sure that prospective shareholders know exactly what type of business activity they are investing in.

1 The name of the company is Straight & Narrow Ltd.

2 The registered office of the company will be 10 Straightline, Narrowbed, Narrowshire.

3 The objects for which the company is established are to design and manufacture computer software.

4 The liability of members is limited.

5 The share capital of the company is £40,000 divided into 40,000 shares of £1 each.

Memorandum of Association

Information which must be included in the Memorandum of Association is shown above. It would also include details of the number of shares which the subscribers are prepared to buy.

Articles of association

This document deals with the internal administration of the company; it is like a company rule book. It specifies the arrangements for holding and conducting the annual general meeting (AGM; see Chapter 2), the voting rights of the shareholders and the powers and duties of the company's directors.

When complete, both documents are sent to the Registrar of Companies for examination and approval. If everything is in order and to the satisfaction of the Registrar, a certificate of incorporation (see opposite) is sent to the company. Upon receipt of this certificate, a private limited company can start trading. A certificate of incorporation is like a birth certificate – once a company has been incorporated, it becomes a legal entity, and its debts and liabilities are its own and separate from those of its members.

CERTIFICATE OF INCORPORATION

OF A PRIVATE LIMITED COMPANY

Company No. 98765432

The Registrar of Companies for England and Wales hereby certifies that

STRAIGHT & NARROW LIMITED

is this day incorporated under the Companies Act 1985 as a private company and that the company is limited.

Given at Companies House, Cardiff, the 31st April 1994

J.D.M. STEPHENS

For The Registrar Of Companies

COMPANIES HOUSE

Certificate of Incorporation

In the case of a public limited company there are additional legal requirements which must be met before it can begin trading. This is because of the large sums of money and the amount of people involved. The company must issue a prospectus advertising the new shares for sale. It must also sell enough shares to convince the Registrar that it has sufficient capital to carry out its plans as specified in the memorandum of association.

When the above procedures have been completed successfully to the satisfaction of the Registrar of Companies, the Stock Exchange Council must approve the company. Then the Registrar will issue a trading certificate upon receipt of which a plc can begin trading.

Raising finance

Limited companies raise finance not only by selling shares but also by selling debentures. A debenture is a long-term loan to a company which gives its owner a fixed rate of interest each year. Like shares they can be bought and sold on the stock exchange. However, debenture holders are different from shareholders as they are creditors of a company, not part-owners, therefore they do not have a say in the running of the business. Interest has to be paid to debenture holders whether the company makes a profit or not even if assets have to be sold to do so, and this makes debentures a safer investment than shares.

The disadvantage is that, although debenture holders are paid prior to shareholders, if the company has a successful year, the shareholders are likely to receive a high dividend, but debenture holders will receive the agreed rate of interest and no more.

Issuing of shares

When a public limited company wishes to raise finance to start up the business it will advertise its shares for sale. Interested parties will then send for a prospectus before deciding whether or not to buy. However, it is not only private individuals who buy shares, many company pension funds and insurance companies, for example, invest their members' money by purchasing shares in plcs.

Once a plc is up and running, if it wishes to raise more capital the most popular way of doing so is by a rights issue. This involves selling more shares to *existing* shareholders. This means there is no need to advertise nationally for new shareholders and prospectuses do not have to be sent out, both of which are expensive to do. Therefore, it is a cheaper method of raising extra capital.

Types of shares

Not all shares are the same, nor do they carry the same benefits or risks.

Ordinary shares

When dividends are paid out, ordinary shareholders (equity shareholders) are paid last of all. These shares carry the greatest risk as it is possible that no profit will be left after everyone else has been paid. However, the advantage of this type of share is that its owners have voting rights – for each share held the owner is allowed one vote.

If the company makes a large profit and dividends are high ordinary shareholders will also benefit from this. Directors of a company, usually major shareholders, prefer to own this type of share as they consider voting power to be more important than the certainty of receiving a dividend.

Preference shares

This type of share pays out a fixed dividend and, provided the company makes a profit, these preference shareholders are paid first. Obviously they carry less risk than ordinary shares, but as the dividend is fixed, if the company makes a large profit there is no extra benefit for shareholders.

Cumulative preference shares

These are similar to preference shares except that if a company does not make a profit one year, the dividend is paid in future years when it does.

How much can you remember?

1 Who owns limited companies?
2 Why is a Public Limited Company so called when it belongs in the private sector?
3 Do shareholders of private and public limited companies have unlimited or limited liability?
4 Briefly explain the legal procedure which has to be followed when setting up a limited company.
5 Suggest why the procedure for setting up a plc is more complex than that of a private limited company.
6 Who or what is the Registrar of Companies?
7 Some shares carry more risk than others. Explain why.
8 Explain the difference between a share and a debenture.
9 What is a multi-national company?

Activity 1.4

Using the format given on page 22 prepare a chart to compare a private and a public limited company. Try to include as many similarities and differences as you can. One similarity and one difference have been completed for you.

LIMITED COMPANIES

Private limited companies	*Public limited companies*
Similarities:	
1 Both types of company form part of the private sector.	
2	
3	
4	
5	
...	
Differences:	
1 A private limited company has the letters Ltd after its name.	1 A public limited company has the letters plc after its name.
2	2 ....
3	3 ....
4	4 ....
5	5 ....
...	...

Activity 1.5

(a) Using a 'quality' newspaper, follow the share prices of any two companies of your choice over 10–12 weeks and show the changes on a graph. Using the same axes for both companies, compare their performance and explain what has happened to the shares during your period of study.

(b) If you had invested £500 in each company, what would have happened to your money and how much would you have now if you sold your shares?

Activity 1.6

case study

Read the case study and then answer the questions following.

Peter Waterhouse and Bill Thornley have owned and run a plumbers merchants supplies business for the past four years. Business has dropped off so much over the past six months that they have decided to close the business down before they get into financial difficulties. All the stock on the premises is paid for and their actual debts are quite small. They have placed the following advertisement in the local newspaper.

• CLOSING DOWN SALE • ALL STOCK MUST GO •
• BATHROOM SUITE BARGAINS •
• ONE PEACH SUITE £100 • ONE ONLY • OTHERS FROM £120 •
MUST BE SEEN
RADIATORS AND PLUMBING MATERIALS ALL 50% OFF.

task

Now answer these questions:

1 Classify the ownership of Peter and Bill's business.
2 Explain why you think it is that so many businesses have closed down over the past few years and why you think Peter and Bill's business is now in trouble – why no one is buying their goods.
3 Explain what is meant by 'before they get into financial difficulties'.
4 Why do you think Peter and Bill have decided to sell off their stock cheaply and close the business down? Why don't they wait a little longer?
5 How may Peter and Bill benefit from selling off their stock now, and what advantages might this have for their future?

Activity 1.7

Read the case study and then answer the questions following.

case study

Window Fit Ltd is a private limited company which has been trading for the past 15 years. It is a small family business with ten shareholders, four of which actually run the company. During the first five years business was good and profits were high. The company expanded during its seventh year and began to install uPVC windows in addition to its wooden range. Materials are stored and manufacturing takes place in a small workshop on an industrial estate outside the main town. The showroom and office are located here, too. The rent is reasonable and there is plenty of space to make and display windows.

While many other window companies are closing down, Window Fit is keeping very busy. The company has just won two orders to supply and fit two large office blocks from its uPVC range of windows. There are also several other large orders for which it has tendered and which it hopes to win.

It now has a problem. To meet the deadlines specified by its latest customers and fulfil existing orders on time, it needs more staff. The materials are costly and more money is required. The shareholders are considering going public.

task

Now answer these questions:

1 What is meant by 'going public'?
2 What would be the advantages for Window Fit of going public?
3 Why do you think it may not be a wise move to go public?
4 Can you suggest an alternative to going public?
5 If the company does go public, what legal procedure will it have to follow and why?
6 Prepare draft documents for Window Fit for submission to the Registrar of Companies.

The public sector

Private sector enterprise is owned by private individuals; public sector enterprise is owned by the government on behalf of the nation. However, this is not the only difference between businesses in the private and public sectors. The main aim in the private sector is to make a profit, but in contrast many enterprises in the public sector do not make any profit and are not meant to, for example, the army or prisons.

Public corporations

Businesses in the public sector are run as public corporations. The government does not have the time to personally run the businesses which are in the public sector and so a Board of Managers is appointed to do this on its behalf according to policies laid down by the state. A public corporation has a separate legal identity from the government, just like a limited company in the private sector, but it is accountable to Parliament rather than to a group of shareholders.

To nationalise or privatise?

Nationalisation means transferring industries from the private sector into the public sector and therefore bringing them under the control of the government rather than leaving them to be run by private individuals. Nationalisation occurs when an Act of Parliament takes over the assets of an existing firm within an industry and compensates the shareholders by paying an agreed price for their shares.

In contrast, privatisation transfers public sector enterprises into the private sector. As a result of the Conservative government's privatisation programme, there have been a great many changes in the public sector throughout the 1980s and into the 1990s, and many public-owned enterprises, some of them highly profitable, have now been transferred into the private sector – for example, British Telecom, British Gas and the electricity supply industry. One nationalised industry which has attracted much public interest is coal. Many years ago coal mining was a private sector business; it was then brought under government control and became a nationalised public corporation. There are strong arguments for and against privatisation and consequently the Conservative government's pit closure and privatisation programme met with strong resistance from groups inside and outside of the industry.

Coal mining – nationalise or privatise?

Municipal enterprises

The government allocates money to local councils so that services can be provided for local people – for example, fire and ambulance services, refuse collection and parks and leisure facilities. Not all of the money needed to finance these services comes from the government – entrance fees often supplement money from central government. Private individuals and businesses pay local taxes (for example, council tax) and this provides local authorities with additional income for services.

How much can you remember?

1 Explain what is meant by the terms 'privatisation' and 'nationalisation'.
2 Make a list of as many privatised industries as you can think of.
3 What are the main differences between businesses in the private sector and those in the public sector?
4 In addition to those already mentioned in this chapter, identify as many services and facilities as you can think of which are provided by your local council.

Activity 1.8

You have just read in your morning newspaper that 'workers paid from the public purse are receiving only a 2 per cent pay rise. This is because of a squeeze on public spending.'

task 1

Explain what you think is meant by:

(a) 'the public purse'

(b) 'a squeeze on public spending'.

task 2

Identify at least seven groups of people to whom this pay rise will apply.

task 3

Individuals will not be the only casualties of this 'squeeze on public spending'. Explain why and how local communities will be affected.

Activity 1.9

Using the title 'What future for the coal industry?', discuss the following question:

As a result of the reduced demand for coal, do you think the government's decision to close uneconomic pits in preparation for privatisation was correct?

Your discussion must consider both sides of the argument and then reach a sound, definite conclusion.

You may wish to make reference to:

- The nationalisation of coal – why was it nationalised?
- The history of conflict between the Conservative government and the miners since the 1970s.
- Why has British Coal's market declined?
- What were the government's economic reasons for pit closures?
- How did pressure groups manage to get the decision to close the pits postponed? Which were the most influential and why?
- What are the social costs to the mining communities?
- What are the arguments for and against privatisation?

Chapter 2 The structure of business

By the end of this chapter you should be able to explain:

- the difference in internal organisation and structure between a small and a large firm
- the purpose of an organisation chart
- the role and structure of a board of directors
- the purpose of an AGM (annual general meeting)
- the difference between a centralised office services system and a departmental one
- the functions and importance of the main areas of business organisation – personnel, production, marketing and finance.

The need for organisation

At home, telephone calls are received, and letters arrive from relatives, from friends and sometimes from people you don't know. In addition, telephone calls are made and letters are written, some of them in reply to those that have been received.

Business works in much the same way. An electrician might receive a telephone call enquiring about a rewiring job. Before a firm price can be given, the following steps have to be taken:

1 A visit has to be arranged to the place where the wiring is to be installed and a note made of the customer's requirements.
2 Information has to be found – for example, the prices of all the materials required to complete the job.
3 Calculations have to be carried out so the electrician can charge a fair price and make a profit. Most tradespeople charge by the hour or by the day. Bricklayers often charge an amount per 1,000 bricks.
4 A letter has to be sent to the customer giving a total price for the job.

The work the electrician must carry out is clerical work (which is another name for office work). All businesses, however large or small, have clerical work to do and they all have an office of some kind. People working from home often use their sitting room or spare bedroom as an office. An office is any place where clerical work is carried out (see Chapter 3).

In the case of the electrician, all the clerical work and decision making was carried out by one person. This is a good example of the way in which a small business may operate. In a small firm it is not uncommon to find only one person making the decisions and one or two staff dealing with the clerical work – for example, typing, filing, preparing accounts and answering the telephone. However, in larger firms this is not possible.

Decision making in a larger company

In larger organisations there are too many decisions to be made for one person to deal with them all. Similarly the workload is too great for one or two staff to cope with. To be efficient, larger companies need some formal structure. The internal organisation of larger companies varies but there are common features.

Businesses use organisation charts to show the hierarchy of the firm – that is, the rank, order and relationship of job roles (see the sample chart opposite). An organisation chart is like a family tree except that it contains job titles rather than names. The reason for this is that while the title of most posts remains the same, the person doing the job will change as employees leave or are promoted. By omitting the names of the post holders the chart does not become out of date so quickly.

The route by which orders are passed down an organisation is called the chain of command. Orders must be passed down quickly so that firms can react to market change. If the chain of command is too long then decisions made by the board are not implemented quickly as they take time to reach the shop floor. Also, messages which have to travel a long way can become distorted on their journey. If the board of directors decides to reduce the advertising budget by 10 per cent immediately, then this message must be passed down very quickly to the appropriate personnel.

The span of control refers to the number of personnel who report to a particular manager. If a span of control is too wide it is very difficult for the manager in charge to supervise properly the activities of the personnel who report to him or her. The chart opposite shows a span of control of three.

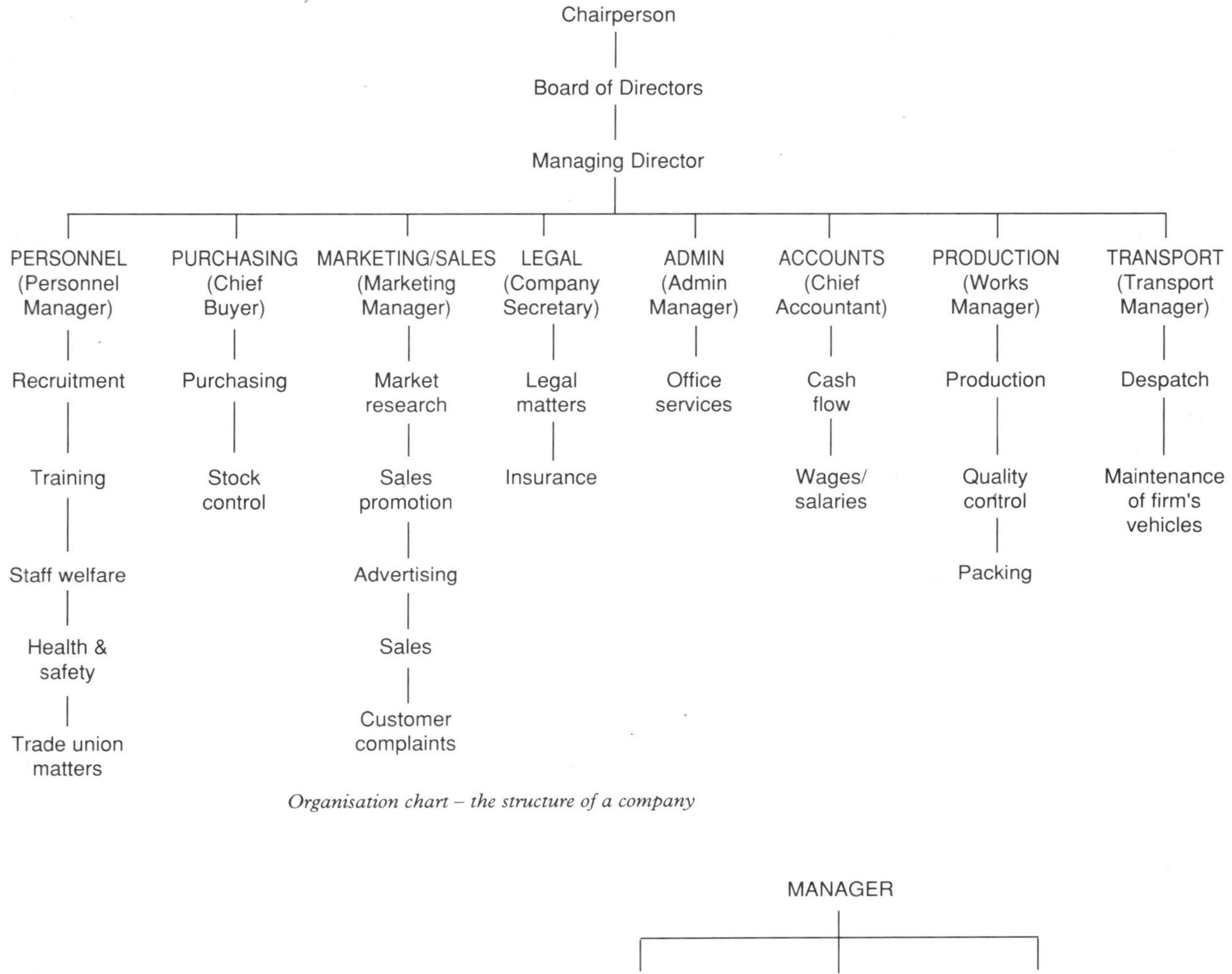

Organisation chart – the structure of a company

Span of control of three

Delegating

Delegating is entrusting someone else to do something or make a decision on your behalf. In small firms only one or two people make the decisions and they take full responsibility for them. In larger organisations, because of the range of responsibilities and the amount of work involved, it is impossible for one or two people to take control of everything, and therefore some tasks are delegated to subordinates who are given the authority to make decisions. However, overall responsibility for any decisions made remains with the manager who has delegated the work.

Board of directors

When a company has lots of shareholders, it is not possible for them all to be involved in the running of the business, so they elect a small group of people called a board of directors to run the company for them. The board of directors is made up of several directors, usually major shareholders, each with expertise in a specific business area, for example, finance or marketing.

Annual general meeting

Although all shareholders cannot take part in the day-to-day running of a company, they do have the opportunity to vote on important matters and to be informed of how the company is performing. It is a statutory requirement that any organisation that is a limited company must hold an AGM and notice of this meeting must be sent to all shareholders. It is at this meeting that the directors are elected and/or re-elected each year and where shareholders have an opportunity to have their say.

Structure of the board of directors

Chairperson

The chairperson (sometimes abbreviated to 'chair') is the most important member of the board of directors. The chairperson is the spokesperson for a company and as such represents the firm to the outside world. Another major responsibility is controlling meetings by keeping order and ensuring that the correct procedures are followed. (These are dealt with in detail in Chapter 9.) For a vote where there are equal numbers for and against, the chairperson has the casting (deciding) vote.

Managing Director

The managing director has a very important role to play in the day-to-day running of a company. As the name suggests, the managing director oversees the management of the whole company. Department managers need to be told of decisions made by the board; similarly, the board must be kept informed of what is happening throughout the company. Thus the managing director forms a two-way channel of communication between the board of directors and the department managers. This ensures that all departments are run effectively in accordance with company policies specified by the board and that the board is aware of any problems being encountered in the company.

Company secretary

Unlike a personal secretary – who types letters, files documents and answers the telephone, together with other clerical duties – the company secretary is usually a member of the board of directors. As part of the job involves dealing with legal and insurance matters, the post holder will be qualified in the necessary legal areas. The company secretary is also responsible for keeping a register of shareholders and dealing with any other matters connected with them.

How much can you remember?

1. What is the purpose of an office?
2. What is another name for office work?
3. Why do all firms need to be organised?
4. Why is decision making more complex in large companies than small ones?
5. Explain the role and structure of a board of directors.
6. What is the purpose of an AGM?
7. Explain the term 'casting vote'.
8. How does a company secretary differ from a personal secretary?
9. What is an organisation chart and what is its purpose?
10. What do you understand by the terms 'chain of command', 'span of control' and 'delegation'?

Activity 2.1
task 1

(a) Using the words listed below write a passage entitled 'The need for organisation in business'. All the words/groups of words listed below must be used and they must not be repeated in the same sentence. When complete, the passage must read clearly and fluently with the information in a logical order.

Words:

Informed	Managing director	Annual general meeting
Chairperson	Duties	Structure
Shareholders	Manager	Efficient
Internal	Decisions	Company secretary
Departments	Office	Clerical
Communication	Span of control	Organisation
Responsible	Board of directors	Price
Profit	Information	Correspondence
Delegation	Legal	Chain of command

(b) Identify any key words you have used in your passage that are not already in the list and add them to it.

task 2 (a) Select two local companies and find out how they are organised. Obtain a copy of each company's organisation structure and identify the similarities and differences.

(b) Prepare an organisation chart for the fictitious company Soft Toy plc. The company specialises in the design and manufacture of soft toys; its customers are nationwide and it has a reputation for personal and prompt delivery.

Departmental organisation

Large companies are divided into departments with each department having certain duties and responsibilities, as well as its own manager. Each department manager is responsible to the board of directors, which makes decisions on behalf of the shareholders.

Departments in a company

Not all companies have the following departments, but most of them will have something similar.

Administration

All departments need office/clerical services to support them in their work. Office/clerical services refers to services such as typing, filing, word processing, mail handling, telephone and photocopying etc. These services are sometimes provided by a separate administration department.

Centralised admin versus departmental admin

CENTRALISED ADMINISTRATION

Many firms centralise their office services. For example, all of the files for the company are kept together in one place and looked after by trained staff, instead of each department keeping their own files. Similarly, the typists all work together in one place and work is completed on a rota basis. This form of organisation can be more economical in terms of staff and equipment, since less equipment is needed and staff are trained in a specific area, which increases the quality of work.

However, there are also disadvantages of having a centralised system. In very large companies, staff may need to go a long way to retrieve a letter from a file and there is no guarantee that the file will be there when they arrive. Also, queues may form and staff may have to wait their turn for typing, photocopying and other services to be completed. With this system, there is a lack of personal contact between the staff carrying out the office service and the person requiring the work, which can slow down the process of having work completed. There is the added problem of how to deal with urgent and confidential work.

Departments in a company

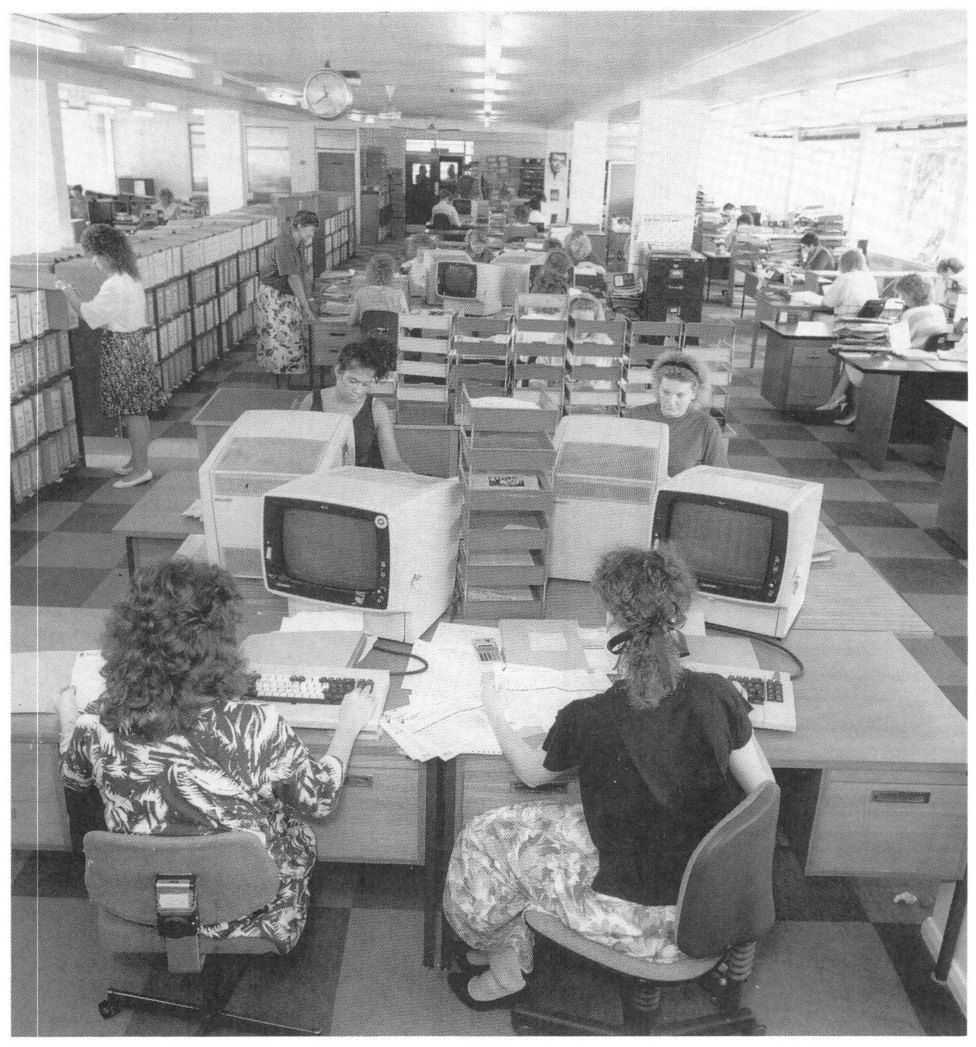

Centralised administration

Departmental administration

The alternative to a centralised system is a departmental one. Many of the disadvantages of a centralised system are the advantages of a departmental one and vice versa. For example, with a departmental system each department has its own typist and filing system. This makes it much quicker to get a letter typed or to retrieve a document from a file. However, as there is no central file, the information will be limited to what is happening within a particular department and problems may develop because of the lack of communication between departments. With regard to typing, as the typist will have lots of other jobs to do, the author may still have to wait to have a letter typed.

When each department looks after its own administration, more equipment is needed around the building and this is costly not only to purchase but also to repair and maintain.

Legal

The Companies Acts lay down strict legal requirements relating to the setting up and running of limited companies and the company secretary has the job of ensuring all legal obligations are met and that the company does not break the law.Other legal matters which may arise are, for example, those connected with property or contracts. It is common practice for smaller firms to employ outside legal experts rather than set up a special department for this purpose.

Personnel

This is one of the most important departments in a company as the success of any business relies heavily on the right person being selected for the job. However well equipped a firm is and however healthy its order book is, if the staff are not well trained and well motivated, the personnel team is not doing its job and the business will not prosper.

The responsibilities and duties of a personnel team are numerous, but they have one common link: they are all connected with people. Some aspects of personnel work are given below:

- Dealing with all staff matters, not only recruiting and resignations/dismissals, but also looking after the health, safety and general welfare of the workforce.
- Liaising in trade union matters when there is a problem – for example, pay negotiations, working conditions or a disciplinary matter.
- Security around the building and grounds.
- Planning and implementing a staff development programme to motivate staff and give them something to strive for. This also helps to prevent a company losing its best members of staff to other firms because there are no promotion opportunities or future prospects.

Recruiting staff can be quite a complex exercise, although most companies follow a very similar procedure to the one shown below:

The vacancy is advertised. If a post carries a large salary and requires a very highly skilled/specialised person it will most likely be advertised nationally. Many jobs, however, are advertised in the local press and job centres.

The employer prepares a job specification. This sets out the qualities and qualifications of the ideal person for the job.

A job description describing the job being advertised is also prepared by the employer. It lists the duties of the post-holder and it is often sent to applicants so that they are aware in advance of what will be expected of them if they are successful.

The job applications in response to the advertisement are examined and a short-list is drawn up. Short-listing is when the most promising-looking applicants are selected from those who have applied and invited for interview. Some applicants at this stage will neither be called for interview nor rejected – if the first group of interviewees is not up to expectations, more applicants may be sent for.

SOMETOWN BOROUGH COUNCIL

JOB DESCRIPTION

Job Title: Saturday Assistant

Directorate: Recreational and Cultural Services

Section: Library Service

Workbase: Central Lending Library

Responsible to: Central Lending Librarian

Responsible for: Public Service and other routines as directed

Job Purpose: To provide service to the public

DUTIES AND RESPONSIBILITIES

1. To be involved in public service routines, including issue, discharge and renewal of books and audio materials.
2. To maintain the Library Stock in good order and condition.
3. To shelve returned books and audio materials.
4. To pack and unpack material.
5. To levy fines on overdue items and collect postal charges on reserved items.
6. To undertake minor repairs, re-jacketing and re-labelling of books.

Job description

The interviews take place and the most suitable person is selected for the post. This is assuming that one of the applicants is suitable; if not, the job may be re-advertised. When this happens there is usually a note at the bottom of the advert which advises applicants who have already applied not to re-apply.

Production

A company will have a production department only if it is a manufacturing business. This department is responsible for making the product – in other words, turning the raw materials into a finished good or part finished good (see Chapter 1). To meet demand, a company must make sure it has sufficient of the three main resources associated with production – labour, materials and machinery. Another important aspect of the production department's work is to check the quality of finished goods and ensure they are despatched to customers on time. Many larger organisations have their own transport department and are able to offer customers a personal delivery service.

A works/production manager will be in charge of this department supported by a team of production supervisors and workers. It is also in a company's interest to employ a team of skilled technicians to keep the machinery and equipment in good working order. Breakdowns cause delays and delays can lead to deadlines not being met and orders being lost. Many production departments operate a 24-hour continuous shift system as it can be very expensive to keep stopping and starting machinery. Each separate shift team will consist of a manager, supervisors, a team of production workers and skilled technicians to deal with breakdowns.

Although there are different versions, many production programmes follow a similar procedure to the one given below:

- Order received from customer specifying a date on which delivery is required.
- A schedule of work is prepared to ensure the deadline can be and will be met.
- Stock levels are checked and raw materials taken out for the order.
- Finished products are checked for quality. Quality control is crucial as inferior workmanship will not lead to further orders.
- While production is taking place, materials are carefully controlled so that wastage is kept to a minimum. This helps to keep costs down and allows firms to be more competitive with their final price.
- Machinery faults or breakdowns are reported and rectified as quickly as possible to minimise any delay in production.

Marketing/sales

It is of little use having a good product or being able to offer a good service if potential customers don't know about it. Usually, the first stage in the marketing process is to find out if there is a demand for the product/service which is to be offered. Depending on what the product/service is, specific segments of the market will be targeted according to age, interests or income etc. and a survey will be carried out. This is the most common way of researching the market and is known as market-orientated research. However, sometimes a product is made first and then tested – this is product-orientated marketing.

Once it has been established that there is a demand for a particular service or product the potential customers must be made aware of it and encouraged to buy. Advertising plays a key role in this process and many firms have a special budget for this purpose. However, it is no good just informing people of a product/service – they must be persuaded that they need it, that it is better than those already on the market, and they must be constantly reminded of its existence so that they keep on buying it.

Sales promotion is the term used to persuade customers to buy and this can be achieved in many ways. Methods often used are: offering increased quantity for the same or less money, two for the price of one, money-off coupons, or a free gift.

Customers will only make repeat purchases if they are impressed with the product/service and feel they have received good value for money. With expensive items, customers will be more encouraged to buy if a firm can offer a good after-sales service. Complaints need to be dealt with quickly and in a proper manner so that customers will remain loyal and still deal with the firm if they have been unfortunate enough to buy a faulty product.

Finance

Sound financial planning is crucial to the success of any firm. Every business needs to have a constant supply of money coming in so that all its debts can be paid. Cash flow is the term that refers to money coming into a business from customers and investments and money being paid out for materials, wages and running costs.

If there is insufficient money coming into a business to pay all debts then a cash flow crisis will occur. If this is not dealt with quickly and resolved it will lead to closure. Many firms use a bank overdraft facility to bridge the gaps which occur between money coming in and money being paid out. (Overdrafts are dealt with in Chapter 13.)

All firms must keep proper financial records. Financial accounts will include a profit and loss account and a balance sheet. The profit and loss account summarises a firm's expenses over a period of time and shows the gross and net profit/loss. The balance sheet shows the financial position of the company at a particular date.

A balance sheet is so called because it is divided into two parts and the two sides have to balance. One side gives details of the firm's assets (all the property and possessions owned by the company – these will include any debts due to it) and the other side shows its liabilities (what the business owes).

How much can you remember?

1 What is meant by office services?
2 Explain the difference between a centralised system of office services and a departmental one.
3 Why is the work of the personnel department important to a firm?
4 What other responsibilities and duties does the production department have besides making the product?
5 Explain the role of the marketing/sales team.
6 Why is sound financial planning crucial to the success of a business?

Activity 2.2

task 1

(a) For each of the advertisements shown on page 40 make a list of the qualities and qualifications required for each job. Present this information in the format of job specifications.

(b) Explain why the qualities and qualifications are so different for each post.

task 2

Examine the advertisements carefully, choose one and prepare a realistic job description.

task 3

(a) Assume the role of interviewer for one of the jobs advertised and prepare a list of questions to ask the interviewee.

(b) Assume the role of interviewee and make a list of preparations which are necessary prior to the interview and a note of any questions you could ask.

(c) Use your notes and carry out a role-play exercise with a partner who has chosen the same job as you have. Do this once as interviewer, and then as interviewee.

(d) Discuss and evaluate with your partner your performance as interviewee. Identify your strengths and weaknesses at the interview and agree how you could improve your interview technique.

PERMANENT FULL TIME SECRETARY/ ADMINISTRATIVE ASSISTANT
Grade 3 (£8440-£9837 plus proficiency allowances per annum).

A vacancy has arisen for an individual to offer secretarial and administrative support to the Quality Assurance Co-ordinator at St Hilda's Hospital. Candidates should possess RSA Stage III Typewriting (or equivalent), 80 wpm shorthand, and a working knowledge of PCs; word processing, preferably WordStar, would be advantageous. Effective communication skills and well-developed office practice abilities are essential criteria for the post.

For a job description and application form, please contact: Miss R Hancock, Secretary to Quality Assurance Co-ordinator, St Hilda's Hospital.

ASSEMBLY OPERATORS

Applicants should be enthusiastic, hard working, possess excellent manual dexterity, a sharp eye for detail and a flexible attitude to work.

Although previous factory assembly experience is desirable, full training will be provided.

Pay initially is £96 per week rising to £112 per week. Further increases are possible beyond this. Shift-working may be required after the initial period.

Application forms are available from your local Job Centre.

This is a re-advertisement, previous applicants need not apply as they are already being considered.

TOP NOTCH
HAIR DESIGN STUDIO
Require
TOP STYLIST
(min 5 years experience)

Exceptional opportunity.
Exceptional salary.
If you're among the best – come and join the best.

Contact:
Mr Morton on 498725 for interview.

Activity 2.3
task 1

(a) In groups of six, design a simple paper product which you can make. Give full details of measurements in your design.

(b) Make a prototype of your proposed product.

(c) Make a list of the equipment and materials you need to make your product.

(d) Time production and find out how quickly each item can be made, remember quantity is no good where there is poor quality and/or lots of wasted materials.

(e) Explain why it is important to monitor production rate, quality and level of wastage.

task 2

You have received an order from a customer for 12 of your paper products. If these are ready within the specified time and of the same quality as your prototype a large order will be forthcoming.

The success of your production team depends on three things:

- the quality of the finished product
- meeting the customer's deadline (to calculate your deadline, consider the time taken to produce one item as detailed in task 1 (d))
- being competitive in price, and that means keeping wastage to a minimum.

(a) Using the specification and time limits prepared in task 1, allocate three members of the group to form the production team and make six of the 12 items required. The remaining three members will be responsible for quality control, timing production and checking wastage.

(b) Change roles and complete the order.

(c) Which team was the most competitive and why? Find out how well or badly the other groups performed and why.

Activity 2.4
task

Working in groups, choose a product/service and plan an advertising campaign. This should include the following:

(a) Details of your product/service together with a suitable slogan which will attract the public's attention.

(b) A poster and an advertisement which give full details of your product/service. The purpose of these will be to inform the public of your product/service, persuade them to buy it and emphasise how different and better it is than similar products/services already on the market.

(c) Try out your advertising campaign on the class and find out: how many people would buy your product/service and why the others would not.

(d) Using the above information, identify how you could improve or adapt your product to make it more successful.

(e) Calculate the likely cost of producing your new product/service. To do this you will need to identify the materials required and take into account labour charges linked with production.

Chapter 3 Introducing the office

By the end of this chapter you should be able to explain:

- the role of the office and the ways in which it deals with information
- the use of a circulation slip
- the differences between an open plan and a traditional type of office
- the term 'flexitime'
- the range of different types of office services and personnel
- the role of the receptionist
- reception records
- how to deal with visitors to a firm
- the use of business cards.

The purpose of an office

An office is a place used for transacting business. It is the nerve centre of every business where information is received, processed, stored and sent out. Businesses need to communicate with each other and with consumers via:

Telephone calls These are made and received when information is required quickly. When the telephone is answered the person on the other end may require some information and this has to be found.

Written correspondence When letters arrive they cannot be ignored, nor can they be filed away and forgotten about. Most letters require a reply or some action taking on them. On occasions, the information contained in the letters has to be circulated around the building to several people, and at other times the information is stored away safely so that it can be found again later if and when it is required. Sometimes before a letter can be answered, information has to be found.

Electronic communication Many modern offices correspond with each other electronically using fax or other forms of electronic mail. In simple terms this is when one computer communicates with another computer somewhere else. (This is dealt with in detail in Chapter 12.) The information sent out and received needs processing in the same way as telephone messages and written correspondence do.

Personal visits The number of visitors a company receives depends on the type of organisation it is. A busy shop will have a constant flow of customers to buy its products and a hospital will have hundreds of people arriving for treatment and to visit sick relatives. A small office might have only the occasional sales representative or a business person from another company coming in to discuss matters with the manager, while a very large office will have numerous visitors attending conferences or on other company business.

Circulating information

When information arrives which needs circulating around several people, there are two ways of dealing with this. If the message is short it can be photocopied and everyone sent their own copy. However, sometimes the information may be quite lengthy, perhaps a detailed report, and providing a photocopy for each individual can be very time-consuming and expensive. If there is no urgency for everyone to read the information at the same time, a circulation slip is attached to the documentation and it is passed around the people concerned.

CIRCULATION SLIP

ITEM BEING CIRCULATED: Proposals for design of new product

ACTION REQUIRED: Read and be prepared to comment at next management meeting

NAME	DEPARTMENT	INITIAL
R Narrow	Finance	RN
D Slade	Marketing	DS
B Tunmore	Production	
S Harvey	Legal	

PLEASE RETURN TO: E A Straight – ASAP

The circulation slip (sometimes called a routing slip) contains a list of names at the side of which is a space for each person to add their signature and the date to say they have read the information and passed it on to the next person on the list (see example on page 43). The major disadvantage with this method is the time it takes to go round everyone. If someone is ill or on holiday it could remain in their 'in-tray' for several days or even weeks before being passed on.

The office building

Depending upon the type and size of the business, an office can be one room, either small or large, several rooms or a whole building. It will contain equipment and machinery suitable for carrying out clerical (office) work. Most staff employed in offices are referred to as clerks or clerical workers.

An office building

When an office consists of a series of small rooms, like the classrooms in a school or college, it is called an enclosed, traditional or corridor office. An office where lots of people work together in one large room is an open plan office. Open plan offices are found mostly in modern buildings and they are often divided up into small sections by furniture or screens.

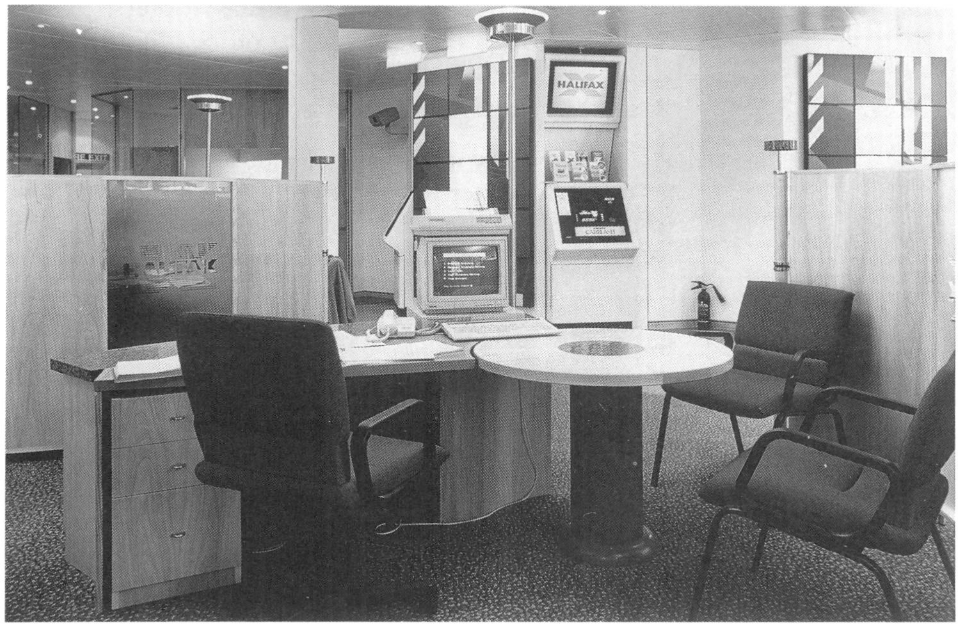

An open plan office

The advantages of an open plan office are:

- ❍ It is bright, spacious and well ventilated.
- ❍ Supervision is easy as everyone is in the same room.
- ❍ Communication is quick as everyone is in close contact with each other and not separated by walls.

The disadvantages of an open plan office are:

- ❍ Working with a lot of people in one room can be very distracting as it can become very noisy with people talking and telephones ringing.
- ❍ Furniture and screens do not allow much privacy.
- ❍ When someone catches a cold, for example, this is easily passed on to other staff in the same room.
- ❍ It is not very secure as there are no walls or doors between where people work and leave their belongings.

How much can you remember?

1 What is the purpose of an office?
2 List and explain the various ways in which communication takes place.
3 What is the purpose of a circulation slip and in what instance might it be used?
4 What is another name for office workers?
5 How does a modern type of office differ from the more traditional one?

Activity 3.1

Read the scenario and then answer the questions following.

As an employee of the local leisure centre which offers a wide variety of activities together with conference facilities you have to deal with all types of enquiries. Your job involves answering the telephone, sending and receiving fax messages, dealing with callers and answering letters.

This morning you took an hour off to visit the dentist and arranged for a colleague to stand in for you and take messages which you would deal with on your return.

It was very quiet and there were only two telephone calls. The first was from a young lady who had left her jumper at the centre the previous evening. She wasn't sure where she had left it as she had spent time in various parts of the centre. The second caller wanted to know what sporting activities were available at the weekend and if he needed to book in advance.

A young mother called in to find out if the children's party afternoons were still available and how much it would cost for her daughter and nine friends to spend her birthday at the centre next Wednesday.

A fax arrived to book the conference hall on the first Monday of next month.

Lastly, a letter arrived from the printer, it contained a copy for the file of the new advertising leaflet.

Fax is explained in chapters 11 and 12.

task

Answer these questions on the scenario above.

1 What, if any, information needs to be found?
2 Is there any information which needs to be circulated and if so, specify what it is and which method should be used and why?
3 Which information if any needs a reply?
4 Does any of the information need storing? If so is it likely to be required in the future?
5 Explain what action you would take in each situation given.
6 Suggest other situations which might arise when you would have to find, circulate or send out information.

Office hours

The days when all people in offices worked 'nine to five' are over. Many firms have now introduced flexible working hours. This does not mean that staff can come and go as they please, but it does offer them some flexibility with regard to when they start and finish work within specified times.

There is a certain time of the day – core time – when all staff have to be at work. Core time is the busiest part of the day, perhaps between 9.30 a.m. and 12 noon and 2 p.m. and 4 p.m. Regardless of what time staff start and finish, they must all work an agreed minimum number of hours per week and be in the office during the core period.

If staff work extra hours over and above the minimum specified they can bank these hours – in other words, save them – and with the agreement of management take time off in lieu at a later date. The hours worked must be within the boundaries specified by a firm.

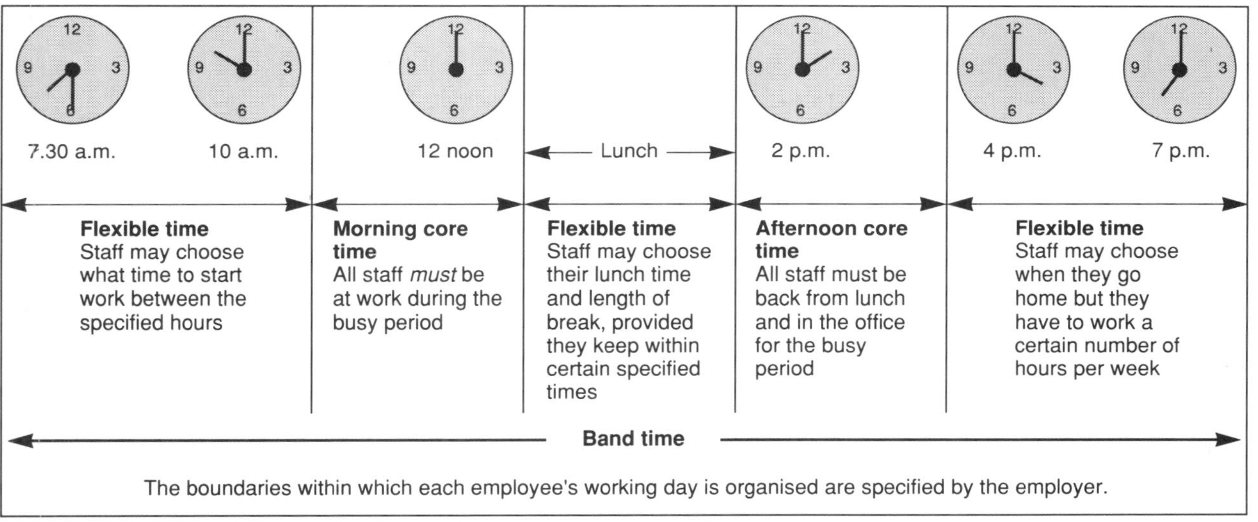

Flexitime working

Employees who work flexible hours are normally required to clock or sign in and out so that records can be kept of the total hours worked. Many local authorities and larger firms have implemented a flexible working arrangement for their staff. The trend towards this way of working is certainly increasing, particularly in today's world of equal opportunities.

Female members of staff no longer have to retire from employment when they have a child. Employees with babies, small children or dependent relatives can now return to or go out to work and, within the limits imposed by their employer, arrange their working day around family commitments.

Office/clerical services

Any office regardless of its size will offer a range of clerical services. Office staff don't just type and answer the telephone, they have many more duties to perform, which may include:

- reception duties
- computing work
- shorthand/typing/audio for business correspondence
- copying/duplicating
- storing and retreiving information
- arranging travel and meetings
- dealing with the mail
- answering and making telephone calls
- handling cash
- processing documents involved in the purchase and sale of goods
- looking after stock
- dealing with petty cash and banking transactions.

Office/clerical personnel

If you look in any local or national paper with a 'situations vacant' page you will see a range of clerical posts being advertised. Offices do not just need typists and filing clerks, they need managers, computer operators, shorthand typists, training supervisors, telephone sales people and many others. As you work through this book you will find out more about what these jobs entail.

How much can you remember?

1 Is it true that employees who work flexitime can come and go as they please, or are there conditions?
2 How are the hours worked by each employee monitored when a flexi-system is in operation?
3 List a minimum of ten different types of clerical post.

Activity 3.2

Each of the people described below will want to vary their working hours in a different way. Using the boundaries and core periods from the diagram on page 47, draw up a timetable for each person which will allow them to fit their working lives around their own personal commitments. The minimum weekly hours specified by the company is 36.

Harold Medway has an invalid mother who he looks after. He pays for a nurse during the day and she works from 7 a.m. to 4.30 p.m.

Rohana Jones has two small children, the youngest of which has just started school. She cannot afford to pay someone to take the children to school so she has to do this before starting work. School starts at 8.30 a.m. Her friend picks them up and is able to look after them until 6 p.m. each evening. It is a 30-minute journey from her home to her work place.

Robert Ellis has a very close friend who is seriously ill in hospital. He travels quite a distance to get to work but the hospital is located within five minutes of the office. Visiting times are 10–11 a.m., 12.30–1.30 p.m. and 7–8 p.m.

Activity 3.3

(a) Study the job titles below and then read carefully the descriptions of the jobs on offer in the adverts on page 50. Match each job title to one of the descriptions.

(b) You should have four descriptions left with no job title. Read them carefully and choose an appropriate job title for each one.

(a) MEDICAL LABORATORY ASSISTANT
Part-Time

(b) PERSONAL ASSISTANT

(c) EXPERIENCED AUDIT ASSISTANTS

(d) ACCOUNTS CLERK
Part-Time

(e) ENTERTAINMENTS MANAGER

(f) MARKETING & TOURISM OFFICER (LEISURE)

(g) TELEPHONE SALES PERSON

(h) PHOTOLIBRARIAN

(i) JOURNALIST

(j) SECRETARY
(Full-time)

(1)

(10 Hours per week)
Pay Scale: £5,299 - £9,294

The clerical worker will be required to provide secretarial and clerical support to Two Welfare Rights Workers. He/she will need typing, recording, and organisational skills.

(2)

Required for high class Ladies Wear Department.
3 Days per week plus holidays.
Please apply in writing with details plus CV to:

(3)

Salary package to c.£21,000 + performance related pay up to 8%
Removal package to £5,000
(Assistance with house purchase may be available and housing for rent in approved cases)
Private health care. Day nursery.

The post provides an exciting opportunity for a qualified and/or experienced Marketing professional to develop the marketing of the Council's Leisure Services and initiate a strategy for the management of tourism in the District.

You will, in conjunction with line management, co-ordinate the promotion and sale of the existing and expanding range of leisure and recreational facilities, services and events, oversee the Council's interests in respect of tourism management and assist with the corporate marketing of the Council. You will have a proven record in the marketing profession, excellent communication and presentation skills, and the ability to effectively manage advertising and promotional budgets.

(4)

... with computer cataloguing and graphics experience, to reorganise and run their photographic library. Please send CV and application to:

(5)

With good accountancy knowledge required by this long established and independent firm of Chartered Accountants.
Applicants should have at least 3 years' auditing experience in a good general practice and preferably be studying for a professional qualification.

Please apply in own handwriting with full C.V. to:

(6)

He/she should be committed, fast working and a quick learner. The job involves writing both hard news stories and informed features for our monthly title. We are looking for a self-starter, who will be able to build up contacts quickly. Some international travel may be involved.

(7)

Duties involve the preparation of day to day accounts, wages, VAT and the operation of a computerised management system. The successful applicant will have previous experience in book-keeping, computerised databases and wordprocessing WordPerfect 5.1. Working hours will be 12 - 15 hours per week by arrangement.

(8)

Preferably with telephone sales experience either in builders merchanting or in some other aspect of the construction sector, you will have a proven record of success in handling customer enquiries and generating sales. A knowledge of the roofing sector is desirable.
An excellent telephone manner is essential along with the personal qualities of a team player, drive and initiative.
An attractive benefits package will reflect the importance of the position and career prospects are excellent.

(9)

... to work 20 hours per week on an Electronic Switchboard.

Applicants must be prepared to cover all shifts, including days, nights, evenings and weekends sometimes at short notice to ensure continuity of the service during times of sickness and absence.

Previous switchboard/reception experience would be an advantage, but not essential. A home telephone is essential.

(10)

Manufacturers of Soft Furnishing Fabrics and suppliers to customers throughout the World. Applicants must be aged 30+, able to work on own initiative, accurate with figures, good standard of typing essential. Experience of Exporting would be an advantage.

Hours 9.00 a.m. to 5.15 p.m.
Salary Negotiable

(11)

Our Policy and Planning Director is looking for a confident and effective PA. Supervising a clerk/typist, the PA will also manage and deliver secretarial services for a team of four.
With at least 2 years' secretarial experience, you will be a well organised self starter, able to develop and run efficient admin systems and communicate well at all levels.
This is a responsible job working for a dynamic charity which is tackling homelessness and community care. Benefits include flexitime, 5 weeks paid leave, and a pension scheme.

(12)

The Students' Union is a lively, developing organisation committed to providing high quality services to students.
Due to the career development of our present Manager, we are seeking applicants for this post with drive, initiative and enthusiasm, who will be committed to our aim of developing and expanding our entertainments programme for students.
Our Entertainments events include formal balls, live bands, discos etc, soon to be re-located in an exciting new venue.
Benefits include a contributory pension scheme and six weeks' annual holiday.

(13)

Duties involve providing a secretarial service to a professional team of surveyors in a busy office. Reception duties will be involved. The successful applicant will be of smart appearance, have a good telephone manner and have a minimum of 3 years experience of wordprocessing WordPerfect 5.1 in a professional environment. Salary and terms of appointment dependent on age and experience.

Applications are invited for the above posts in your own handwriting with full C.V. and the names of two referees to:

(14)

... required to work part-time (20 hours per week) from 9.00 a.m. to 1.00 p.m. Monday to Friday. The postholder will perform basic laboratory work under supervision of qualified staff in the Virology Laboratory. The successful applicant will enjoy working as part of a team.
Qualifications: 4 GCSEs or equivalent essential. 1 Science 'A' level or equivalent desirable.
Salary: £6,535 - £8,284 pro rata

First impressions of the office

When you go into any organisation the impression you form of the firm is usually based on the greeting and help you receive from the person at the reception desk inside the entrance. This person is the receptionist and is employed by a firm to receive and deal with any visitors. It is the responsibility of this employee to ensure that all visitors form a favourable impression of the firm so that they will return and also recommend the firm to their friends and associates.

Qualities of a good receptionist

It is not just the manner of the person at the reception desk that is important – appearance matters too. If the receptionist is smart and well organised this image of the firm will be reflected to the visitor, but if the receptionist is very casual and untidy in appearance even though he or she may possess all the right personal qualities, appearance alone may well create a rather 'slap happy' impression of the firm. For example, jeans and a baggy top will not create a good impression, but a smart suit with matching shirt or blouse will.

However, just as personal qualities without a smart appearance are no good, a smart appearance without the essential personal qualities will not impress either. A smartly dressed but rather rude and abrasive individual will do little to encourage visitors to return.

There are many desirable personal qualities required for this job, the most important of which are being patient, helpful, polite, tactful, friendly and staying calm in all kinds of situations. Some visitors are very difficult to deal with, especially if they have a complaint, while others may be a little confused and unsure of who they want to see. Each type of visitor requires a different approach but both need careful handling.

Firms usually prefer their receptionists to have had previous office experience so that they are used to dealing with people. It is unusual therefore to employ a receptionist under the age of 18. Often a receptionist is someone who has worked their way up in a firm and has a thorough knowledge of its products and services, the people employed in it and where they are located. This is most helpful when telephoning staff to notify them that their visitor has arrived and also when directing people to the right location or taking them there.

Types of visitors

The type and number of visitors who arrive at a firm varies considerably from firm to firm, depending upon the organisation itself, and consequently no two reception jobs are exactly the same. However, one thing is certain: if potential and existing customers are not happy with the service they receive from a firm they will go elsewhere. Visitors are influenced by what they see when they first enter a firm, if the receptionist is unhelpful they will look somewhere else.

It is not just business people who a receptionist has to impress, many services rely totally on the general public for their business. For example, if a family goes on holiday and the hotel receptionist is unpleasant or creates a bad impression it is unlikely that the family will return the following year. Hairdressers, depend on their regular clients and the receptionist is a key figure in helping to keep customers happy and encouraging them to return.

Dealing with callers, although the most important part of a receptionist's job, is not the only duty. Depending on the size of the company, the receptionist will be expected to carry out other duties, too. If it is a very busy reception then answering the telephone and dealing with personal callers may be all that is expected. However, in a very small firm where there are few callers, the receptionist may be expected to type, file and carry out a variety of other office duties.

Reception records

Visitors cannot be allowed to come and go at will. Therefore, records are kept of everyone who has visited and is visiting a firm.

Callers' register/visitors' book

Often there is a visitors' book on the reception desk and all visitors are expected to sign in on arrival. There are several reasons why it is necessary to know who is in the building at any one time, most importantly because of security, fire and insurance.

In large organisations where offices are spread out on several floors it is important to know who everyone is and why they are there. If there is a bomb alert or a fire, the reception register will show how many visitors are on the premises and where they are. Visitors are often given a badge to wear while they are on the premises so that they can easily be identified. In smaller firms this is not a problem, but records are still kept for reference purposes. The record is called a callers' register (see below).

DATE	TIME	NAME OF CALLER	NAME & ADDRESS OF FIRM	SEEN BY
4/12/9-	10.35	W. Cope	Burlington + Cope	Accounts
			54 New Road Newtown	
	10.55	Ms S. Parsons	16 Central Square	Personnel
	12.45	W. Otwell	Otwell Supplies 29 Furnival Street	No appointment
				- to write/ telephone to
				arrange convenient
				time with Chief Buyer

Callers' register

Appointments book

When members of staff make an appointment to see someone from outside the office, they notify the receptionist of the details. The receptionist is then able to enter these details into a diary which is used to record all future appointments. In a small firm, the receptionist may have access to staff diaries and be able to make appointments on their behalf. Many larger firms now make use of a computerised diary for all staff, which is easily accessible by the receptionist and updated.

Staff in/out book

The receptionist keeps a staff in/out book. When staff leave the building they sign out and when they return they sign back in. This saves time being wasted trying to contact someone who is not in the building. Staff who are absent are also recorded in this book.

DATE	TIME OUT	TIME RETURNED	NAME	DEPARTMENT	DETAILS
15/3/9-	10.55	1.15	C. Dodge	Purchasing	hospital appointment

Staff in/out book

Dealing with visitors

When a caller arrives there is a certain procedure which should be carried out to deal with each visitor so that they feel welcome. A receptionist should always greet callers politely and ask for their name. Once the caller has introduced him/herself it is polite to refer to them by name.

While the receptionist notifies the relevant member of staff of their visitor's arrival, it is usual to offer the visitor a seat. If the appointment is delayed for any reason, refreshments should be offered together with an apology for the delay. A receptionist should never leave a visitor waiting after the appointment time without some explanation.

If a caller arrives without an appointment, discretion must be used as to whether to contact the person he or she wishes to see or to persuade the visitor to make an appointment for a future time.

Business cards

TELEPHONE (1302) 47184
ALAN BRENTNALL
Property Repairs
NO JOB TOO SMALL

ASTON SERVICES LTD
Presented by
STEVEN CHAPPELL
Director
T • H • G
Technology House Group Ltd.
Technology House, Ridge Road
Rotherham S65 1NS
TEL: (1709) 320755
FAX: (1709) 320687

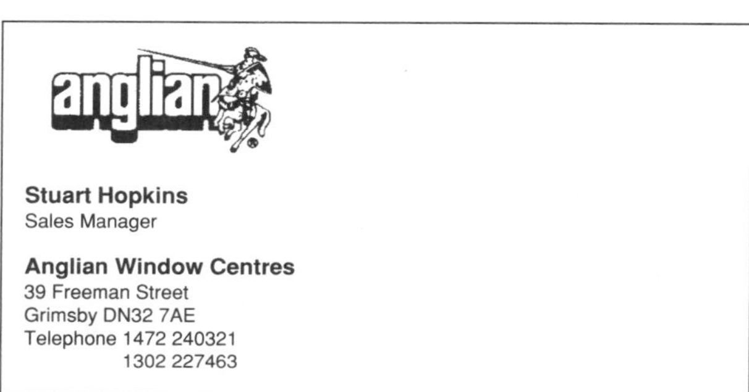

anglian
Stuart Hopkins
Sales Manager
Anglian Window Centres
39 Freeman Street
Grimsby DN32 7AE
Telephone 1472 240321
1302 227463

Many business callers bring with them a business card. This is a small card which gives details of their name, their business, the product/service offered and other items of information like the company logo, fax and telephone numbers. This is useful as it saves the receptionist having to ask questions, it also saves embarrassment when a name has a peculiar spelling or pronunciation. This card is often filed in a card index box and kept on the reception desk for future reference.

How much can you remember?

1 Why is the appearance and manner of a firm's receptionist so important?
2 What personal qualities should a receptionist possess?
3 What are the duties and responsibilities of a receptionist and how do they differ between small and large organisations?
4 What is the accepted procedure for dealing with visitors to a firm?
5 What is a business card and why is it so useful?
6 What records are kept by a receptionist?

Activity 3.4 Your company, a large organisation, requires a new receptionist as the young man presently in the job has been promoted. The company has on average around 250 visitors per week. The post is to be advertised internally and externally. You have been asked to make suitable arrangements.

task 1

(a) Find out how much it will cost to place a classified advertisement in at least two local newspapers.

(b) Design suitable advertisements for:
- (i) the internal noticeboards
- (ii) the staff magazine
- (iii) the local newspaper(s).

(c) It is intended that each applicant will undergo a practical reception test and you have been asked to make the necessary arrangements. You will need to:
- (i) prepare a callers'/visitors' register
- (ii) invent five imaginary visitors, write the details on cue cards. These must include at least one difficult customer and one who does not have an appointment. An example of a cue card is given below. At least one visitor must have a business card to present to the receptionist
- (iii) take the part of receptionist and try the role play with other members of your group
- (iv) make a list of the criteria which the interview panel will use to measure the suitability of each applicant.

MR NEVILLE CHARMER

You are a sales representative. You want to see Miss Sugden the Chief Buyer but you do not have an appointment. Interrupt the person chatting to the receptionist, present your business card and try to persuade the receptionist to let you see Miss Sugden.

Example of a cue card

task 2

There are so many different types of people coming and going, the receptionist has to be fully prepared to deal with a variety of situations. Many callers can be quite rude and awkward for various reasons and many situations have to be handled very carefully.

(a) Read the situations below and explain how you would deal with each one.

(b) Make a list of the qualities you would need to display when handling each situation.

Situation 1: A young man has arrived in a panic. He was expected at 10.30 for a job interview but after setting off in ample time there was a very serious accident on the motorway and traffic was halted for two hours. Even though he allowed extra time for hold-ups he is still one hour late. Interviews are still going on and the time is 11.30. He is in a terrible state as he really wants this job.

Situation 2: The office window cleaner has called in for payment after finishing cleaning all the windows. He won't go away and insists on telling you the latest jokes he has heard and generally chatting about anything and nothing. Your next visitor, a very important caller has just walked through the door.

Situation 3: One of your firm's products was bought by the man standing at the reception desk. He has one arm wrapped up in a bandage, and he is using his other arm to wave the faulty product in the air. You assume from his shouting and the way he is carrying on that his arm injury has been caused by the appliance and that he has brought the product back to complain. He is rather red in the face and shouting very loudly at you. People are staring.

Chapter 4 Computing in the office

By the end of this chapter you should be able to explain:

- the factors a business will consider before choosing a computer system
- the terms 'hardware' and 'software'
- the different types of computer
- the parts which together make up a computer system
- the purpose of secondary storage devices
- the formatting of a disk
- the difference between a hard disk and a floppy disk
- the range of printers available to suit the needs of different businesses
- how to care for computer equipment and materials
- the need for good housekeeping
- the most common software applications for business use
- the skills and qualities of word processor operators.

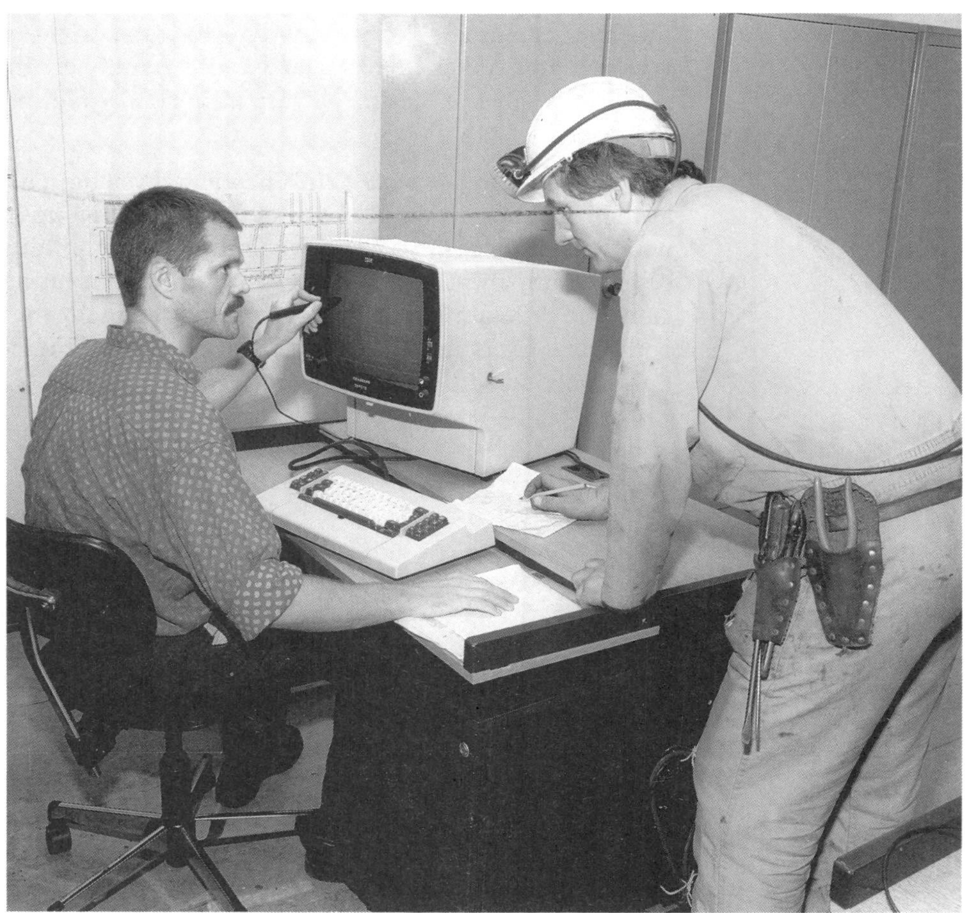

Technology in the office

Computers

The use of new technology in business is increasing and the office is no exception. You rarely enter any office and fail to see at least one computer, a telephone with the latest facilities, a fax machine or some other item of new technology. With the wealth of software (the computer programs – the instructions that tell the computer what to do) now available, many firms are using computers to assist them in a variety of business activities. The requirements of a business vary depending on the type of work it carries out and its size. For instance, it is unlikely that the needs of an individual trader will bear much resemblance to those of a larger organisation. However, the wide range of both hardware (the actual parts you can see and touch) and software available means that the needs of any business can easily be met.

Before buying a computer system, a firm will consider:

- What type of work the computer will be used for – graphics, text, statistics etc.
- The quantity of work it will have to deal with.
- Whether or not it will be a good investment – will it earn its keep?
- How quickly the output will be needed.
- How much money the firm can afford to spend.

Choosing a computer

There are three types of computer from which a business can choose:

- a mainframe, which is by far the largest, most powerful and expensive type of system available
- a mini-computer, which offers many of the advantages of the mainframe but is smaller, cheaper and less powerful
- the microcomputer, which at one time was used only by schools, colleges and home computing enthusiasts. Nowadays this type of hardware is becoming increasingly popular with small to medium sized businesses, which do not have the need or resources for a mainframe or mini system.

Mainframes are used mainly by larger organisations. It will have many terminals (which consist of a keyboard and screen) connected to it and they can access and use the large amount of information the computer stores. A mainframe works so fast that it appears to be carrying out many tasks at the same time and it usually has a room to itself because it requires special environmental conditions. A mini-computer cannot handle as much information as a mainframe and has fewer terminals connected to it.

Mainframe computer system

The size, power and price of the latest microcomputers make them an asset to even the smallest business. While they are constantly being improved in terms of how powerful they are, they remain small enough to sit on most desk tops and cheap enough for the small business to buy. There is a variety of software available which can be used for many different tasks.

Lap-top and notebook computers are becoming increasingly popular for the business executive. These are self-contained portable machines which can be carried around easily from place to place. Most are designed to run industry-standard software packages such as word processing, desk-top publishing (DTP), databases and spreadsheets (these terms are explained later in this chapter). They offer many facilities, such as calendar/diary scheduler with reminder function, address and telephone book and spell-checker. They can be linked up to a wide range of printers and peripherals. (Peripherals are explained later.)

Storing information

Information can be stored temporarily in a computer's internal memory or more permanently using a secondary storage device such as a magnetic disk. Computers have two types of memory, one permanent and one temporary. The permanent memory is referred to as a ROM (read-only memory) and the user cannot access this memory to store information. The ROM contains the programs which tell the computer what to do and how to do it, and when the power is switched off the contents of it are not affected.

The other memory is the working space where work is stored temporarily while the power remains switched on, and this is the RAM (random-access memory). However, once the power is switched off the memory empties and any work in the RAM is lost unless it has been saved on to a secondary storage device.

Computers have different size internal memories – generally the larger the memory, the more expensive the computer. To help clarify how much work can be stored it may be helpful to know that the computer's internal memory capacity is measured in bytes, kilobytes, and megabytes and that each byte roughly represents one character. One kilobyte is actually equal to 1,024 characters; therefore, a machine which is advertised as having a 28K memory will store 1,024 x 28 characters or bytes, while a machine with one megabyte (Mb) will store approximately one million bytes.

Secondary storage devices

Secondary storage devices, such as cassettes and disks, are used in computer systems for various reasons. Often the internal memory is not large enough, but more importantly, the contents of the volatile memory (RAM) can be preserved and backed-up on these devices. Some home computers use cassettes but these are very slow in comparison to disks and do not hold very much information.

The more expensive microcomputers as well as using floppy disks often have a hard disk. Floppy disks are quite cheap, but most are limited in the amount of information they can store, although very high capacity floppy disks are available. This type of storage device is quite fragile and requires careful handling.

Mini and mainframe computers which store large amounts of information use hard disks and also magnetic tape for off-line storage. Floppy disks would be totally inadequate in terms of the amount of information they hold, for many of the larger organisations. Users of the more expensive micros which have a hard disk back up their work on to a floppy disk for safety. Cheaper, less powerful micro-computers use floppy disks only.

Preparing a disk for storing information

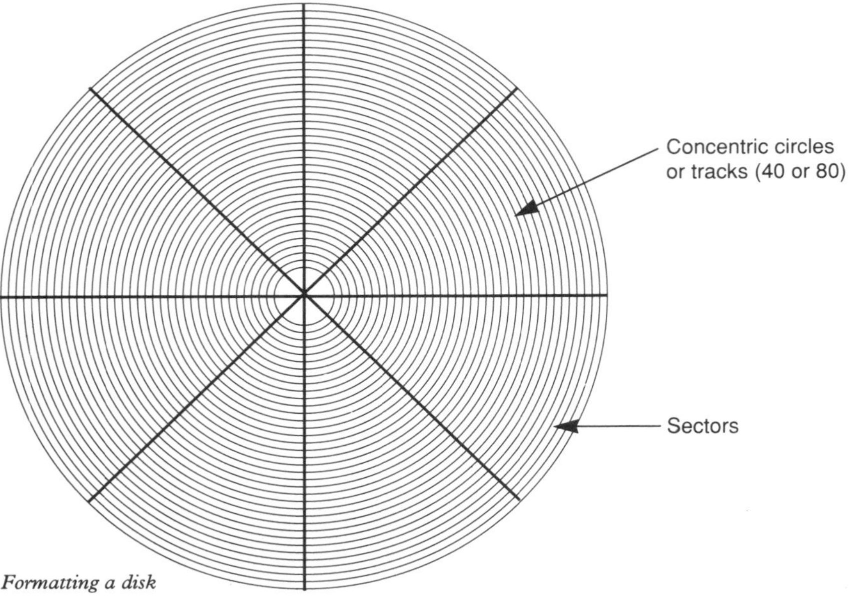

Formatting a disk

Before information can be stored a disk must be prepared and this process is known as formatting. Trying to use a disk to store information prior to formatting would be like trying to put documents into a filing cabinet without drawers. An impossible task! The computer divides the disk up into separate tracks (40 or 80) and sectors like pieces of cake (see above). Each file saved is stored on a certain track in a particular sector. The disk is like a filing cabinet, and the sectors and tracks are the drawers and files used for storage.

How much can you remember?

1 Explain what is meant by the terms 'software' and 'hardware'.
2 What will a business consider before choosing a computer system, and why?
3 Briefly explain the difference between mainframe, mini and micro computers.
4 A computer has two memories: what are they called and what is the difference between them?
5 What are secondary storage devices used for?
6 What are characters referred to in computer jargon?
7 Using a diagram to illustrate your answer, explain what happens when you format a disk and why it is necessary to carry out this process.
8 What is the difference between a hard disk and a floppy disk?
9 Why is the use of computers in business becoming so popular?

Parts of a computer system

Just as we humans cannot function without a brain, neither can a computer. The 'brain' of the computer is known as a central processing unit (CPU). The CPU enables a computer to carry out the instructions of a program. All the other parts of a computer system which are attached to the CPU are called peripherals – for example, the keyboard, visual display unit (VDU), disk drive and printer.

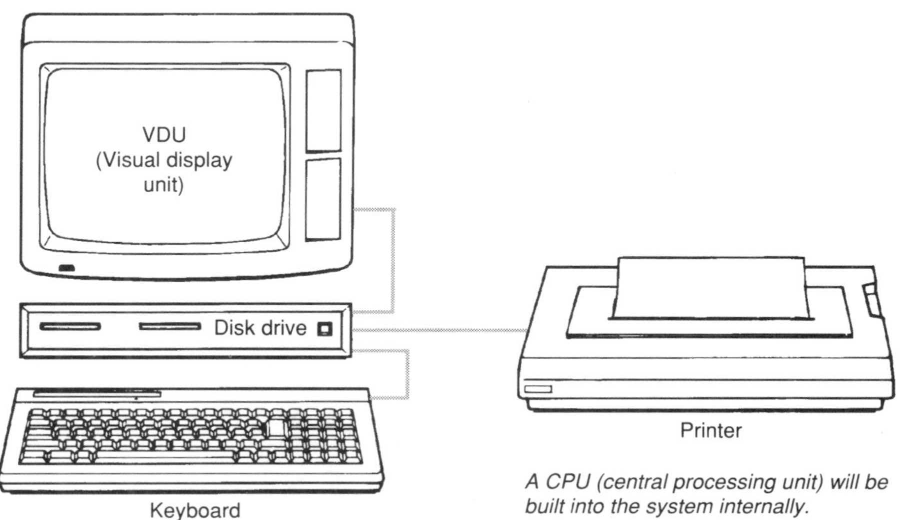

A CPU (central processing unit) will be built into the system internally.

Parts of a computer system

Each computer system requires some way of inputting text and the most common is the QWERTY keyboard, which is similar to a typewriter keyboard, except that it has additional function/command keys. Another common input device is a mouse.

When information is put into the computer it appears on the VDU (or monitor, as it is sometimes called). Most modern systems come with colour monitors as many organisations use computers for graphic design and desk top publishing, for which a colour screen is very useful.

There are various types of disk drive, but the one most commonly used is one which will accommodate floppy disks. These can be single or double sided, but the single-sided drives can only access one side of the disk while double-sided drives can access both, thus enabling more information to be stored. Larger organisations may make use of fixed or exchangeable hard disks.

Printers

Most users require a printed (hard) copy of their work and there are printers on the market to suit different needs and all pockets. Before buying a printer, a business will consider:

- *Output:* Choice will depend on the type of work the business carries out. The output required may be text, graphs, charts or figures.
- *Speed:* A slow printer will be of little use when a large amount of information has to be printed out in a limited time.
- *Quality:* Business correspondence will need to be of a much better quality than internal data processing.
- *Cost:* The latest printers are very fast and offer excellent quality output, but are very expensive. Some printers are very cheap but do not offer the same quality or speed as the more expensive models. Some models have the additional facility of colour printing.

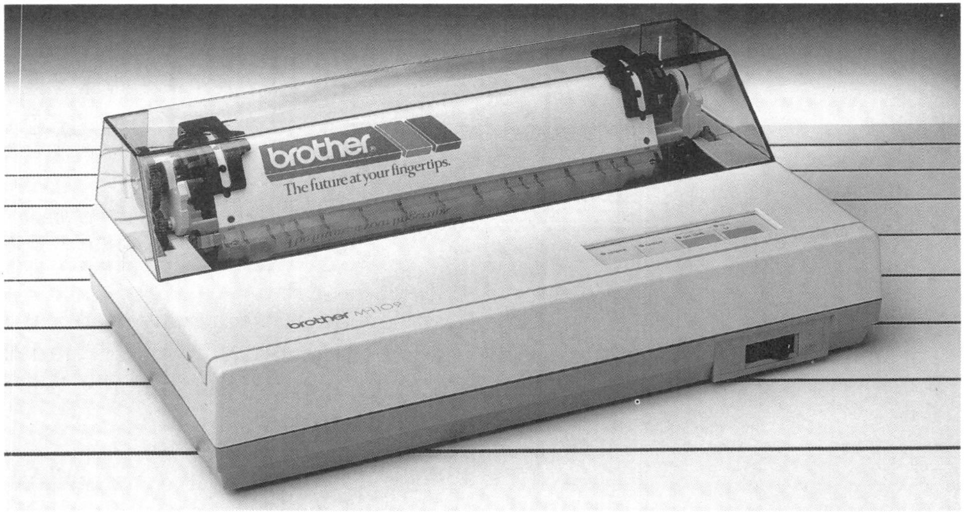

Printer

Printers fall into two main groups: impact and non-impact.

Impact printers

With impact printers, the printhead strikes the ink ribbon to make the impression of a character on the paper, like a typewriter; consequently, they are noisy. Examples of this type of printer are the dot matrix and the daisy wheel.

Each character printed by a dot matrix printer is made up of dots formed by a series of steel pins. The greater the number of steel pins, the better the quality of type (the dots are closer together), and the more expensive the printer (see illustration at the top of the next page).

Dot matrix letters

Some models are fairly cheap and do not offer particularly good quality print, but they are ideal for internal data processing. The more expensive models, however, offer near letter quality (NLQ) work and are used for business correspondence. This type of printer is fast and prints both uni-directionally (left to right only) and bi-directionally (left to right and then right to left) and it is ideal for producing graphics as well as text. More expensive models offer a black and multi-colour facility.

The daisy wheel printer produces excellent quality print similar to a typewriter and it is used for the production of text-based documents as it is not suitable for graphics. It is slower than most printers, but much faster than a typist. It prints uni-directionally and can be fairly expensive.

Non-impact printers

With non-impact printers, no pressure is placed on the ink ribbon to form the characters and therefore this type of printer is very quiet. Its main disadvantage is that carbon copies cannot be produced as there is no pressure applied to the paper. An example of a non-impact printer is a laser printer. This is the ultimate in technology. It is a quiet printer suitable for text and drawings and, although expensive, offers speed together with superb quality print. The output from a laser printer has a really professional look about it.

Paper handling

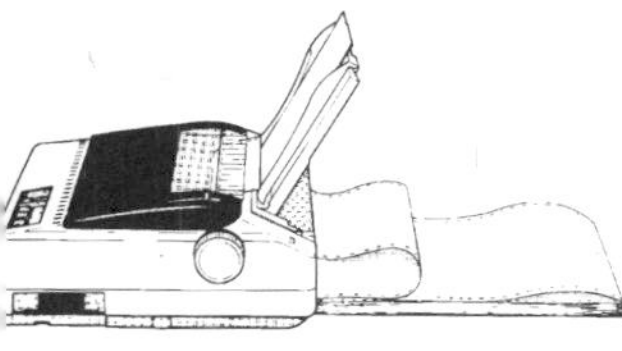

Continuous stationery

Many printers use continuous stationery, which saves time inserting and removing paper. A tractor mechanism feeds the paper through the printer and once printing has been completed the edges of the paper containing the punched holes can be peeled away. Continuous stationery is most suitable for internal data processing as it is cheap and convenient to use. For business correspondence and other A4-type documents each continuous roll is separated into page lengths and is referred to as fanfold paper.

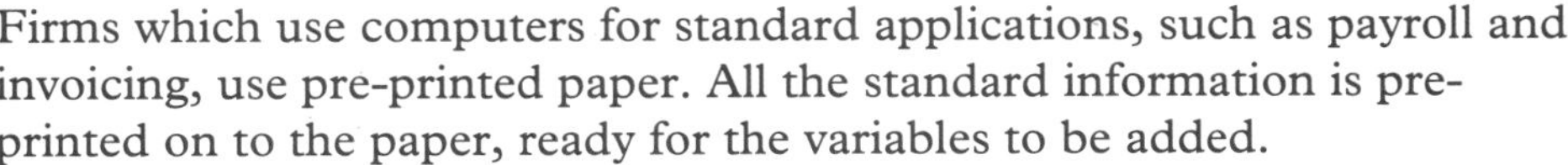

Firms which use computers for standard applications, such as payroll and invoicing, use pre-printed paper. All the standard information is pre-printed on to the paper, ready for the variables to be added.

Cut sheet

Cut sheet refers to individual sheets of paper. When single sheets of paper are being used each sheet has to be fed into the printer separately. To speed the process up a cut sheet feeder can be attached to the printer and this automatically feeds one piece of paper at a time into the printer. Laser printers use a cut sheet feeder that is similar to the paper trays on photocopiers.

How much can you remember?

1 What is a CPU?
2 What is meant by 'peripherals'?
3 What is the main difference between an impact and a non-impact printer?
4 What is hard copy?
5 What is continuous stationery and why is it so popular?
6 Explain what is meant by:
   (a) Fanfold paper
   (b) Cut sheet paper
   (c) Cut sheet feeder
   (d) Pre-printed paper.

Activity 4.1

Your college is considering offering a short basic introductory course to information technology (IT). It is felt that if students understand more about the theoretical aspects of IT, it will give them confidence when carrying out practical computing tasks on related courses.

task

The course starts in two weeks' time and it is to be held each Wednesday evening between 7 and 8 o'clock. You have been asked to:

(a) Make a list of topics to be covered by the course and decide how long it will take to cover these. You may wish to add to your list once you have completed this chapter.

(b) Design an advertisement for the local press which gives full details about the course, including its duration.

(c) Prepare handouts which can be used in forthcoming lessons to cover the basic points of theory for each topic on your list. Use a wide variety of resources to complete this task so that the handouts you produce are up to date, interesting, well presented and accurate.

Choosing a configuration

A configuration is the term used to describe the way in which a computer and its peripheral devices are arranged. Different configurations are described below.

Stand-alone

This system consists of a keyboard, CPU, VDU, disk drive and printer (see the illustration at the top of the next page). It is a self-contained unit and as it does not communicate with other machines it is good for confidential work. More expensive computers will have a hard disk; otherwise floppy disks will be used for storing data. The disadvantage of this system is that as one of each part has to be purchased, it is expensive. Some machines are dedicated, which means that they carry out only one type of work, for example, word processing.

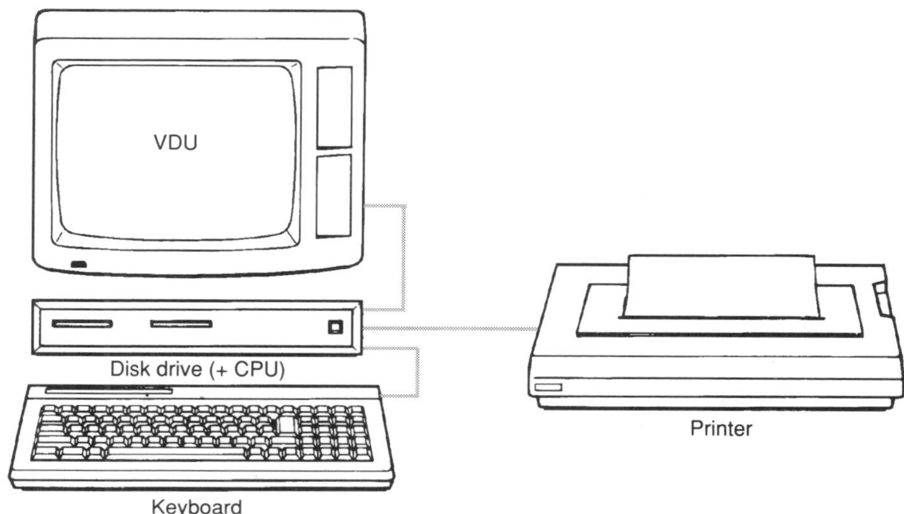

Stand-alone system

Sharing resources

This is similar to a stand-alone system except that the peripherals – for example, the disk drive, disk storage and printer – can be shared (see illustration below). This set-up is cheaper to buy than several stand-alone systems. When computers are linked together over a small area, it is called a local area network (LAN). When they are linked together over a wider area, it is known as a wide area network (WAN). To maintain confidentiality when a network system is being used, passwords are introduced to restrict access to files.

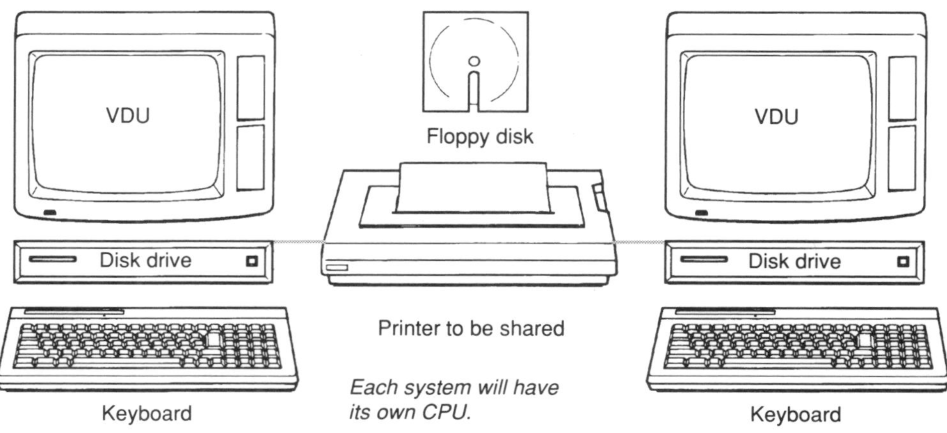

Shared resources

Terminals can also share the same CPU and this is most commonly associated with a mainframe system which uses hard disk storage and has a large CPU. When terminals share the same CPU it is referred to as shared logic. The terminals connected to the mainframe may be dumb terminals, which means that they cannot perform independently of the mainframe computer as they have no individual processing power. To reduce the cost it is common to share some of the peripherals as well as the CPU.

Remote computers can be linked to a large mainframe computer using the telephone network. This is very useful for a company which has several offices around the country which need access to the same files. If the terminals connected to the CPU are intelligent (that is, they are capable of doing a limited amount of processing themselves), the computers can also be used locally as stand-alone systems and use a floppy disk for storing word processing files etc.

Caring for equipment and materials

Computing equipment and materials can easily be damaged if proper care is not taken of them.

Floppy disks

A floppy disk can easily be damaged if it is mis-handled. Replacing it would not be too expensive – the problem may be replacing the work which was on it. Sensible users will ensure that all work is backed-up on to a second disk in case the original disk becomes damaged in any way.

A floppy disk is made of plastic which is coated with magnetic material, and, as its name suggests, it is fairly flexible. This is not true of the 3.5 inch floppy as it is encased in solid plastic and not so easily damaged, because the magnetic surface is better protected than on the 5.25 inch disk.

The magnetic surface, however, is the most sensitive part of both types of disk and if this is handled by the user, it is likely that the disk will be damaged and work lost. Similarly, if a disk is bent or left too near to radiators or other hot appliances this can also corrupt it; the same is true of electrical equipment and telephones because of the magnetic fields created by such appliances. Following the list of simple rules below will help to keep disks in good condition and avoid work being lost.

Caring for your floppy disks:

1 Do not handle the magnetic surface.
2 Keep away from radiators or other hot appliances.
3 Avoid using or storing disks near to a telephone or other electrical equipment.

4 Remove from disk drive prior to switching off the power.
5 At the end of each work session, place the disk in the correct disk sleeve and store in a protective box.
6 Do not leave disks lying around where they can become dusty.
7 Label all disks using a soft felt tip pen and never apply too much pressure.

Hard disks

Hard disks are not as easily damaged but care needs to be exercised when using them. If a hard disk is damaged then it can be very serious as not only is it expensive to repair or replace but there is likely to be a large amount of information stored on it and this may be lost. Considerable care should be taken when moving a computer which is fitted with a hard disk. If a move is really necessary, the heads of the hard drive should be parked first (a simple procedure – often you need only type the word 'park' prior to switching off the machine) and sudden jolts or bumps avoided at all cost. A sudden burst of power or a power cut can cause a hard disk to malfunction and it is wise therefore to back-up work whenever possible in case this happens.

Equipment

When equipment is not in use, it should be covered to prevent it becoming dusty. You should use anti-static cleaner for screens.

Food and drink must be kept away from computing equipment at all times, as drinks can easily be spilled and cause damage to equipment, which may be very expensive to repair or replace.

Good housekeeping

To a computer enthusiast the term good housekeeping will refer to disk maintenance. However, it can also mean much more than that. In the home, if someone is a good housekeeper, one assumes that the individual concerned puts items away after use, keeps furniture and carpets clean and dust free, the house tidy and ensures that there are adequate stocks of food, household cleaners and toiletries kept at all times.

When this term is applied to computer equipment it means much the same. Computing equipment needs to be kept clean and dust free, disks require backing up regularly and at the end of each work session they should be put away in the correct container for future retrieval. Adequate stocks of disks, cleaning materials, ribbons for printers and so on need to be kept so that materials do not run out. Good housekeeping keeps the system working well and helps to give a good quality service.

How much can you remember?

1 Explain what is meant by a computer configuration.
2 Using diagrams to illustrate your answer distinguish between a stand-alone and a shared resources system.
3 When might a lap-top or notebook PC be very useful and why?

Activity 4.2

You work in a computerised office and your manager is becoming increasingly concerned about the lack of care being exercised by staff when they handle computing equipment and materials. As a result of this carelessness, money is having to be spent repairing equipment and replacing consumables which have been damaged. You have been asked to speak to staff about this matter.

task

(a) Prepare a talk entitled 'Caring for equipment and materials' in which you are to emphasise the consequences of careless handling of equipment and materials in terms of the risk of losing work, and also the financial cost of replacement and/or repair.

(b) Give your talk to the class.

(c) Prepare an illustrated poster for the noticeboard which will support the points you made in your talk. Use the title 'Are you a good housekeeper?'

(d) Prepare a leaflet about caring for equipment and materials which can be handed out to staff.

Software applications

Word processing

Perhaps the most common software application used by businesses, schools, colleges and home workers is word processing. This refers to using a computer to input text, edit it as required and produce a hard copy. It is used mainly to produce business documents such as letters, reports and memoranda. Detailed examples of the different types of business correspondence which can be produced using a word processor are dealt with in Chapter 6. This chapter deals with word processing in a more general sense as it looks at how a word processor can manipulate text and the preferred and essential skills of word processor operators.

What is word processing?

Word processing is similar to typing but much easier. When you type a letter you will follow a procedure similar to this:

1 Put a piece of paper into the typewriter.
2 Line the paper up and set a margin.
3 Type the letter.
4 Proofread for errors.
5 Correct any errors, if the typewriter does not have a memory this will involve erasing or using correcting fluid.
6 Remove from the typewriter and present it to the author for approval and signature.
7 If incorrect in any way, retype as necessary repeating steps 1–6 as often as required.

To word process a letter you will follow a similar procedure:

1 Load the software
2 The margin is set by default (automatically) with many software packages.
3 Key-in the text.
4 Proofread for errors.
5 Correct any errors before printing.
6 Print a copy and present it to the author for approval and signature.
7 If incorrect in any way, insert changes and repeat steps 4–6 as required.

As you will appreciate, the main difference between the typing and word processing procedures above is the correction of errors. Word processing a letter provides much more opportunity to check for errors before committing work to paper as all the keyed-in text is available for viewing and easily changing prior to printing.

Many typewriters also have some memory and are in a sense mini word processors. Some machines have a small window facility for displaying text and are similar to a word processor but on a much smaller scale, and therefore correction of errors can be carried out before the work is committed to paper. However, unlike a word processor, the whole document is not available at one time for proof-checking prior to printing.

Word processors offer many other advantages – for instance, if more than one copy is required you simply repeat the printing process and each copy looks like an original. Just in case you have missed an error and committed your work to paper, the file can be stored permanently on disk until you have no further use for it. Retyping a whole document becomes a thing of the past.

Word processing allows the user to manipulate text in many ways. Some common word processing terms and their meanings are:

Cut and paste is when a piece of text is moved to a different part of the document, or sometimes into a different file.
Emboldening is a command which is given so that when a document is committed to paper, the print heads will strike certain words/letters twice to make them stand out.

> **This sentence has been emboldened.**
> This sentence has not been emboldened.

Justified is when all lines end at the same point. The computer automatically inserts extra spaces across the width of the line to ensure that this happens.
Merging enables files to be joined together. Mailmerging allows addresses which are kept in one file to be merged with a standard letter in another file. This reduces the need for repetitive typing.
Search and replace instructs the computer to search through text looking for specific words/phrases giving the user the opportunity to change them if necessary – for example, change 'computer' to 'word processor'.
Word wrap allows the user to keep typing at the end of each line. When the line is full the computer carries the next word forward to a new line.

Word processor operators

The most significant part of a word processor's job is to key text into a computer, and therefore keyboarding skills are essential. Without them it would take too long to produce the quantity of work that many organisations have to deal with each day. However, it is of little use putting text into a computer quickly if it is not done accurately and checked carefully before printing. Accurate proofreading, therefore, is just as important as keyboarding skills and to fulfil this part of the job an operator needs to have good language skills. Many programs have the added facility of a spell check and although this makes the task of checking for spelling errors a little easier it should not be relied upon to replace spelling and language skills.

Word processing is about following instructions and being able to use the commands and facilities of the program to produce work which is both accurate and well displayed. These are additional qualities which any good word processor should possess.

Databases

A database refers to a store of information which can be kept in a manual or electronic system. The advantage of using a computer database is that it can access, sort and extract previously stored information in a matter of seconds. Manual and electronic systems and the ways in which they are used to store and retrieve information are dealt with in more detail in Chapter 8. However, this chapter provides a basic introduction to databases and their structure which will help you to understand the applications which are included in Chapter 8.

You will see from the illustration below that the computer represents the electronic filing cabinet. If you pull out a drawer from an office filing cabinet you will find inside it lots of files; similarly, a disk in an electronic database is equivalent to a filing cabinet drawer as it too holds lots of files.

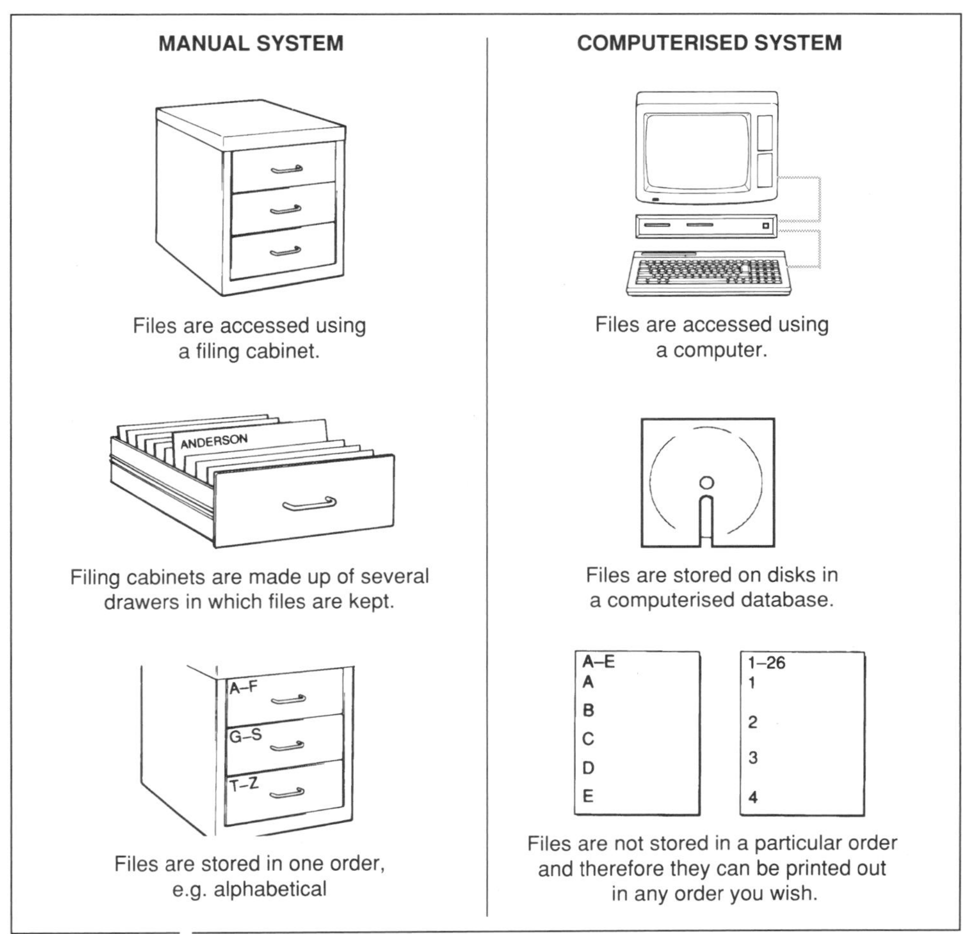

MANUAL SYSTEM
COMPUTERISED SYSTEM
Files are accessed using a filing cabinet.
Files are accessed using a computer.
ANDERSON
Filing cabinets are made up of several drawers in which files are kept.
Files are stored on disks in a computerised database.
A–F
G–S
T–Z
Files are stored in one order, e.g. alphabetical
A–E
A
B
C
D
E
1–26
1
2
3
4
Files are not stored in a particular order and therefore they can be printed out in any order you wish.

Comparison of manual and electronic databases

To create an electronic database it is necessary to understand how it is structured. It will consist of several fields and numerous records (the illustration below shows these in more detail).

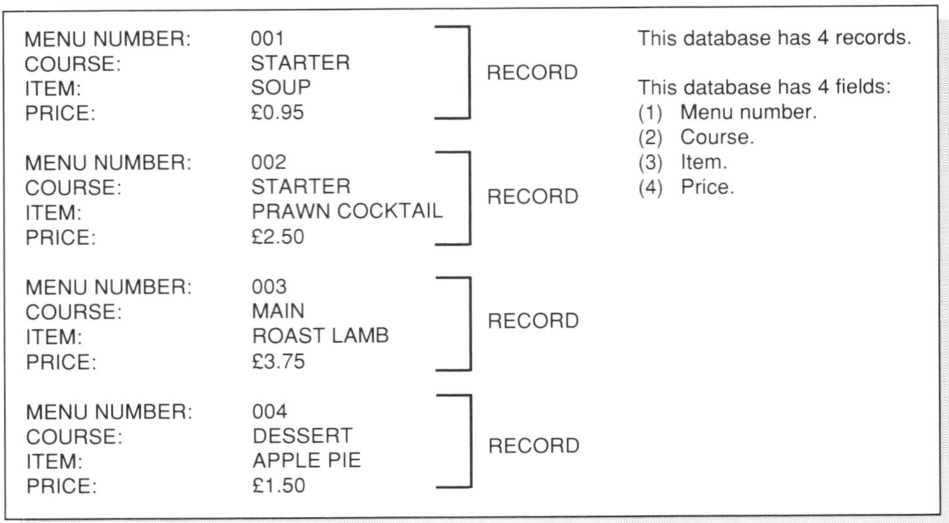

MENU NUMBER: 001
COURSE: STARTER
ITEM: SOUP
PRICE: £0.95
RECORD
MENU NUMBER: 002
COURSE: STARTER
ITEM: PRAWN COCKTAIL
PRICE: £2.50
RECORD
MENU NUMBER: 003
COURSE: MAIN
ITEM: ROAST LAMB
PRICE: £3.75
RECORD
MENU NUMBER: 004
COURSE: DESSERT
ITEM: APPLE PIE
PRICE: £1.50
RECORD
This database has 4 records.
This database has 4 fields:
(1) Menu number.
(2) Course.
(3) Item.
(4) Price.

The structure of a database

Spreadsheets

Spreadsheets are electronic worksheets which perform calculations quickly and easily. They are most commonly associated with payroll, invoice and stock applications. A simple activity is included in this chapter to demonstrate the potential of this type of program, but more realistic business applications are included in later chapters at appropriate places.

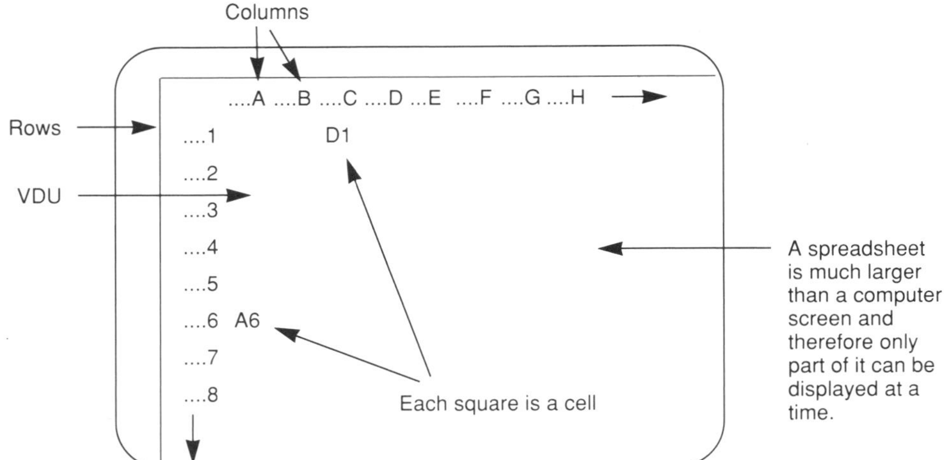

Spreadsheet

You can see from the illustration at the foot of the previous page that a spreadsheet is made up of rows and columns, each with its own heading for identification purposes. Spreadsheets are quite large and it is impossible to show the whole sheet on the screen at any one time.

Calculations which can be performed using a spreadsheet include adding, subtracting, division, multiplication, percentages and averages. Perhaps the most useful application of a spreadsheet program is for future planning – that is, 'What if' situations. For example, if a business is considering a pay rise for its employees but is not sure what overall financial effect this will have on the firm, it only takes a few seconds to feed the information into the computer and change different variables and find out. The same manual calculations will take a great deal of time. You need only change one variable and all calculations can be done automatically. Another example is if a supplier notifies a firm that it intends to increase prices by 5 per cent. The buyer can experiment using a spreadsheet to determine whether or not it needs to increase its prices to consumers or if it can afford to absorb the price increase or part of it in its costs. If just one figure is to be changed, this can be keyed in and all the subsequent calculations done automatically.

Desk-top publishing

DTP is a professional way of presenting documents using a variety of fonts (typefaces) and it has the added facility of integrating pictures and text. It is ideal for newspapers, posters and any application which comprises text, pictures or both and which requires a professional looking finish. This form of reproducing material is widely used by printing firms and publishers. It is becoming increasingly common for firms and educational establishments to use it to produce their own booklets, prospectuses and brochures rather than going to external agencies.

How much can you remember?

1 What is word processing?
2 Make a list of both essential and preferable skills which a word processor operator should possess.
3 What is a database?
4 Using a diagram explain why a spreadsheet is like an electronic calculator.

Activity 4.3 TEST YOUR SPEED AND ACCURACY

task 1 See how quickly you can key-in to a word processor the following passages.

Passage 1
Once you learn one word processing system, you can easily transfer your skills and learn another. Although each system has different commands, they all offer similar facilities for manipulating text. A good word processor will be able to key-in text quickly and proofread accurately, just like you should be doing now. If errors are not spotted prior to printing then paper is wasted and therefore checking work on the screen is a very important skill.

Passage 2
There are many different printers on the market. Some of them offer superb quality printouts while others, usually the cheaper models, are more suitable for internal work only. Printers which are used for internal data processing do not need to produce high-quality work, but those which are used for business correspondence must produce good-quality printouts. When a firm sends a letter out it is advertising its business – if a letter is poorly presented and contains lots of errors it will create a very bad impression of the firm.

task 2 TEST YOUR PROOFREADING SKILLS

See how accurately you can proofread the following passages.

Passage 1
New techology is being used far more freqently in the office than ever before. Computer operators requires new skills as more and more software become avialable. Although many peopple are under the imppression that we are fast aproaching the paperless office, I firmly beleive that this is some way off. It is intresting to note the quanty of paper which is acummulated by firms which use computers for large amounts of work.

Passage 2
Desk top publishing is a very immpresive peice of software and it is becoming increesingly popular. With it's facillity to intergrate text and illustratins, its a most useful facility to have. Many schools; collages and business establishments are printing there own in-house magazines and Posters. This is saving them a great deal of money by not having to use outside proffesional printing Firms.

Activity 4.4

task

CREATING AND INTERROGATING A SIMPLE DATABASE

This task is designed to provide an introduction to setting up and interrogating a simple database.

(a) Using software available to you, collect the necessary information (as detailed below) from colleagues in your class and create a database, using the format given:

Filename:	CLASS
Number of fields:	8
Number of records:	(Number of students in class)

Details of Fields:

LASTNAME:	Last name
FIRSTNAME:	First name
ADD1:	First line of address
ADD2:	Second line of address
ADD3:	TOWN
PCODE:	Postcode
TEL:	Telephone number
DOB:	Date of birth XX.YY.ZZ

(b) Interrogate your database using the sort facility. Some suggested sort tasks are:

(i) In alphabetical order of last name.
(ii) In DOB descending order.
(iii) In DOB ascending order.

(c) Information can be extracted from a database using the search facility. Some suggested searches are given below, but these will require adapting to suit your database:

(i) Produce a list of everyone under/over 18.
(ii) Print a list of student names and telephone numbers.
(iii) Produce a list of everyone who lives in area 'X'.

(d) Information in a database can be changed, added to or deleted:

(i) Add three extra records to your database.
(ii) Delete two records from your database.
(iii) Change one address and telephone number.

Activity 4.5 CREATING AND USING A SPREADSHEET TO PERFORM BASIC CALCULATIONS

task

(a) Using the format given in the example below insert the details into your spreadsheet program and then calculate:
- (i) The total mark for each student.
- (ii) The average mark for each student.
- (iii) The average mark for each examination.

	.......A	.......B	C	.......D	.......E	.......F	.......G
.......1	EXAM	RESULTS					
.......2	STUDENT						
.......3	STUDENT	EXAM 1	EXAM 2	EXAM 3	EXAM 4	TOTAL	AVERAGE
.......4							
.......5	Adams	84	61	72	40		
.......6	Smith	67	51	74	72		
.......7	Finch	74	64	81	90		
.......8	Harris	61	69	42	53		
.......9	Cook	41	39	45	36		
.....10		------	------	------	------	------	------
.....11	AVERAGE						
.....12	MARK						
.....13							

(b) Using the format given below, insert the details and then calculate:
- (i) The total amount spent on each household item.
- (ii) The estimated amount to be spent on each household item next year assuming an increase of 6 per cent.
- (iii) The total expenditure for each month.
- (iv) The total expenditure for each month next year, assuming an increase of 6 per cent.

	.......A	.......B	C	.......D	.......E	.......F	.......G
.......1	BUDGET						
.......2							
.......3	ITEM	JAN	FEB	MAR	APR	TOTAL	TOTAL + 6%
.......4							
.......5	Rent	160	160	160	160		
.......6	Rates	30	30	30	30		
.......7	Gas	54	38	23	12		
.......8	Water	18	18	0	20		
.......9	Coal	88	67	54	23		
.....10		------	------	------	------	------	------
.....11	TOTAL						
.....12	TOTAL + 6%						
.....13							

Chapter 5 Legislation and workers

By the end of this chapter you should be able to explain:

- that there are a number of Acts in force relating to employment
- the effect of European directives and regulations on UK law
- the role of industrial tribunals
- the reason for contracts of employment
- the complexity of the law and trade unions
- the implications for employers and employees as a result of health and safety legislation
- the need to include new technology in current health and safety legislation
- the rights of non-smokers at work
- the purpose of the Data Protection Act.

The law relating to employment

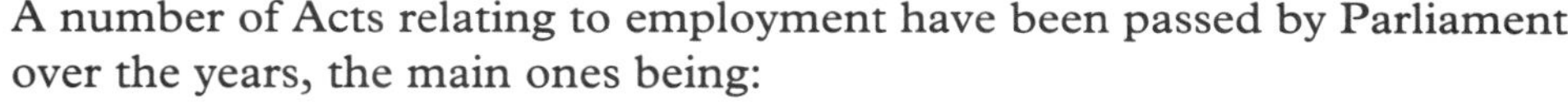

A number of Acts relating to employment have been passed by Parliament over the years, the main ones being:

- Employment Protection (Consolidation) Act of 1978
- Trade Union and Labour Relations (Consolidation) Act 1992
- Trade Union Reform and Employment Rights Act 1993.

The latter gives employment rights to many more workers, such as part-time employees, who were not covered by previous Acts, and makes further reforms of the law relating to trade unions and industrial relations. It also amends the law relating to employment rights and abolishes the right to statutory minimum remuneration. Some of the main areas covered by this Act are given below, together with an example of one of the requirements specified in each area.

Trade unions:

- Ballots – for example, in relation to election and political fund ballots, an independent person must be appointed to store and distribute the voting papers and count the votes cast in the ballot.
- Financial affairs – for example, the Annual Return must contain additional information such as details of salary paid to each member of the executive, the president and the general secretary.
- Rights in relation to union membership – for example, the right not to be excluded or expelled from a trade union unless the member does not satisfy an enforceable membership requirement contained in the union rules, such as employment in a specified trade/industry/profession.
- The organisation of industrial action – for example, the requirement for a postal ballot where voters are sent a voting paper to their home address and given the opportunity to vote by post.

Employment:

- ❍ Maternity rights.
- ❍ Right to written particulars of employment.
- ❍ Right to itemised pay statement.
- ❍ Industrial tribunals.
- ❍ Employment protection in health and safety cases.

The Acts referred to are far too lengthy and complex to deal with in entirety in a book of this nature, however, some key areas which relate to office workers are dealt with to provide a general background knowledge of employment legislation.

Legislation in the UK

In addition to the law of the land, the UK as a member state of the European Community, has agreed to conform with Community law. The Council of Ministers in Europe, a decision-making body comprising of ministers from the government of each member state, issues regulations and directives. Regulations are binding without ratification; in other words, they must be recognised by the courts of member states. Directives do not automatically become law, they have to be incorporated into national law within a prescribed time limit. Where there is conflict between the two laws, Community law prevails.

Industrial tribunals

Industrial tribunals were set up by Parliament around the country to resolve disputes relating to employment such as claims for redundancy payments, equal pay and complaints of unfair dismissal. They are made up of three members: a legal chairperson (who must be either a barrister or solicitor with at least seven years' experience), a representative for the employee and one for the employer. If an applicant is not legally represented, the chairperson will assist him or her.

It is much cheaper for a case to be heard by an industrial tribunal than in the ordinary courts as the procedure is more informal, much simpler and quicker. The Trade Union Reform and Employment Rights Act has amended the constitution of industrial tribunals so as to permit an industrial tribunal chairperson to sit alone without lay members in a wider number of circumstances. It has also extended the jurisdiction of industrial tribunals to complaints about breach of contract of employment.

Contract of employment

A job is advertised in some way, an interview takes place, the main terms of employment are explained, an offer of a job is made and at the point where the offer is accepted a contract exists even though it is not in written form.

Once you become an employee you have a contract of employment with your employer: you provide working skills for which the employer pays a wage or salary. There is no legislation which enforces employers to supply employees with a written contract of employment, but since 1963 there has been a statutory requirement for employers to set out a summary of the terms of employment in a written statement to be received by the employee within 13 weeks of starting work, but at that time some employees were not included in this legislation.

This area of employment law has now been updated by the Trade Union Reform and Employment Rights Act 1993 which gives every employee who works eight hours or more a week, and whose employment lasts for at least a month, the right within two months of starting work, to a written statement of his or her main terms and conditions, including details of entitlement to pay, hours and holidays.

The terms of employment do not necessarily have to be all contained in one document, the employee may be referred to other sources such as a disciplinary procedures booklet. The details which must be written down are given on page 82.

In the event of a dispute where an employer has not put the terms of employment into a written statement, the employee is entitled to refer the matter to an industrial tribunal.

Paying employees

There are specific requirements with regard to the payment of workers. An employee should be able to calculate how his or her net pay has been arrived at, and so employers must provide a payslip which itemises gross and net pay, together with details of any deductions made. The Trade Union Reform and Employment Rights Act removes the qualifying period of five years which relates to employees working between eight and sixteen hours per week, except for employers who employ fewer than 20 workers.

The Equal Pay Act of 1970 specifies that where men and women are doing the same or similar work, they should be paid the same wage. This Act is quite complex and it is not always easy to establish whether a man and a woman are actually doing the 'same/similar work' or work of 'equal value', as it is stipulated in the Equal Pay (Amendment) Regulations 1983.

The statement of terms and conditions will have to cover:

- the names of the employer and the employee
- the date when the employment (and the period of continuous employment) began
- remuneration and the intervals at which it is to be paid
- hours of work
- holiday entitlement
- sickness entitlement
- pensions and pension schemes
- notice entitlement
- job title or a brief job description
- where it is not permanent, the period for which the employment is expected to continue or, if it is for a fixed term, the date when it is to end
- either the place of work or, if the employee is required or allowed to work in more than one location, an indication of this and of the employer's address
- details of the existence of any relevant collective agreements which directly affect the terms and conditions of the employee's employment – including, where the employer is not a party, the persons by whom they were made.

If an employee is normally employed in the UK but will be required to work abroad for the same employer for a period of more than one month, the statement must also cover:

- the period for which the employment abroad is to last
- the currency in which the employee is to be paid
- any additional pay or benefits
- terms relating to the employee's return to the UK.

Where there are no particulars to be given for any of the items covered in the statement, this will have to be indicated.

The statement will have to include, in addition, a note containing details of the employer's disciplinary and (except in firms with fewer than 20 employees) grievance procedures, and stating whether or not a pensions contracting-out certificate is in force for the employment in question.

The contents of a terms and conditions statement

Source: Dept of Employment Guide to Industrial Relations and Employment Law Provisions.

Sex Discrimination Act 1975

This Act makes it unlawful to discriminate against a person on grounds of sex in relation to education, recruitment, provision of housing (including right to obtain a mortgage), promotion and training.

When advertising a job it is illegal to word an advert in such a way that it discriminates against a person because of his or her sex.

Race Relations Act 1976

The terms of this Act are similar to those laid down in the Sex Discrimination Act. You cannot discriminate against a person because of his or her colour, race or creed, or ethnic or national origin.

Pregnancy

Until the Trade Union Reform and Employment Rights Act there was no statutory right to maternity leave but women who met certain qualifying conditions had the right to return to work after a period of maternity absence. New legislation has now changed this situation and the following information taken from the Act explains the new rights.

WHEN THESE PROVISIONS TAKE EFFECT, all pregnant employees, regardless of their length of service or hours of work, will have a right:

- to take a period of 14 weeks' maternity leave;
- to benefit during that period from all their normal terms and conditions of employment, except for wages and salary; and
- to be offered a suitable alternative vacancy, where available, if they would otherwise have to be made redundant at any point during that period.

In addition, employees who meet the established qualifying conditions described above will still have the right to return to work following a longer period of maternity absence, lasting from the end of the maternity leave period until 29 weeks after the week of childbirth. The same protection as previously will apply in relation to a redundancy situation arising at the point when the woman seeks to exercise this right.

****

In order to exercise her maternity right at least 21 days before she begins her leave, or as soon as practicable, a woman must give her employer:

(a) Written notice of the fact that she is pregnant and of the expected week of childbirth which must be confirmed with a medical certificate if requested by the employer.

(b) Notice, if requested by the employer, of the date when she intends to begin her leave which may be no earlier than the beginning of the eleventh week before the expected week of childbirth. However, if the child is born early, the maternity begins on the date of the birth even if this is prior to the eleventh week.

Extract explaining new maternity rights

Source: Dept of Employment Guide to Industrial Relations and Employment Law Provisions.

Redundancy

In order to compensate redundant workers upon losing their jobs a redundancy payments scheme was introduced in 1965, but this does not cover all workers. The amount of the redundancy payment varies depending on the age of the employee and his or her length of service from the age of 18. Redundancy payments are not taxable but any accrued holiday pay is. To make an employee redundant, an employer must show that either the labour the employee is doing is no longer required or that fewer workers are required for a particular task. The definition of redundancy for consultation purposes has now been widened to include any dismissals for reasons not related to the individual so that it now reflects the wording of the EC Directive on Collective Redundancies. An extract from the Act to clarify this new definition is given below. The changes will not affect redundancy payments.

Definition of redundancy for consultation purposes

> The existing definition is basically dismissal because there is no longer work for the employees to do or because the employer needs fewer workers for a particular task or ceased to carry on business. The new definition is dismissal for any reason not related to the individual workers concerned. This reflects the wording of the EC Collective Redundancies Directive.
>
> The main 'reason not related to the individual' would still be redundancy because of lack of work. But there might be other circumstances where an employer was considering dismissing employees, for example if there were a reorganisation or reallocation of duties which did not result in there being a diminution in the needs of the business for workers to carry out work of a particular kind. In this case the new definition makes clear that the employer would have to consult recognised trade unions in accordance with the Directive.

Source: Dept of Employment Guide to Industrial Relations and Employment Law Provisions.

Unfair dismissal

The Industrial Relations Act of 1971 introduced legislation covering unfair dismissal. Until that time the only obligations placed on employers were that they had to give an employee notice and pay any redundancy payment due.

Nowadays, an employer must be able to justify any dismissal to an industrial tribunal if necessary. If after hearing both sides, a tribunal decides a dismissal was unfair, an employer may have to pay compensation to the employee or re-employ him or her.

A woman cannot be dismissed on the grounds of pregnancy. Also, where an employee would have been suspended from work for health and safety reasons on maternity grounds, suitable alternative work (if available) must be offered and an employee who is suspended must be paid during her suspension.

Trade unions

The law on trade unions is quite complex. Much of the Trade Union Reform and Employment Rights Act 1993 deals with this subject. Details of some of the areas covered by this Act are given at the beginning of this chapter.

Employees have a legal right to join or not to join a trade union, and it is unlawful for anyone to interfere with this right. The only time individuals may be excluded or expelled from a trade union is when there is a permitted reason – for example, union rules restrict membership to workers employed in a specific trade or industry or a specialised skill.

When a trade union is recognised by an employer, union officials must be given time off work for union duties and activities.

Picketing when on strike is legal only when an employee does so peacefully outside his or her own workplace. Secondary picketing – when an employee from one workplace pickets outside another workplace – is now illegal.

How much can you remember?

1 How does being a member of the European Community affect the UK in relation to the law?
2 What is the legal position in relation to written particulars of employment and what does this document contain?
3 What is an industrial tribunal?
4 List and explain briefly the Acts which relate to employment legislation.

Activity 5.1 SUGGESTED ASSIGNMENTS/ESSAYS

1 Investigate and comment on the implications employment legislation has on any business.
2 It is essential that workers are fully protected by the law – investigate and discuss.

Union march

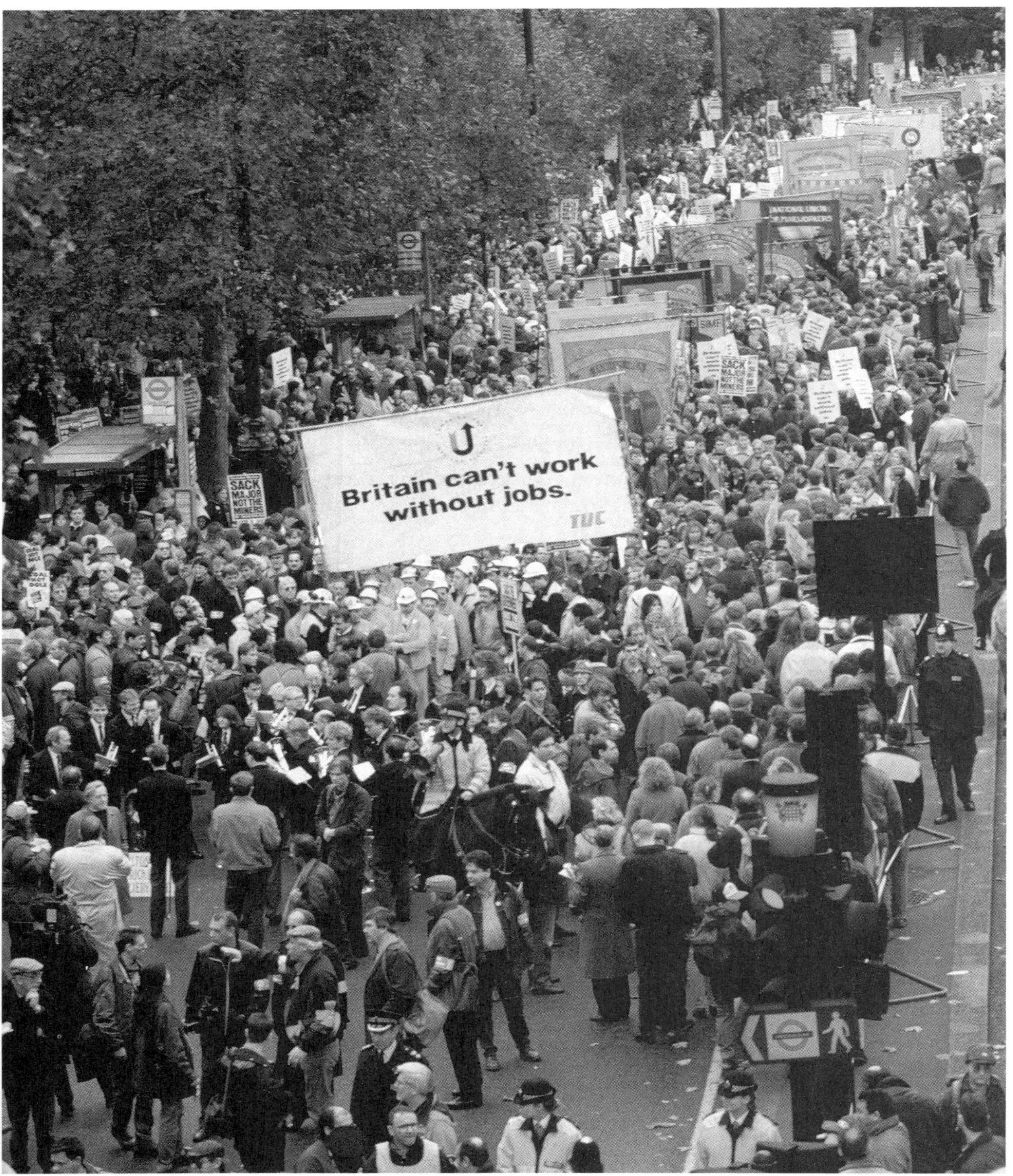
Britain can't work
without jobs.
TUC
SACK
MAJOR
NOT THE
MINERS

Activity 5.2

task 1

1 Describe three situations in which you would consider the dismissal of an employee to be unfair.
2 Describe three situations in which you would consider the dismissal of an employee to be fair.

task 2

In a group of three set up either as:

- an industrial tribunal (Group A), or
- a group of employees who have been dismissed and have decided to make a case for unfair dismissal (Group B).

To complete task 3 each Group A will need to pair up with a Group B.

Group(s) A – industrial tribunal(s):
(a) Decide who will be the legal chairperson and who will represent the employee and the employer.

(b) You will hear three cases on which you must decide whether the dismissal was unfair or not. When each case begins listen carefully to the circumstances, ask sensible questions and then reach a decision which must be by majority vote.

Group(s) B – dismissed employee(s):
In task 1 you each suggested six situations, three of which you considered could be justified as unfair dismissal and three which couldn't. Each member of the group should choose one suggestion from either category and prepare a case to put before an industrial tribunal (Group A).

task 3

Carry out the role-play exercise – each industrial tribunal will hear three cases and reach a decision by majority vote.

task 4

As a class discuss the situations and decisions made.

Health and safety at work

The health and safety of employees is protected by law and employers have a legal duty to protect their employees and to keep them informed about health and safety matters. Where there are five or more employees, employers have to put these arrangements in writing. However, it is not only employers who have responsibilities, employees are expected to take good care of themselves and ensure that no one gets injured because of their actions.

Whenever an accident occurs it is important to record accurate details of it as soon as possible, in case there is later a dispute or claim by the employee for compensation. A special accident report form or book will be provided by the organisation for this purpose. The information recorded will include: the date and time of the accident, the cause, details of injuries sustained and any treatment required. This information will be kept for future reference.

In 1963 the Offices, Shops and Railway Premises Act was passed to try to improve the working conditions for employees. Minimum standards were specified and employers were required to provide a safe and healthy working environment for their employees. The minimum standards related to:

- the amount of space per worker
- the provision of clean, well-lit and well-ventilated premises
- a comfortable working temperature
- the provision of drinking water, toilets and washing facilities
- the provision of safe machinery with adequate supervision and proper instruction on its use for staff.

This Act did not apply to schools and colleges and it was not until 1974 when the Health and Safety at Work Act came into force that staff who worked in these establishments were covered.

In January 1993, new Health and Safety at Work Regulations which reflect the European Community directives on health and safety came into force and these apply to almost all kinds of work activity in Great Britain and offshore. While the more modern law has been kept, these regulations update or replace out-of-date health and safety issues and include some new legislation.

The new regulations cover six important areas:

- health and safety management
- work equipment safety
- manual handling of loads
- workplace conditions
- personal protective equipment
- display screen equipment.

An extract from the new regulations, relating to workplace conditions is given below.

Workplace (Health, Safety and Welfare) Regulations 1992

These regulations too will tidy up a lot of existing requirements. In fact they will replace a total of 38 pieces of the old law, including parts of the Factories Act 1961 and the Offices, Shops and Railway Premises Act 1963. They will be much easier to understand, making it clearer what is expected of you.

The regulations will cover many aspects of health, safety and welfare in the workplace. Some of them are not explicitly mentioned in the current law though they are implied in the general duties of the HSW Act. The regulations will apply to all places of work except:

- means of transport;
- construction sites; and
- sites where extraction of mineral resources or exploration for them is carried out.

Workplaces on agricultural or forestry land away from main buildings will also be exempt from most requirements. Only the requirements on toilets, washing facilities and drinking water will apply. The regulations will set general requirements in four broad areas:

Working environment

- temperature in indoor workplaces
- ventilation
- lighting including emergency lighting
- room dimensions and space
- suitability of workstations and seating

Safety

- safe passage of pedestrians and vehicles, eg traffic routes, must be wide enough and marked where necessary, and there must be enough of them
- windows and skylights (safe opening, closing and cleaning)
- transparent and translucent doors and partitions (use of safety material and marking)
- doors, gates and escalators (safety devices)
- floors (construction and maintenance, obstructions and slipping and tripping hazards)
- falling a distance and into dangerous substances
- falling objects

Facilities

- toilets
- washing, eating and changing facilities
- clothing storage
- drinking water
- rest areas (and arrangements to protect people from the discomfort of tobacco smoke)
- rest facilities for pregnant women and nursing mothers

Housekeeping

- maintenance of workplace, equipment and facilities
- cleanliness
- removal of waste materials

You will have to make sure that any workplace within your control complies with the regulations. For existing workplaces you will have until 1996 to do so. Other people connected with the workplace – such as the owner of a building which is leased to one or more employers or self-employed people – will also have to make sure that requirements falling within their control are satisfied.

The regulations will be supported by an Approved Code of Practice.

A separate booklet giving more information on these regulations is due to be issued towards the end of 1992.

Display screen equipment

The legislation introduced for display screen equipment is new and does not replace old law. As it is such an important area of office work, it is dealt with in this chapter in some detail. Although working at a display screen is not considered to be a high risk, it is acknowledged that it can lead to muscular and other physical problems, for example, backache and tired eyes.

Under the new regulations, employers will have duties to:

- Assess display screen equipment workstations and reduce risks that are discovered.
- Make sure that workstations satisfy minimum requirements which are set for: the display screen itself, keyboard, desk and chair, working environment and task design and software.
- Plan display screen equipment work so that there are breaks or changes of activity.
- Provide information and training for display screen equipment users.

The regulations also state that 'Display screen equipment users will be entitled to appropriate eyesight tests by an optician or doctor and to special spectacles if they are needed and normal ones cannot be used. It will be the employer's responsibility to provide tests and special spectacles if needed.'

There are numerous suggestions as to the cause of the physical problems associated with the use of VDUs, some of which are:

- inadequate ventilation
- badly designed workstation
- working for long periods of time without a break.

A number of recommendations have been made which if implemented may help to alleviate and prevent some of the health problems from which VDU operators suffer and generally provide a much more comfortable working atmosphere.

Glare can be greatly reduced by decorating rooms in pastel colours with a matt finish and fitting blinds or an anti-glare surface to windows. However, it is not only glare which helps to induce a headache – noise can be a problem also and acoustic ceiling tiles cushion noise from printers. In addition, if an impact printer has to be located in the same room as an operator, it can be fitted with an acoustic hood which makes it much quieter.

Static can present problems for the VDU user and also cause the computer to malfunction. Fitting a room with an anti-static carpet and cleaning screens with an anti-static cleaner will help to prevent it building up.

Furniture must be chosen very carefully. Desks at the wrong height for an employee can be very uncomfortable. Two important features to check when choosing a desk are that there is an adequate amount of space underneath for legs and that the height is at a comfortable working level. Chairs are equally important and an adjustable backrest will help to prevent the worker suffering from backache.

If you look closely at any computer system you will see that the screen and keyboard are detached or that the screen will move independently of the drive to which it is attached. This is so that the VDU can be manipulated to suit individual requirements. Modern screens have adjustable controls for brightness and come in colours which are particularly restful for the eyes. Keyboards have a matt finish and a gentle slope, this is quite different from the old typewriters which had steep sloping keyboards and made typing for long periods very uncomfortable on the wrists.

It will be of little use buying equipment and furniture to help reduce health problems for workers if special attention is not given to the layout of a room. Even though windows can be fitted with blinds to protect workers from some glare it is still sensible to position a screen away from a window to remove the glare altogether.

Last, but most important of all, is the operator. Although there is no medical evidence to prove that the use of a VDU has a long-term effect on either eyes or eyesight, it is acknowledged that VDU users do suffer from eye fatigue. Many firms even prior to the new regulations operated a system whereby operators have frequent breaks away from the VDU, thus reducing the risk of eye strain.

Overleaf is an extract taken from the Health and Safety Executive 'Working with VDUs' and it gives advice on how you can help yourself if you are working at a VDU.

Employers have until the end of 1996 to upgrade existing equipment but new equipment being used for the first time must comply with the new regulations immediately.

Adjusting your workstation to suit you

WHAT CAN I DO TO HELP MYSELF?

Lots! You should make full use of the adjustment facilities for your VDU and work environment to get the best from them and avoid potential health problems. If the Regulations apply to you, your employer must cover these things in training. If the Regulations don't apply to you, using these facilities is still important. Here are some specific tips.

- Adjust your chair and VDU to find the most comfortable position for your work. As a broad guide, your arms should be approximately horizontal and your eyes at the same height as the top of the VDU casing.
- Make sure there is enough space underneath your desk to move your legs freely. Move any obstacles such as boxes or equipment.
- Avoid excess pressure on the backs of your legs and knees. A footrest, particularly for smaller users, may be helpful.
- Don't sit in the same position for long periods. Make sure you change your posture as often as practicable. Some movement is desirable, but avoid repeat stretching movements.
- Adjust your keyboard and screen to get a good keying and viewing position. A space in front of the keyboard is sometimes helpful for resting the hands and wrists while not keying.

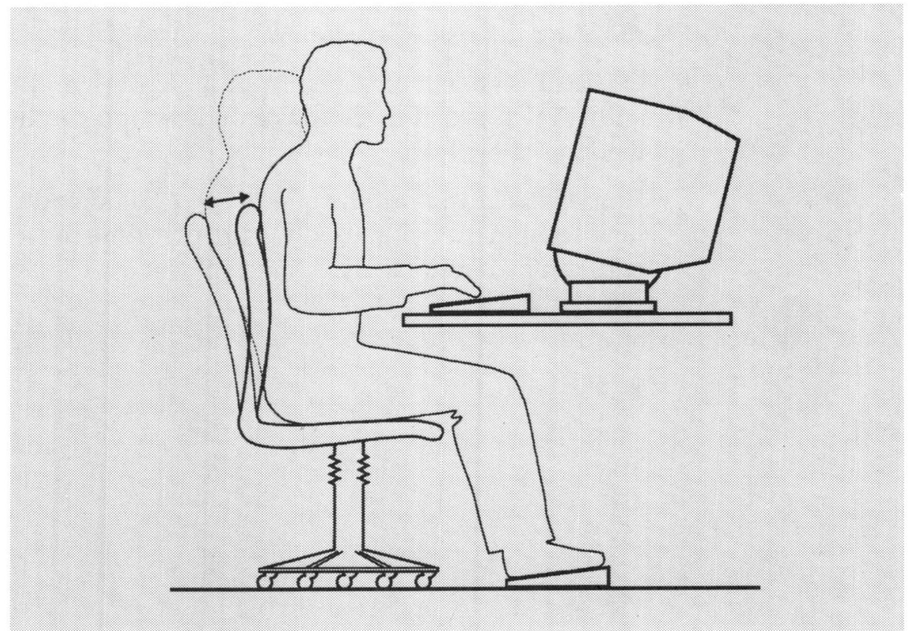

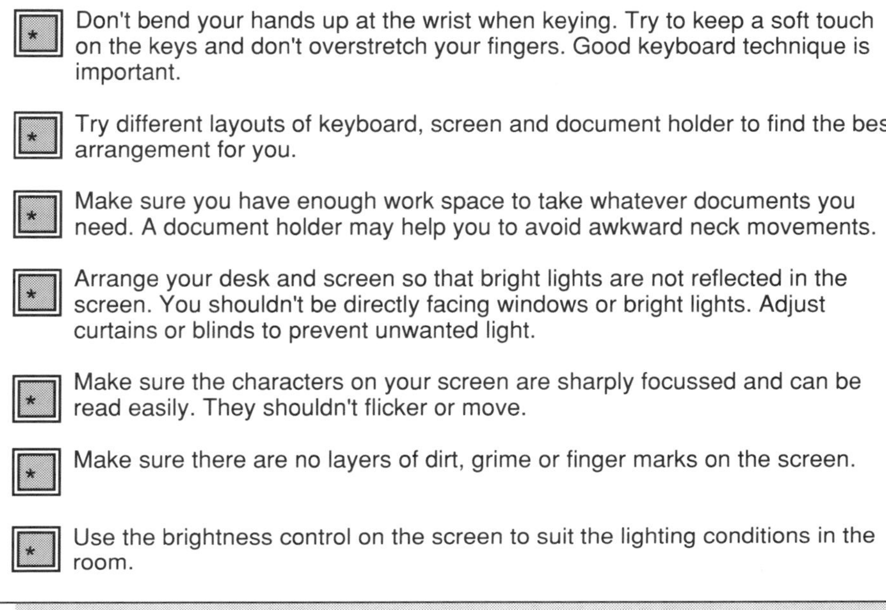

* Don't bend your hands up at the wrist when keying. Try to keep a soft touch on the keys and don't overstretch your fingers. Good keyboard technique is important.
* Try different layouts of keyboard, screen and document holder to find the best arrangement for you.
* Make sure you have enough work space to take whatever documents you need. A document holder may help you to avoid awkward neck movements.
* Arrange your desk and screen so that bright lights are not reflected in the screen. You shouldn't be directly facing windows or bright lights. Adjust curtains or blinds to prevent unwanted light.
* Make sure the characters on your screen are sharply focussed and can be read easily. They shouldn't flicker or move.
* Make sure there are no layers of dirt, grime or finger marks on the screen.
* Use the brightness control on the screen to suit the lighting conditions in the room.

Source: Health and Safety Regulations 1993.

Passive smoking

Passive smoking, particularly in the workplace, is a topic which many people feel very strongly about and it causes much concern. The new regulations recommend that all employers should introduce a policy to control smoking in the workplace following full consultation with their employees. For interest, as this affects all office workers, an extract explaining the legal situation with regard to passive smoking is shown below.

WHAT IS THE LEGAL SITUATION

Under section 2 of the Health and Safety at Work Act 1974 employers have to ensure, so far as is reasonably practicable, the health, safety and welfare at work of all their employees.

This means that if a risk to health can be demonstrated, for example if a worker with a respiratory condition is forced to work in a very smoky atmosphere which may make that condition worse, the employer must take action to deal with the risk. Health and safety inspectors can take enforcement action if necessary in these circumstances, but ultimately it would be for the courts to decide in a particular case whether the risk to health was significant.

Employers also have a common law responsibility to provide a safe place and system of work. They should act to resolve complaints from employees that their health may be at risk from a smoky environment.

Under proposed new health and safety Regulations, due to come into force in 1993 for new workplaces and in 1996 for existing workplaces, employers will have to ensure that there are arrangements to protect non-smokers from discomfort caused by tobacco smoke in rest rooms or rest areas.

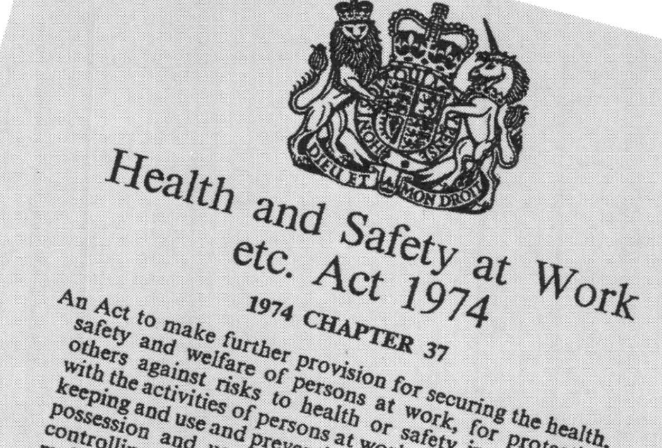

Health and Safety at Work etc. Act 1974

1974 CHAPTER 37

An Act to make further provision for securing the health, safety and welfare of persons at work, for protecti… others against risks to health or safety in … with the activities of persons at work, f… keeping and use and preventi… possession and use … controlling …

Source: Health and Safety Regulations 1993.

How much can you remember?

1 Outline the main areas covered by the 1963 Offices, Shops and Railway Premises Act making reference to those employees to whom it did not apply.
2 Explain why the Health and Safety at Work Act 1974 was introduced.
3 Who is responsible for the safety of employees at work?
4 When did the new Health and Safety at Work Regulations come into force and what is the purpose of this Act?
5 Why is there now a need to include the use of new technology in health and safety legislation?
6 What is the legal position for non-smokers at work?

Activity 5.3 SUGGESTED ASSIGNMENT/ESSAY TITLES

1 Are the new Regulations for the health and safety of employees using computers adequate? Discuss.
2 Choose a local business and investigate to what extent health and safety legislation has helped/hindered the employer.
3 Are the new regulations on passive smoking at work adequate?

Data Protection Act

Why was this Act introduced?

In today's world of technology, more and more firms are using computers to store and process information of all types. Medical, education and employment details are examples of the type of information which may be stored by a computer. In order to try to control the use and accuracy of information such as this, legislation in the form of the Data Protection Act was passed and came into force in July 1984.

Who does it protect?

All living persons; this Act is concerned with personal data and therefore the information has to relate to a living person. Consequently any living person (including sole traders) is covered by this legislation. As a limited company is a *legal* 'person' but not a *living* person the Act does not apply to information held about the company itself. Also the Act does not cover information which is kept manually in ordinary paper files.

What if the information held doesn't include the person's name?

Where a person can be identified from data which is kept about them either from a name, address, pay number or other source, then this is personal data. It is not only factual information which is covered by this Act but also expressions of opinion about an individual.

Does this Act apply only to information kept on computers?

No, the Data Protection Act does not cover data held only on computers, it includes other equipment which has some ability to process information automatically, for example, electronic flexitime systems, telephone logging equipment and automatic retrieval systems for microfilm and microfiche (more details of microfilm and microfiche are given in Chapter 8).

What/who is a data user?

The definition given of a 'data user' by the Data Protection Office is 'a person who holds data'. As a data user does not have to be a living person only a legal 'person', a limited company can be a data user because it is recognised in law as a legal 'person'.

Do you have to own a computer to be a data user?

No. To be a data user the legal person must control the contents and use of the data. Therefore, if you don't own a computer but use a computer bureau to process information for you, you are still a data user as you are in control of what is kept and how it is used.

What is a computer bureau?

Computer bureaux are firms which either provide a service by processing data for others or allow others to use equipment to process their own data.

Do data users have obligations?

Yes. Data users have certain obligations placed on them under the Data Protection Act:

- Data should be accurate and kept up to date.
- Access to personal files should be restricted.
- Data should be processed fairly and lawfully.

What about word processors – does the Act apply to them?

Sometimes – it depends upon what they are being used to do. The Data Protection Act does not apply to word processors which are used to prepare text even though when a document is printed it may contain details about a living person.

To clarify the position a little more, if 50 names and addresses are kept on file and the same standard letter is sent to all of them, the Data Protection Act will not apply. However, if only *certain* living persons are *selected* from the list to receive the standard letter, then the Act applies. In other words, if it is a general letter which applies to anyone regardless of who they are and where they live, the Act will not apply as everyone is being treated the same and receiving the same letter. Where individuals are being selected – that is, singled out – for some reason, the Act comes into force.

What is a data subject?

The definition given of a 'data subject' by the Data Protection Office is 'an individual who is the subject of personal data'. We already know that the data must refer to a living person, but this is not restricted just to individuals who are of UK nationality; it relates to every individual regardless of his or her nationality or residence.

Does a data subject have any rights?

Yes, every data subject has certain rights under the Data Protection Act. These rights are:

- The right of access – data subjects are entitled if they wish to a copy of the personal data held about them by a data user.
- The right to take action for compensation – if he or she is damaged by inaccurate personal data or disclosure of personal data.
- A right to take action to have inaccurate personal data corrected or erased.
- A right to complain to the registrar – that any of the Data Protection Principles or any other provision of the Act has been broken.

What if the registrar doesn't know about the data user?

All data users who hold personal data must apply for registration unless the data which is held is exempt. The details which must be supplied include:

- who the data user is
- what personal data is held and how it is being used
- where the data user obtains information from
- who the data user may disclose information to
- details of any overseas localities to which the data user may transfer personal data.

Individual names are not listed in the register, but the relationship between the data user and data subject is – for example, 'customer' or 'employee'.

What if a data user breaks the rules?

Once registered, a data user has to operate within the terms set out on the register entry. The details can be changed if necessary but the data user has to apply to alter them. Registration lasts for one, two or three years depending upon the preference of the data user.

If a data user holds information which is not detailed in the register entry or does anything with it that is not detailed in the register entry then he or she is committing a criminal offence. Similarly, it is unlawful to hold personal data which is not exempt if an application for registration has not been made.

Who can look at the register?

Anyone. Details submitted by the data user are kept by the registrar and are available for public inspection free of charge. Once the information in the register has been examined by an individual, he or she can make a subject access request to a data user. The data user must respond and say whether any personal data is held about that person and if it is what the information is.

What is the purpose of the register?

The purpose of the register, apart from providing individuals with access to information, is to help the registrar enforce the Act.

Are there any exemptions?

Yes. A brief summary is given below:

- Personal data held for domestic or recreational purposes.
- Information that the law requires to be made public.
- National security.
- Payroll, pensions and account purposes.
- Unincorporated members clubs.
- Mailing lists.

How much can you remember?

1 Why was the Data Protection Act introduced?
2 What is the difference between a data subject and a data user?
3 What obligations are placed upon data users?
4 List the rights data subjects have under this Act.
5 In which instances does the Act not apply?
6 Explain the role of the data registrar.
7 What is the data register?

Activity 5.4 SUGGESTED ASSIGNMENT/ESSAY TITLES

1 Failure to control the use of personal data may have serious consequences for some individuals. Discuss.
2 The Data Protection Act is an adequate and effective way of controlling personal data. Discuss.

Chapter 6 Business correspondence

By the end of this chapter you should be able to explain:

- the uses for the many different forms of written business documentation
- the importance of well-presented and accurate business correspondence
- the range of different types and sizes of paper and envelopes
- the importance of correctly addressed mail
- the purpose and use of proof correction signs
- the advantages and disadvantages of shorthand and audio work
- the skills of shorthand writers and audio transcribers
- the main types of audio system.

Despite the increasing use of new technology and the availability of electronic mail, traditional methods are still widely used for business correspondence.

Letters

Writing letters is an everyday occurrence in business and firms have special letterheadings designed on which to send out their letters. A typical letterhead will contain a firm's name, address, telephone and fax numbers and, if appropriate, VAT number. Many firms add a logo which immediately identifies them – for example, when you see a black horse you immediately know it represents Lloyds Bank. All external correspondence is typed or printed on to a firm's letterheading and therefore good-quality paper is used. Using pre-printed letterhead not only saves time as the firm's details do not have to be inserted at the top of each letter, it is a good way of advertising.

What's behind the Black Horse?

The horse has been the symbol of Lloyds Bank for over 100 years.

The Black Horse was originally used as a banking symbol in 1677 by a goldsmith with premises in Lombard Street, where Lloyds Bank now has its head office.

That was 88 years before the Quaker ironmaster Sampson Lloyd founded his bank in Birmingham.

For the first 100 years, until 1865, he had only one office and no branches.

Then the firm began to expand across the Midlands, followed by London in the 1880s, when it took over the Lombard Street premises. Then in the early part of this century the Bank began to expand overseas.

For a time, the bank had another symbol – the beehive – but the horse began to dominate from the 1890s. However, it was not until 1980 that the beehive finally disappeared when Beehive Life Assurance Company was renamed the Black Horse Life Assurance Company.

It is of little use spending money having an impressive letterhead printed if special attention is not also paid to the content and display of each letter. It is crucial that all letters are well presented and that typed/word processed work is carefully checked and errors corrected prior to posting.

Spacing and punctuation

The modern way of punctuating a letter is by using a method known as open punctuation. When this method is adopted, punctuation is used only in the main body of the letter (see example below), there is no punctuation in any of the information prior to or after the main body of the letter.

Straight & Narrow Ltd, 10 Straightline, Narrowbed, Narrowshire.
Telephone: 9823 652314

Our Ref AI/TI

23 December 1994

FOR THE ATTENTION OF THE MANAGER

The Bank
21 High Street
LOCALTOWN
Local County
LO1 4TH

Dear Sirs

BUSINESS SERVICES

We are considering buying premises in your town as we intend to expand our business. Could we please arrange to come in to see you to discuss opening a business account with your bank.

Could we arrange a meeting next Monday or Tuesday when I will be in the area looking for a suitable location.

Yours faithfully
STRAIGHT & NARROW LTD

E A STRAIGHT
Managing Director

Acceptable spacing is two spaces after punctuation at the end of a sentence (to represent a long pause) and one space after any punctuation mark elsewhere. The example shows a fully blocked style letter layout where all lines begin at the left margin. Some firms, however, prefer to use a different format. They may choose to indent the first line of each paragraph and use punctuation throughout the letter including the address. Where paragraphs are indented it is usual to begin the first line of each paragraph five spaces in from the left margin.

Types of letters

Circular letters

When the same letter needs to be sent to a number of people, a circular letter is used. There are several ways of setting out a circular letter and one of these is shown in the example below.

Straight & Narrow Ltd, 10 Straightline, Narrowbed, Narrowshire.
Telephone: 9823 652314

Our ref: AI/TI

February 1994

Dear Sir/Madam

SAVING MONEY ON FUEL

In these days of rising inflation and unemployment, money just does not go far enough. However, we have found a way to make it stretch just that little bit further. A revolutionary system of heating can be yours, installed and working in a matter of days. It is guaranteed to cut heating bills in half.

If you would like our representative to call, complete the reply slip today and we will arrange a time convenient to you.

Yours faithfully
STRAIGHT & NARROW LTD

Please send me full details of your new heating system.

Surname: .... Forename(s): ....

Address: ....

.... Tel No: ....

Note: There are acceptable variations to the layout shown.

1 The date can be included as 'date as postmark'.
2 Not all circular letters have a tear-off portion.
3 Space is sometimes left after the date so that an address can be added.
4 Space is sometimes left at the bottom so that the letter can be signed before being sent off.

Standard/form letters

Sometimes, much of the information contained in a letter is the same for a number of people, with just some parts differing. For example, the same letter will be sent to a number of people selected for interview, but the time and date of their appointment will differ. In this situation a standard or form letter is prepared and space is left for the variables to be added prior to the letter being sent out (see example below). A merging facility on a word processor is often used to merge names and addresses into a standard letter.

Straight & Narrow Ltd, 10 Straightline, Narrowbed, Narrowshire.
Telephone: 9823 652314

Our ref: BI/TI

Dear Sir/Madam

Thank you for your letter of enclosing Invoice No.
on which we wish to make payment in the amount of

Yours faithfully
STRAIGHT & NARROW LTD

B IALOT
ACCOUNTS MANAGER

Memoranda

It would be rather pointless and too expensive to use company letterheading for internal communication and so memoranda (memos) are used instead. They are often printed internally on cheaper paper. A memo differs from a letter as it has no details of the firm at the top and the writer does not begin with a salutation (Dear ...) or end with a complimentary close (Yours ...). (See example below.)

Memorandum

FROM: Sales Manager

TO: Transport Manager

DATE: 23 August 1994

DELIVERIES

We are constantly receiving complaints from customers that delivery dates are not being met. One of our best customers has threatened to stop doing business with us unless the situation improves immediately. Can you please let me know exactly what the problems are so that steps can be taken to remedy the situation.

AI/TI

Compliment slip

When a firm is sending something to someone externally, but a letter is not really necessary, a compliment slip is used. This is a small slip of good-quality paper which contains the same details as the firm's letterheading but the words 'With compliments' are added (see example on page 104). The slip tells the recipient where the enclosure has come from. Often, there is a space for the sender to write a short message if an explanation is needed. Using compliment slips in this type of situation saves time and reduces paperwork.

Straight & Narrow Ltd, 10 Straightline, Narrowbed, Narrowshire.
Telephone: 9823 652314

With compliments

Reports

Letters and memos are not the only written documentation used by businesses – reports have an important role to play, too. Reports in schools and colleges are used to record an individual's progress – they identify strengths and weaknesses, draw conclusions and make recommendations for improvement. The same is true of a business report, except that it records the progress of a business situation rather than an individual. Sometimes a report is the product of an investigation and its findings, conclusions and recommendations are used to assist management to make a decision. In this type of report the terms of reference should be clearly stated.

There are different types of report and consequently there are alternative ways of setting them out. However, several common features are detailed below.

Title: All reports have a title, which indicates what the report is about.

Introduction: The introduction will indicate who the report is from, who it is for and its purpose. Where appropriate, this section will also include how the information was obtained and/or the investigation carried out.

Main body: The main body will be divided into sections and sub-headings should be used to help the reader follow it through. These also help the author to keep the report in a logical order. Paragraphs should be short, kept to the point and not detract from the main issue(s) being discussed/investigated.

Conclusion: All reports must have a conclusion. This is the place where findings/discussions are summarised and where the writer's own opinions are included.

Recommendations: Where an investigation has been carried out the writer will have gathered enough evidence/information to examine critically the situation being reported upon. Recommendations based on evidence collected will be included at this point.

Signature and date: The person who has written the report will sign and date it at the bottom.

How much can you remember?

1. What is a letterheading?
2. What is a logo and what is its purpose?
3. Explain the difference between open and full punctuation.
4. What is a blocked style of letter?
5. What are the spacing rules in relation to punctuation marks?
6. Describe a circular letter and identify a situation for which it might be suitable.
7. How does a standard/form letter differ from a circular letter?
8. What is the difference between a memo and letter and in what instance would a memo be used in preference to a letter?
9. What is the purpose of a report and how is it structured?

Activity 6.1
task 1

Inventing a firm of your choice, design and prepare documentation as detailed below for use in the next task. Use the same firm for all documentation.

(a) A letterheading which must include an appropriate logo. (You will require two copies.)

(b) A compliment slip.

(c) A memorandum.

task 2

You are an employee of the firm you chose in task 1. One of the other secretaries has left suddenly and you have been asked to act as 'stand-in' until he is replaced. Moira Baker, the director who he worked for, is away on business at the moment but she has sent you a message on tape:

> Please sort out the following correspondence as quickly as possible and have everything arranged for my return early next week.

Make arrangements with personnel to send for the best ten applicants for the secretarial post which we advertised last week. Prepare a suitable letter but leave personnel to complete the names and addresses etc. As the new employee will be working for me, I'd like to interview the applicants myself next Wednesday and Thursday. Set up suitable times and make sure you allow at least 20 minutes for each applicant and don't forget I have a business lunch at 12.30 on Thursday.

Ask Alec Rodgers, personnel manager, to be available for the interviews and let his secretary know that we will need to use the meeting room.

Oh, while I remember, I left a file of papers with Cynthia Downing before I left, can you collect them and send the file to Messrs Garth & Hodges at 65 West Lane, Parkside, Leeds LS1 8JN – no letter is necessary, he's expecting it, just put a note in to remind him of our business lunch next Thursday.

Sort out a suitable letter to let our customers know that we are moving premises next month. I'd like a reply from them so that I know they have received the letter.

Please use fully blocked style for all letters and open punctuation. I'll be back Monday morning around 7.30 if anyone asks.

Using your stationery, do what Moira Baker has asked.

Paper and envelopes

Paper sizes

The size of paper most commonly used for letters, reports and longer memos is A4. For short memos and letters A5 is more appropriate. Details of the different sizes of paper are given in the illustration below.

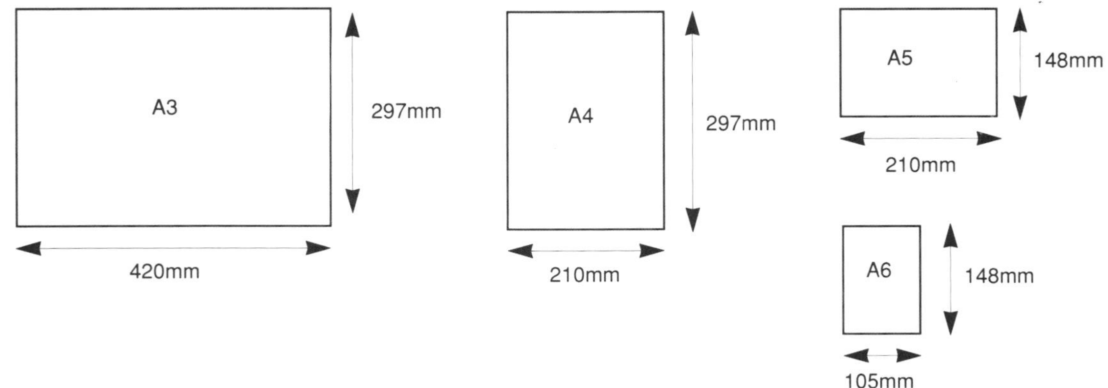

Paper quality

Good-quality paper, 'bond' paper, is available in various colours and is used for any task that requires quality paper, mainly external documents and letters. As it is quite expensive, it is not often used for internal work other than reports.

'Bank' paper is also available in various colours but as it is of a poorer quality and much cheaper, it is more commonly used for internal tasks, mainly file copies of letters and memos.

Envelopes

The use of labels for addressing envelopes is becoming increasingly popular. Addresses can be stored and labels printed from a computer. However, whatever method is used, it is the correct insertion of details on to the envelope that is important if a letter is to reach its destination.

When addressing envelopes, the address should not be abbreviated, it should be written/typed in full including the postcode. It is good practice to include a return address on the back of the envelope so that the mail can be returned if there is a problem with delivery. A correct postal address will consist of:

- the addressee's name
- the addressee's designation
- the addressee's company
- a building number (or a name if it doesn't have a number)
- a street name
- locality name (if there is one)
- POST TOWN (in block capitals)
- the county name (where necessary)
- postcode (very important).

A correctly addressed envelope is shown on page 108, where you will notice there are no punctuation marks. Addresses without commas and full stops are much easier for Royal Mail machinery to read.

Ensuring that the contents of an envelope remain in good condition is as important as addressing the envelope correctly. It is of little use to a firm if an envelope arrives at its destination without its contents, or with the contents damaged. Therefore, you should take care in choosing the correct type, style and size of envelope. Although Royal Mail will accept most sizes, shapes and colours of envelope, certain types can be processed more easily than others. Royal Mail recommend maximum and minimum sizes of envelope that are most suitable for electronic sorting. Sizes above and below those specified are dealt with manually as they cannot be handled by electronic sorting equipment.

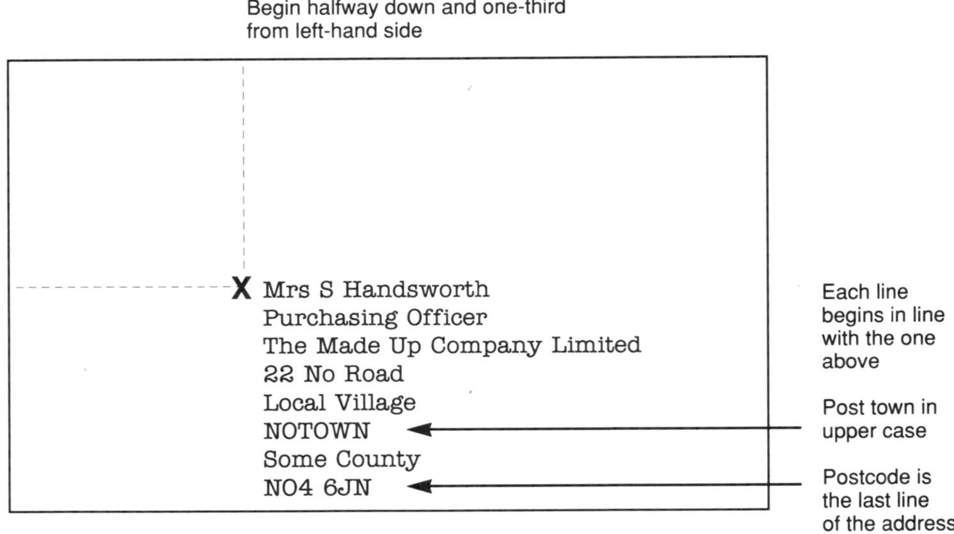

Begin halfway down and one-third from left-hand side
X
Mrs S Handsworth
Purchasing Officer
The Made Up Company Limited
22 No Road
Local Village
NOTOWN
Some County
NO4 6JN
Each line begins in line with the one above
Post town in upper case
Postcode is the last line of the address

How much can you remember?

1 What size of paper is most commonly used for business correspondence and documentation?
2 What is the difference between bond and bank paper?
3 Draw a diagram to show how an envelope should be addressed, and explain why it is important to follow this procedure.
4 Why does Royal Mail recommend certain types and style of envelope?

Activity 6.2 Prepare suitably sized and correctly addressed envelopes for:

(a) The letter on page 100.
(b) The file of papers in Activity 6.1.
(c) Yourself as an applicant for the post detailed in Activity 6.1 (SAE).
(d) The firm of your choice as detailed in Activity 6.1.

Preparing business documentation

Letters and documents which require typing/word processing may be given to the typist in one of several forms:

- They may be written in longhand, which the typist/operator simply copies using a typewriter or computer.
- They may be shorthand (dictated to the person who is to type the text), which the typist/operator converts to longhand while typing/word processing.
- They may be recorded on a tape, which the typist/operator listens to and produces a typed/word processed document while doing so. This is referred to as audio typing.

Written work

When work is written it is common for the author to make changes to the original script. The reader uses proof-correction marks to show what amendments have to be made and where. The most common of these are shown in Table 6.1.

Shorthand and audio

Audio work is becoming more widely used than traditional shorthand dictation as it is more flexible for the author. First, let us examine the role of the shorthand writer.

Shorthand

When this method is used, the shorthand writer and the author of the business documentation must both be present during dictation. The author says what he or she wishes to say and the shorthand writer writes down in shorthand what is said word for word. Shorthand is a quick way of writing, and words, vowels and phrases are represented by a series of dots, dashes and thick and thinly written strokes (see below). When the dictation is finished, the shorthand writer uses a typewriter or word processor to transcribe the notes into longhand.

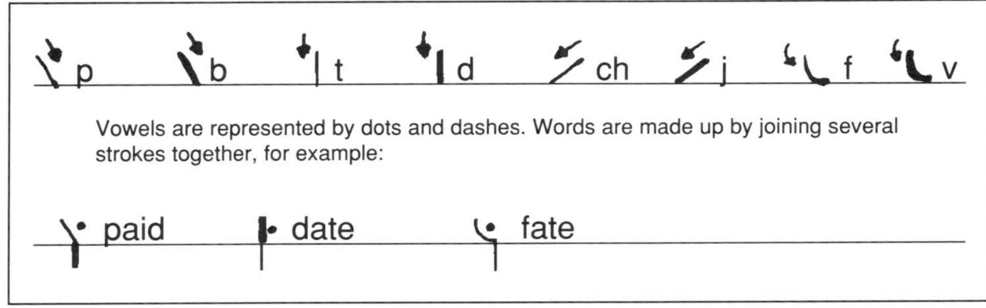

p
b
t
d
ch
j
f
v
Vowels are represented by dots and dashes. Words are made up by joining several strokes together, for example:
paid
date
fate

Sign in margin	What it means
u/c or CAPS	Upper case (capitals). The word or letter to be changed is underlined in the text.
l/c	Lower case (small letters). The word or letter to be changed is underlined in the text.
Stet or ✓ (circled)	Let it stand. Leave in the word which has been crossed out. If there are two words crossed out, the one which is to be left in will have a broken line underneath it.
Trs	Transpose (change the order of). Numbers are used in the text to indicate in what order the words should appear.
NP or [or //	Start a new paragraph. A square bracket or two obliques is placed where the new paragraph is to start.
Run on	Do not start a new paragraph. ⌐⌐ is used to show how the text should run on.
∂	Delete. The word to be deleted will be crossed out.
⋏	This symbol is a caret and it is placed in the text to show that something needs to be added. Details of what needs adding will be in the margin or somewhere appropriate. The addition may be a punctuation mark, a word, a sentence or a whole paragraph.
#	Insert space. A caret, ⋏, will be inserted to show where the space is to be added.
⁐	Close up. There is an extra space, take it out.

Table 6.1 Proof-correction marks

Firms which advertise for shorthand writers often ask for speeds of between 80 and 120 wpm (words per minute), although many well-trained shorthand writers can reach speeds much greater than this. The only equipment needed by a shorthand writer for dictation is a notepad and sharp pencil or special shorthand pen.

Advantages of shorthand dictation:

- There is direct personal contact between the author and the shorthand writer and this is particularly useful for confidential work.
- Shorthand notes can be kept for future reference as a record of what was dictated.
- Any unclear instructions, queries or technical terms can be clarified at the time of dictation.

Disadvantages of shorthand dictation:

- Authors can dictate only during normal working hours, when the shorthand writer is available.
- Shorthand writing ties up the author and the shorthand writer at the same time while dictation is taking place.
- It is difficult to share the work load.
- A shorthand writer may have difficulty transcribing some notes if they have been written down incorrectly.

Audio

The role of the audio transcriber is a little different from that of a shorthand writer. Shorthand has to be written down and transcribed, while the audio worker has only to transcribe the work as there is nothing to write down. The author speaks into a microphone and his or her voice is recorded on to a tape which the audio typist transcribes. An audio transcriber will require a special transcribing machine, earphones and a foot pedal to control the tape. The tape can be started, stopped or rewound using the foot pedal. Audio transcribers should always have their own set of earphones and these must be kept clean to reduce the risk of ear infection.

Advantages of audio dictation:

- The workload can be spread evenly between audio workers as each tape is typed in turn
- Authors can dictate the tapes at any time, even at home during the evening or while they are away from the office on business. Some tapes are so small that they can easily be posted into the office and the work can be typed up immediately. However, this is no longer necessary with

the latest systems, as they allow dictators to link up by telephone to a dual-purpose dictating/transcribing machine, which is housed on the audio transcriber's desk.

- Authors can dictate while audio transcribers type up previously recorded work.
- The latest systems allow direct personal contact between author and transcriber. This enables unclear instructions, queries and complicated technical terms to be cleared up quickly.

Disadvantages of audio dictation:

- Listening carefully through headphones for a long period of time requires a great deal of concentration and is tiring.
- The dictator's voice may be unclear and difficult to hear.
- Background noise is often picked up, either from outside or inside the office.
- If several typists are sharing the work, confidentiality is difficult to keep.
- When tapes have been wiped, no record remains of what was recorded.

Skills of shorthand writers and audio transcribers

Although the roles of the two workers are different, many of the skills they require are very similar:

- All work which is transcribed has to be typed or word processed, so they must both possess keyboard skills.
- Work must be displayed in a proper business format and therefore either word processing or typewriting qualifications are necessary.
- As there is nothing to copy from, correct use of punctuation, good spelling and language skills are essential.

Audio systems

This chapter discusses two types of audio system: bank and secretarial.

Bank system

The bank system is used in large organisations that have a central typing pool and all of the typists/word processors are located in one place. Each dictator is connected directly by a special telephone/microphone to the audio bank machine (see diagram opposite), which he or she accesses by dialling the bank system number. When dictation has been completed, the person supervising the machine removes the tapes and distributes them to the typists.

This type of system takes up a great deal of supervisory time and does not allow the audio typist any personal contact with the author, either before or during transcription.

T T
T T
T T
T T
Supervisor
Bank machine
M M
M M M
M M
M = Manager (Dictator)
T = Typist (Transcriber)

Audio bank system

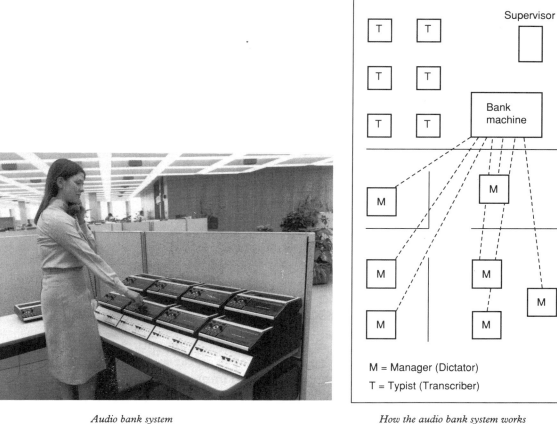

How the audio bank system works

Secretarial system

The current trend seems to be away from central pools and more towards smaller groups, 'puddles', which are made up of two or three audio transcribers. Many firms prefer this system as it has a more personal touch. Audio units are housed within each audio transciber's workstation and as these are accessed in strict rotation by authors using the telephone, it ensures an even distribution of the workload.

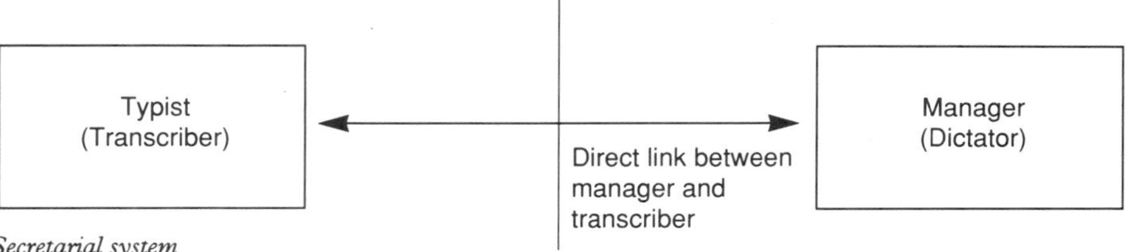

Secretarial system

With this system the audio transcriber can speak to the dictator before, during and after dictation by means of a microphone which is built into the transcription headset. As authors are linked up directly with transcribers (see diagram on page 113) and not to a bank machine, no manual distribution of tapes is required. This speeds up the work process and allows queries to be dealt with quickly. Minimal supervision is required as the supervisor has a master machine which shows exactly which audio typist is busy and who is waiting to receive the next piece of work.

Many organisations are now making use of digital technology. Voice systems are available which eliminate the need for tapes, as authors' voices are recorded digitally and stored centrally on a PC. From here powerful software prioritises all jobs automatically and distributes them instantly to the secretaries and typists. The latest systems eliminate many of the disadvantages of audio work.

How much can you remember?

1 List the three forms documentation comes in for typing/word processing.
2 What are proof-correction signs and why are they useful?
3 Using diagrams to illustrate your answer, explain the meaning of at least six correction signs.
4 What is shorthand writing?
5 How does audio work differ from shorthand?
6 What special equipment is needed for audio work?
7 List the advantages and disadvantages of both audio and shorthand
8 What skills should shorthand and audio workers possess?
9 Describe the two most common audio systems and identify the main differences between them.

Activity 6.3 The written work below needs to be changed as per the proof correction signs shown. Type the amended version.

Passage 1

<u>The Importance of Well-Presented Business Letters</u>

When a firm sends out letters it is advertising the business. A badly presented letter containing several errors will not give a good impression. In contrast a beautifully set out and accurate letter free of errors will impress. A firm is only as good as its employees. Its secretarial support service is also its advertising service and it can create a good or bad impression for the firm.

, NP

Passage 2

ENSURING MAIL REACHES ITS DESTINATION

Most Firms take a great deal of time and trouble ensuring that letters going out to customers are of the highest quality. It is a great pity therefore that of them some never reach their destination.
This is often due to the fact that envelopes have been badly addressed or that bulky correspondence has been pushed into an envelope which is obviously too small. When the latter happens the envelope splits and parts company from its contents. This inevitably delays or sometimes prevents it reaching its destination.

Good secretarial and mail room staff will ensure that all envelopes are of a suitable size and correctly addressed. This will prevent any delay in mail reaching its destination.

Activity 6.4 The firm you work for has in the past used shorthand as a method of dictation. Audio is being used on a limited and trial basis but both authors and transcribers are complaining.

Authors are complaining that transcribers are not listening carefully enough to the dictation and that part numbers and technical terms are incorrect. They are saying that the wrong sized paper is being used and work is not being checked properly for errors. Also that they are having to wait too long for work to be completed.

Transcribers are complaining that authors are not being very thoughtful when dictating. Background noise is being picked up, they are not giving clear instructions or spelling out complicated terms and this is causing unnecessary delays in completing work. Some authors are not dictating very clearly, they keep changing their mind and some parts of their tapes are muffled.

Management is considering replacing shorthand with audio, but acknowledges that this issue must be examined carefully particularly in view of the recent complaints from both authors and transcribers.

task Prepare a report which will assist management to make a decision on whether to replace shorthand with audio on a permanent basis, revert to shorthand or use both. Investigate the complaints made by both authors and transcribers and put forward recommendations which may, if implemented, resolve these problems.

Chapter 7 Making copies

By the end of this chapter you should be able to explain:

- the use of carbon paper
- the care of carbon paper
- the advantages and disadvantages of 'no carbon required' paper
- the suitability of particular methods of duplicating and copying.

Copying/duplicating

We will first clarify the difference between copying and duplicating: copying means producing copies from an original, and duplicating refers to the production of copies from a specially prepared master.

File copies

When letters and memos are typed, it is common practice to keep a copy for the file for future reference. The use of carbon paper provides an exact copy of the typed original.

Carbon paper

There are different types of carbon paper and the type used will depend on the number of copies and the quality required. Some carbon paper can be used only once. Carbon is referred to by its weight – light, medium and heavy. Lightweight carbon enables you to produce the most copies at one time as you can use several sheets because it is less thick, but it does not last for very long. The heavier weight of carbon allows you to produce fewer copies each time because it is thick, but it lasts much longer. Heavyweight carbon is the best quality, but it is more expensive.

NCR (no carbon required) is paper that has been treated with invisible chemicals and this is frequently used for forms where several copies are required. Forms are usually made up in sets with each copy having a different colour. When information is written or typed on the top copy, an impression is formed on the copy or copies underneath which, unlike carbon copies, do not smudge.

Its major disadvantage, apart from being more expensive than carbon paper, is that it is easy to accidentally mark the paper and you cannot correct mistakes once they have been made. However, as there is no necessity to place carbon paper between copies and remove it after completion, it is much quicker to use and cleaner to handle.

Caring for carbon paper

Care has to be taken when using and storing carbon paper. If it is not inserted carefully into the typewriter or printer, it will crease and the copies will not be very clear. After use, carbon paper should be stored flat in a box away from radiators or other heat.

Methods for copying/duplicating

Making copies of documents and letters is a daily necessity in most offices. Various methods can be used and the one chosen will depend upon:

- the number of copies required
- the quality (external or internal destination)
- the content – whether text, drawings or both
- whether colour is required
- whether an exact copy or likeness is required
- the cost.

Word processing

Text is keyed into a word processor and each printed copy of the work looks like an original. It is so easy to make alterations and minor adjustments before printing that this method is becoming extremely popular for external correspondence. Its popularity has increased even more due to the latest high speed printers, which offer superb quality print. However, word processing is suitable only for text and it is not practical to print very large quantities using this method. Where large quantities are required, one copy is printed (and signed if appropriate) and this is then reproduced using one of the methods detailed below.

Producing copies from the computer

Producing copies from the computer refers here to the printing out of any material, text and drawings, from programs other than word processors, which is dealt with separately above. Sales forecasts, pie and bar charts can all be prepared using a computer and printed out when complete. Many printers offer a multi-colour facility, which can be useful for printing graphics. Apart from not being restricted to the production of text only, this method has the same advantages and disadvantages as word processing.

Photocopying

Photocopying is by far the quickest method of producing many copies of a document. The copy quality of most photocopiers these days is excellent, and there is no limit to the number of copies that can be produced. Each printout is an exact copy of the original and this makes it ideal for reproducing any type of material including text and/or drawings.

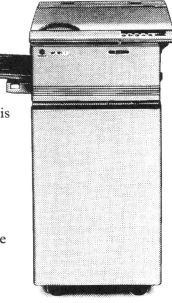

However, some of the latest machines which offer colour reproduction and a reduction/ enlargement facility are quite expensive. This method is fast and clean but it is not always the most economical way of reproducing material.

Ink duplicating

Ink duplicating is sometimes referred to as stencil duplicating. A stencil is a thin but tough fibrous sheet with a wax surface and behind the stencil lies a backing sheet. A piece of carbon paper is situated between the stencil and the backing sheet and this provides a carbon copy which makes checking much easier.

It is very difficult to write or draw on a stencil and therefore this method is more often used for text which is typed directly on to the stencil. The typewriter ribbon is disengaged and the keys cut out the shape of the letters in the stencil. Errors can be corrected using a special correcting fluid and if a signature is required, a special pen called a stylus is used.

The advantages of ink duplicating are mainly the low cost of duplicating and the high number of copies which can be produced from one stencil. The quality of copies produced is good but not of the same standard as a photocopy and therefore many firms use this method for internal rather than external work.

One disadvantage of this method is that a thermal copier or an electronic scanner must be purchased if diagrams or other illustrations are required. The cost of the additional equipment needed to reproduce drawings makes this method much more expensive.

To prevent smudging, semi-absorbent paper has to be used to soak up the ink used for duplicating. Copies can be produced with more than one colour, but the process involved is not straightforward: a fresh drum has to be put on the duplicating machine and a new stencil prepared. This is both messy and time-consuming.

Offset lithography

Offset lithography works on the principle that grease and water do not mix (see illustration below). Masters are prepared on special metal or paper plates which are covered by a greasy substance. Text, drawings, diagrams and photographs can be put on to the plate to be reproduced. While the duplicating process is taking place, water is sprayed on the master to keep it clean and the typing or drawing is inked. The ink is not washed away by the water because it is oily. Good-quality paper is used, which makes this method suitable for letterheadings, price lists and staff magazines.

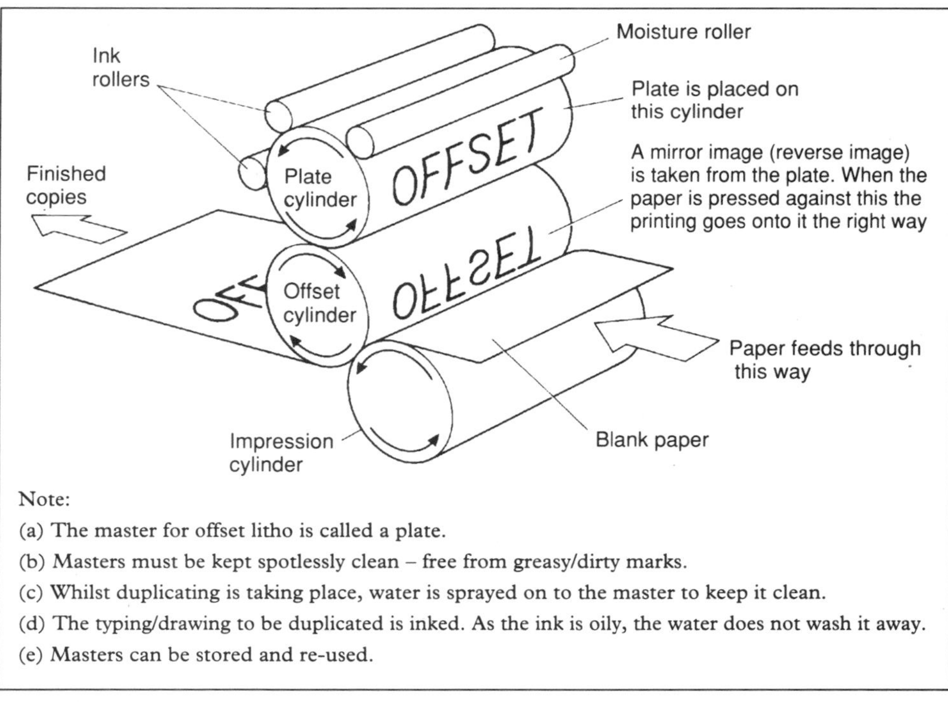

Note:

(a) The master for offset litho is called a plate.

(b) Masters must be kept spotlessly clean – free from greasy/dirty marks.

(c) Whilst duplicating is taking place, water is sprayed on to the master to keep it clean.

(d) The typing/drawing to be duplicated is inked. As the ink is oily, the water does not wash it away.

(e) Masters can be stored and re-used.

Principles of offset lithography

Offset lithography has many advantages, including very good quality print, which makes the copies suitable for external work. Several thousand copies can be obtained from a paper plate and tens of thousands from a metal plate. This method is very cheap when large quantities are required but it is not suitable for small amounts.

Machine operators need special training and the machinery is expensive to buy initially. However, the long-term costs are much cheaper if a firm regularly needs large quantities of printing. Many professional printing firms use this method, and businesses often send their work out to printing firms rather than buying the very expensive machines themselves.

How much can you remember?

1 For what purpose is carbon paper most commonly used?
2 What is the difference between heavyweight and lightweight carbon paper?
3 What can you do to prevent carbon paper becoming damaged/spoilt?
4 What will a firm consider when deciding which method to choose for copying/duplicating.
5 Which method produces copies which look most like the originals?
6 What is the most popular method of copying/duplicating?
7 What is stencil duplicating?
8 Describe, using a diagram, the offset lithography process.

Activity 7.1

A publicity campaign is being mounted for a new multi-screen cinema which is due to open in seven days' time on the outskirts of town. There is a range of material to go out to various people. In addition to the latest computing equipment, management has access to a variety of equipment for reproducing materials.

task 1

Investigate and choose the best method of reproducing the documents detailed below. Consider quantity, quality, content, colour and whether there is a requirement for an exact copy. The cheapest method may not be the best. Give reasons why the other methods available are not suitable in each case.

(a) To arouse the interest of the local community, 100 illustrated posters are to be placed in shop windows to advertise the grand opening of the cinema.

(b) Management have decided to target the immediate local area and offer free entry to the first 100 customers who return the reply slip on the bottom of the circular letter which they receive. 2,500 circular letters with reply slips are to be prepared and sent out.

(c) Most new staff have already started work but there are still five employees who will be joining the company on the opening day. They require a 'welcome aboard' letter which is to be signed personally by the manager.

(d) The directors require three copies of the projected sales forecast, so that they can monitor income each month and compare actual sales with forecasted figures. The information is stored on disk.

(e) Details of the films to be shown at the cinema, together with prices where appropriate, are to be given to customers when they visit. Initially, 5,000 copies are required but a further 10,000 will be needed in the near future.

(f) A number of 'one-off' letters and memos to staff and suppliers need to be sent out. A file copy is to be kept of each one.

(g) Six interesting posters have already been prepared but a further four copies of each one are now required.

task 2 Prepare ready for copying/duplicating, a master/original of at least two of the above documents.

Chapter 8 Filing

By the end of this chapter you should be able to explain:

- the main forms of classification for storing information
- the alphabetical filing rules
- filing procedures
- electronic filing
- the duties of a filing clerk
- the different types of filing and indexing equipment available.

Sorting information

Offices have lots of paperwork; the paperless office is still a long way off, even with today's computerised systems. Letters and documents cannot be put away anyhow – they need to be stored away safely and in some sort of order so that they can be found quickly and easily when required. Information can be classified and stored in one of five ways: alphabetical, numerical, geographical, subject or chronological.

Alphabetical filing

Alphabetical filing is perhaps the most popular classification used, but although it sounds quite straightforward, there are certain rules which must be followed.

A summary of the main alphabetical filing rules are as follows:

Where there is a last name (surname), use it as a filing point – for example, Rebecca **L**angford would be filed under **L**.

If there are several surnames the same, take the first name(s) into account – for example, 1 Langford **Da**vid, 2 Langford **De**borah, 3 Langford **R**ebecca.

Some surnames are hyphenated, file them as if they are one word only – for example, **D**avies-Jones Arthur would be filed under **D**.

Some surnames have a prefix (letters before them), treat such names as if they were one word only – for example, **V**an-Eijk George would be filed under **V**.

Where surnames are similar, file short names before long ones – for example, 1 Woo**d** John, 2 Woo**ds** Geoffrey, 3 Woo**dside** Carol.

Sometimes there are no surnames or first names, only the name of the company. Use the first word of the company name – for example, **W**estfield Removals Ltd would be filed under **W**.

If a company has two or more names in its title, for example a partnership, use the first name for filing papers – for example, **M**illar & Sagar would be filed under **M**.

Some names are prefixed by Mac, Mc and M'. When filing treat them as if they all read Mac and use the 'fourth' letter as the filing point – for example, 1 Mc**A**voy Jennifer, 2 M'**C**lintock Desmond, 3 Mc**P**herson Alexandra.

Ignore the words 'A' or 'The' at the beginning of a company name and any title at the beginning of an individual's name – for example, The **D**oncaster Star file under **D**, A **F**ictitious Co Ltd file under **F**, Sir Stephen **M**orrison file under **M**, Professor Maureen **G**alloway file under **G**, Dr Norman **S**udsworth file under **S**.

When there are initials as part of the company name, file initials before full names – for example, 1 **S P L** Limited, 2 **S R J** Co Ltd, 3 **S**mith & Jenkinson Ltd.

Change numbers into words – for example, **21st** Century Windows & Doors, file under **T**.

Numerical filing

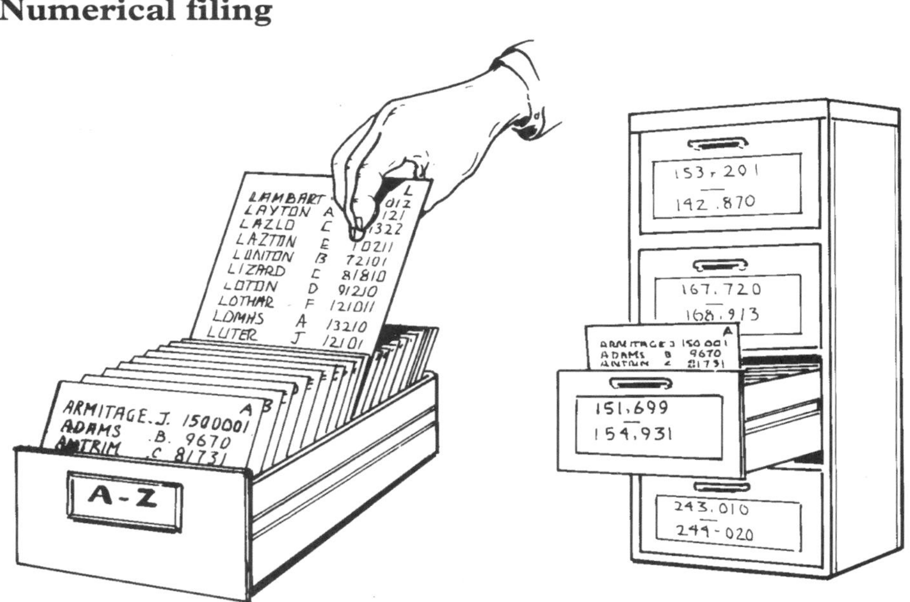

When a numerical filing system is in operation, each new file is given the next number. Unfortunately, with everything having a number and no name, trying to find a document unless you can remember the number becomes a very difficult task. Therefore, a numerical filing system will be accompanied by an alphabetical index. You look in the alphabetical index for the name and this will give you the number the document has been filed under (see illustration on page 123). The main advantage of a numerical index system is that it is easy to open files as each new file is given the next available number.

Numerical filing will, of course, be used for documents that are referred to by a number, such as invoices etc.

Geographical filing

Information is sometimes filed by area, road, village, town, county or even country. Travel and estate agents are two types of organisation which may use this method of classification. A firm that has several branches around the country may use this system. The places under which files are stored and sub-sections within them are usually arranged in alphabetical order.

Subject filing

This is a useful system for personal filing, for example keeping household bills safe. It is also useful in schools and colleges for storing information under subjects, for example Geography, History, and Business Studies. Some firms which like to store information relating to particular subject matter together may choose this type of classification. For example, a market gardener may wish to keep details about different products in separate sections (see illustration below).

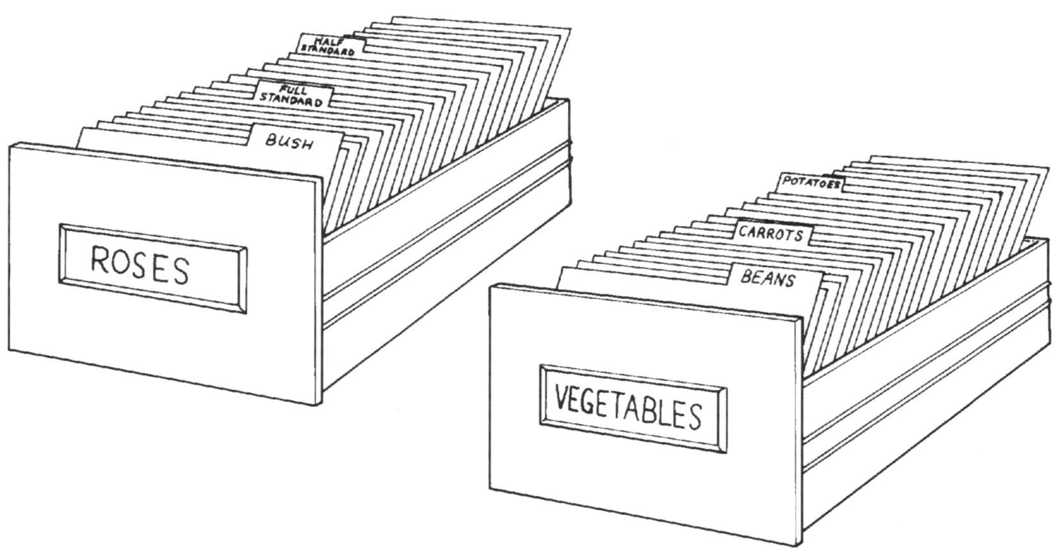

Chronological filing

This is when files are placed in date order, but chronological filing systems are not common. This is because as a filing system it is in most circumstances not very practical. If a firm was to use a chronological filing system, all the letters etc. received bearing the same date would be filed away together using the date as the filing point.

Imagine what would happen if very large quantities of mail were received regularly. The letters would be easy to put away – all the ones bearing the same date would stay together – the problem would be when a letter needed to be retrieved, particularly if it was required urgently. It would take a great deal of time searching through bulky files which contained daily correspondence. It would take even longer if the person looking for it did not know the date under which it was filed.

Consequently, letters are kept in date order *within* a filing system, with the latest correspondence at the top. This means that whether the filing system is alphabetical, numerical, geographical or subject, inside each individual file the letters will have been placed in date order. This is not the same thing as having a chronological filing system.

Miscellaneous files

Sometimes there are not enough papers to make it worthwhile opening a new file for a particular category. If this is the case, such papers are stored together in alphabetical order in a miscellaneous file.

Dead files

Once a file is no longer required it is taken out of the main system and archived – that is, stored away in a box somewhere safe where it can be accessed if necessary. Such files are referred to as dead files. It is usual to keep these files for several years after they are archived in case they are needed at some time in the future.

Electronic filing – database

A database is any place where information is stored, although the term 'database' is normally associated with a piece of software which enables a computer to store information so that it can be edited, sorted and retrieved quickly when required. A whole file or part of one can be printed out in a matter of seconds. Electronic filing is now becoming widely used for the storage and retrieval of information.

With a manual system, information is stored using one type of classification only, for example alphabetical. The major advantage of an electronic system is that information is not stored in one particular order and therefore it can be sorted using any classification at the touch of a button.

To illustrate this point, if in a manual system files are kept in geographical order and the filing clerk is asked to find details of all customers who live in a specific area, this would be a relatively easy task. However, if a firm's personnel records were stored in alphabetical order and the filing clerk was asked to find all of the employees who were aged over 55 on 31 December 1995 and therefore eligible for early retirement, this would involve searching through the whole filing system. A database program could respond to either of these requests in a matter of seconds.

How much can you remember?

1 Name the five ways of classifying information.
2 What action would you take if there were insufficient paper to justify opening a new file on a particular company?
3 What are dead files?
4 What is the main advantage of storing information electronically as opposed to using a manual system?

Activity 8.1

At the school where you work as a clerical assistant, the day begins with assembly. The sixth form have their own assembly once a week on a Tuesday morning, which is normally taken by the head of the sixth form, Miss G Branton. However, Miss Branton feels that other members of staff should also be involved and host some of the assemblies. When she approached the staff she found they were interested in her proposal and agreed to take part. It was agreed that from next month, each assembly which falls on the first Tuesday of the month will be taken by the head of sixth form but the remaining ones will be hosted by the sixth form tutors on a rota basis. The sixth form tutors are:

Miss G Branton	Miss J Smithurst
Mr C Hodge	Mrs P Webb
Mrs M Peel	Mr K Lincten
Mrs B Fernwood	Mr I Isaac
Mr S Tilton	Ms B Ridgewood
Miss D Saltern	Mr L Hugh
Mr A Oliver	Mrs M Gordon
Mr R Clayworth	Mr L Wilson

task 1 (a) Prepare an assembly rota for the Tuesday morning assemblies in chronological order. This should cover a full school year.

(b) Prepare an alphabetical index and cross reference it to the assembly rota.

task 2 Eighteen students (listed below) in the sixth form are in the process of taking extra GCSE subjects. In addition to the subjects detailed, some are re-sitting Maths (M) and/or English (E) to try to improve upon their previous grades. From the details given, manually prepare three lists:

(i) in candidate number order for the examinations officer

(ii) in alphabetical order of last name, also for the examinations officer so that he can cross-reference with the numerical list when he needs information quickly

(iii) in subject order, a copy of which is to be sent to each head of department for checking and reference.

The information you need is as follows:

Candidate numbers	Candidate names	Subjects	Resit(s)
1028	Jayne Wilson	Art, German, History	M
1866	Lesley Hulley	Office Technology, Art, Geography	M & E
1370	Louise Cutts	History, German, Geography	E
1252	Lee Bellway	Office Technology, History, Geography	E
1226	Janice Hickson	Art, German, Geography	M & E
1034	Steven Langden	German, Office Technology, Art	M & E
1556	Jonathan Craven	History, Geography, Art	M & E
1112	Giles Smart	Office Technology, Art, History	E
1448	Wendy Vernon	History, Geography, German	E
1286	Charles Anderton	History, German, Office Technology	E
1130	Darren Parks	Art, Office Technology, German	M
1152	Paul Simmonds	German, Art, History	M & E
1687	Rachel Byrnes	Geography, Office Technology, German	M
1085	Michael Halliday	Office Technology, History, Art	M & E
1193	Amjad Jadhav	History, German, Art	M
1219	Shelly McMahon	Geography, History, Art	E
1317	Shane Wood	German, History, Geography	E
1420	Miriam Shaw	Office Technology, Art, History	M

task 3

The school has a database program which is ideal for this type of work. Unfortunately you were not aware of this until after you had completed the lists. You feel very strongly that a lot of time was wasted sorting and presenting information which could have been done in less than half the time using a computer database.

(a) Using the database software available to you, transfer the above details on to the computer.

(b) (i) Using each candidate's last name, sort the information into alphabetical order and print out full details.
(ii) Using each candidate's number, sort into numerical order with the lowest number first and print out full details.
(iii) Print out a separate subject list for each head of department giving full details of which candidates have been entered for the examination in his or her subject.

(c) Send a memo to the head with a copy to the examinations officer explaining the advantages of computerising the examination details.

Filing procedures

There is much more to filing than simply putting away letters and documents into a filing cabinet. Although it can be a boring job, it is a very important one. The filing clerk is responsible for ensuring that filed copies can be found quickly whenever they are needed. Loose papers can easily become attached to others and placed in the wrong file. A filing clerk needs to take great care to ensure this does not happen.

Storing files

It is important to check that letters can be filed after they have been dealt with. A release symbol will usually confirm this. This varies from business to business, for example the word 'file' may be written or stamped on the document; alternatively, a large tick or a line through the paper will signal that the letter/document has been dealt with and requires filing.

Filing points

When filing a letter, the filing point must be identified. This is the number or letter under which the document is to be filed. For example take a copy of an invoice, number 10345 which has been sent out to Booth & Craven. If a numerical system is used, the filing point will be 10345, but if an alphabetical system is in operation then the invoice will be filed under 'B' for Booth.

Follow-up systems

Often firms need to reply to letters which have been sent out and a follow-up file can be used to serve as a reminder that certain replies have not yet been received.

A follow-up file will be divided into 31 sections and each section is given a number, 1–31 to represent a day of the month. If a letter is sent out on, say, the 4th of the month, an extra copy of the letter is produced and this will be filed in number 11 section (one week after the letter has been sent out by which time a reply should have been received). Every day the filing clerk will check the 'tickler system' to see if replies for that day have been received. If they have, the extra copy is removed; if not, they can be chased up.

Pending tray

A pending tray is used for work which is awaiting attention.

Borrowing files

If someone wishes to take a file away, they must complete an outcard (see illustration below). This is necessary in case the file is needed urgently by someone else. An absent wallet is left in place of the file and any loose papers which arrive while the file is out are kept in the absent wallet. The outcard gives details of who has borrowed the file, when it was borrowed and the intended date of return. This is useful to locate a file if it is required urgently and is missing from the filing cabinet.

FILE NAME	BORROWER	DEPARTMENT	DATE OUT	DATE RETURNED
BARKER	S. JONES	SALES	5/6	6/6

Outcard

Cross-referencing

When you look in one place for a file and it directs you somewhere else, this is called cross-referencing (see illustration below). This might arise because firms sometimes change their name, perhaps after being taken over by another company; women usually change their name when they get married; in some instances an item fits into two categories and is therefore referred to in both files with the cross-reference to the other file or to whichever is the main file.

Duties of a filing clerk

1 Check all papers are finished with and can be filed.
2 Check enclosures are firmly fixed to the correct document and that there are no extra pieces of paper from another file attached.
3 Sort into order.
4 File away carefully in filing cabinet in correct place. File regularly, preferably each day – this prevents a stockpile of filing.
5 If there are any missing files, check an outcard has been completed and that there is an absent wallet in place of the file for loose papers.

Indexing

Sometimes firms need to keep separately small amounts of information, such as important telephone numbers. It would be pointless opening a file just to store a telephone number and so an index system is set up as a quick-reference guide. There are different types available – for example, box, rotary, strip, visible edge and slot (all shown opposite). Information is written or typed on to index cards which are kept in order so that they can be referred to when necessary.

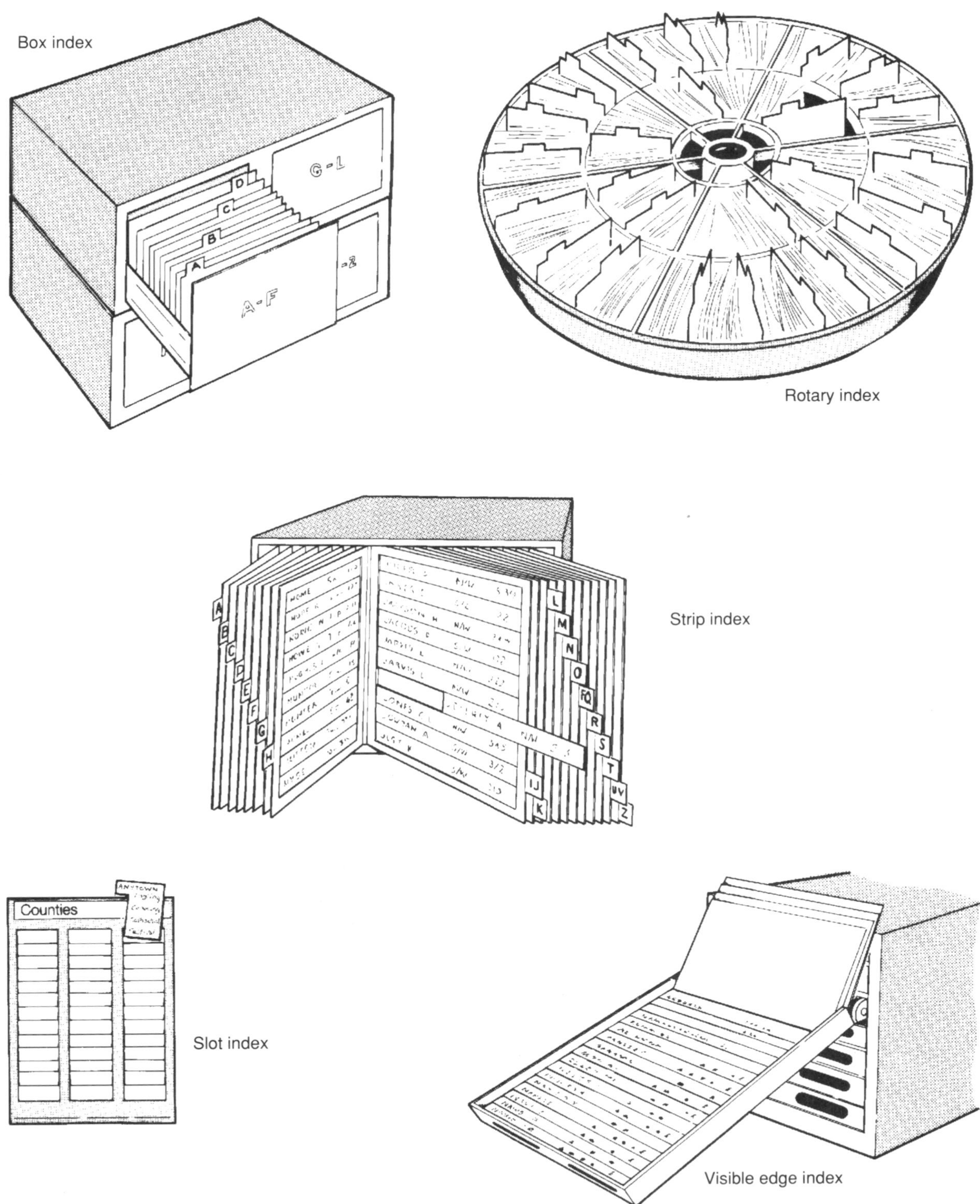

Box index

Rotary index

Strip index

Slot index

Visible edge index

Filing equipment

Filing cabinets

Files are housed in an assortment of cabinets. The type used will depend on the space available and type of information to be stored. Vertical suspension cabinets containing two, three or four drawers are used by most establishments. Files are inserted into filing pockets which are supported by metal rods. The file headings can be read clearly and papers can easily be inserted or removed. The main drawbacks of this type of equipment is the space needed to pull out the drawers, and if too much is stored in the top of the cabinet it could topple over.

Lateral filing is a space-saving way of filing as there are no drawers to open. Cabinets do not take up much floor space and can be extended upwards if required. The files are suspended in pockets in the same way as in vertical cabinets and they look similar to books on a shelf. However, the file headings can be difficult to read.

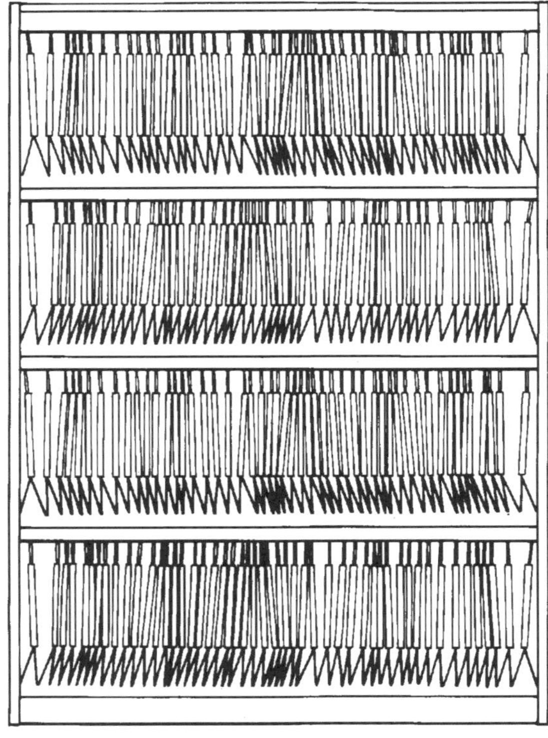

Microfilming

Microfilming reduces documents in size and so offers a good alternative to large storage (plan) chests. However, it can be expensive to set up initially as special equipment is required. The equipment needed consists of a camera and some film, a jacketing machine (which puts a protective coating around the microfilm) and a reader/printer. Very old and valuable papers are microfilmed to reduce the risk of damage when handled. Microfilm comes in various forms – microfiche, roll of microfilm and aperture cards (all shown below).

Microfilm

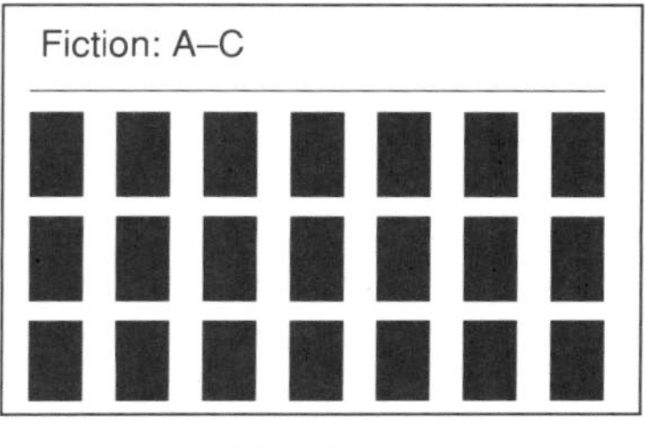

Microfiche

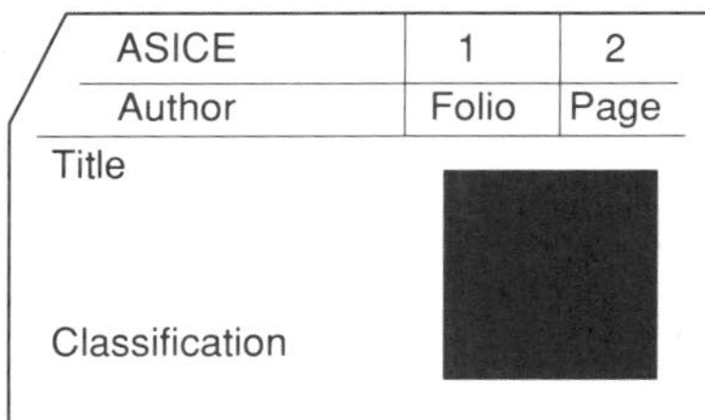

Aperture card

How much can you remember?

1 What special procedures have to be followed when filing papers away?
2 What happens when there are two possible places a file could be stored?
3 How can borrowed files be traced?
4 What is a filing point?
5 Explain the purpose of a release symbol.
6 What is a follow-up or tickler system?
7 In what instance would an indexing system be used?
8 List the different types of indexing system available.
9 What are the two most commonly used filing cabinets?
10 What are the advantages and disadvantages of a microfilming system?
11 What is electronic filing?

Activity 8.2

(a) Prepare a detailed job description for the post of filing clerk.

(b) Prepare a job specification for a filing clerk.

(c) (i) Design a one-day training programme for a filing clerk, with emphasis on practical work such as correctly completing documentation, which is an important part of the job.
(ii) Prepare any necessary documentation for the training session.
(iii) Evaluate your training programme by working through it and making any adjustments which you feel necessary.

Activity 8.3

SUGGESTED ASSIGNMENT/ESSAY TITLES

1 Investigate and compare the different types of conventional filing systems available to business.
2 Compare and evaluate an electronic database to a conventional filing system.
3 A microfilm system is very expensive to buy and limited in its use. Discuss.

Chapter 9 Meetings

By the end of this chapter you should be able to explain:

- the meaning of basic meeting terms
- the main types of meeting
- the preparations required prior to holding a meeting, including making travel arrangements for participants where necessary
- the purpose of an agenda and minutes
- the procedure during a meeting
- the duties and responsibilities of the chairperson and secretary
- teleconferencing
- the preparations involved in arranging travel at home and abroad.

What is a meeting?

Meeting in progress

If a group of people get together to discuss something, then it is a meeting. Some meetings are informal – for example, a friendly chat or group discussion where everyone joins in and has a say with no specific rules or regulations. However, in business, some meetings are more formal and they have to follow set procedures and rules (constitution).

When a meeting is called (convened), a certain number of people have to be present (quorum) to make decisions before it can go ahead. Sometimes a small committee is formed to discuss a special event – for example, 'a retirement celebration' – this is called an ad-hoc sub-committee.

Types of meetings

Meetings can be divided into two main types. The first is one where information is disseminated, the other is where decisions are made. In the case of the latter type of meeting, goals are set and then discussions follow as to how to achieve those goals.

Meeting with audience

The setting up and carrying out of both types of meetings involves different procedures. When information is being given out there can be a large number of people attending; these are seated as an audience with the person in control at the front. There is usually an opportunity at the end for questions.

When discussions are necessary it is essential to impose a limit on the number of participants who are invited. It is important, therefore, when selecting participants to choose people who can contribute to the meeting. The more people who are involved in the discussions, the longer and less effective the meeting will be as decision making will become very slow. Participants are normally seated facing each other around a large conference table.

Preparing for a meeting

Before a meeting can take place there are certain preparations which have to be made:

- A room must be booked and refreshments arranged. The room should be large enough for the number of participants and comfortable, that is, have adequate heating, lighting and ventilation. Many companies have purpose-built conference rooms in which they hold regular formal meetings.
- Audio-visual equipment should be available for use during a meeting, for example flip chart, video, cassette recorder and overhead projector.
- About two weeks prior (or the time stipulated by a constitution) to a meeting, a notice should be sent out to the people who are invited to inform them: *who* is holding the meeting (for example, IT working party), *what* the meeting is about (IT – Key Stage 4), *where* it is to be held (small conference room), *when* it will take place (Friday 3 December 1994).
- An agenda must be prepared and sent out (see example below). The word 'agenda' is a Latin word and it means 'to be done', hence, an agenda is a list of items to be discussed at the meeting. The most effective type of agenda is one that participants of the meeting have contributed towards.

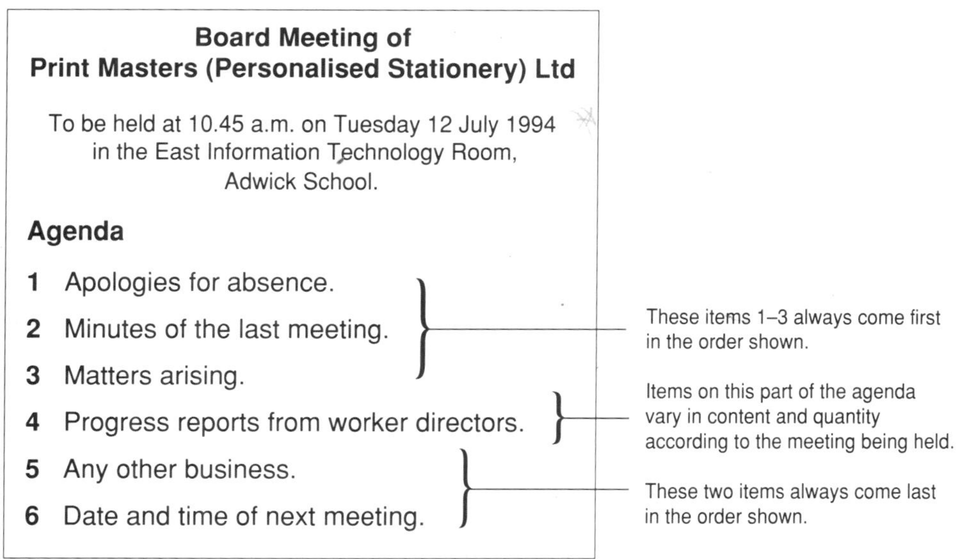

Board Meeting of
Print Masters (Personalised Stationery) Ltd

To be held at 10.45 a.m. on Tuesday 12 July 1994
in the East Information Technology Room,
Adwick School.

Agenda

1 Apologies for absence.
2 Minutes of the last meeting.
3 Matters arising.
4 Progress reports from worker directors.
5 Any other business.
6 Date and time of next meeting.

These items 1–3 always come first in the order shown.
Items on this part of the agenda vary in content and quantity according to the meeting being held.
These two items always come last in the order shown.

Once the notice of meeting has been circulated, participants have the opportunity if they wish to put forward ideas for the agenda. It is usual for the agenda to be sent out prior to the meeting so that participants know what to prepare for it and what material to take for the discussions. Sometimes the agenda is added to the bottom of the notice.

A special agenda is also prepared for the chairperson; this has a wide right margin, so that notes can be added during the meeting.

Travel arrangements and accommodation booking may also be necessary for participants attending meetings away from base.

During the meeting

A meeting should always be opened on time and have a scheduled ending time. Apologies for absence are read out at the beginning of the meeting. It is important to send apologies if you are unable to attend a meeting, because if you are a member of a committee and you miss more than a specified number of meetings without sending apologies you can lose your place on the committee.

The meeting proceeds with items being discussed in the order given on the agenda. Everyone should have the opportunity to give his or her point of view during the meeting without interruption from other participants. During the meeting notes are taken of the main points discussed and any decisions made. These notes are later typed up in the form of minutes (see example opposite) and read at the next meeting.

As minutes can be lengthy documents they are often circulated prior to the meeting to give participants the opportunity to read them thoroughly. If they notice discrepancies, these are mentioned in the next meeting under Matters Arising. If they have not been distributed in advance of the meeting they are read out. If everyone agrees that the minutes give a fair and true account of what happened at the previous meeting, they are signed by the chairperson as read (agreed).

At a meeting, a person may make a proposal – for example, that the forthcoming retirement party for Cyril Windbourne should be held at the Earl Hotel and not in the staff social club. If someone else seconds this (supports the proposal), it becomes a motion and is voted on. If there is a majority vote for the motion, it is said to be carried and it becomes a resolution. Sometimes no one votes against a motion, but this does not mean that eveyone has voted *for* it. Some people cannot decide and so do not vote at all (abstain). When this happens, it is called nem-con, which means 'no one contradicting'. If everyone votes for a motion, it is said to be unanimous.

When all the matters on the agenda have been discussed and dealt with, the meeting is closed. If time runs out before some matters have been dealt with, then the meeting is adjourned (temporarily closed).

When members cannot attend personally, they sometimes vote by proxy. This allows them to send in a postal vote or get someone else to vote for them.

Minutes

Minutes of a meeting of the Board of Directors of Print Masters (Personalised Stationery) Ltd held at 10.45 a.m. on Tuesday 12 July in East Information Technology Room, Adwick School.

Present	C. Shillito	(Managing Director)
	C. Parnham	(Company Secretary)
	D. Brown	(Production)
	R. Simpkin	(Packaging & Distribution)
	M. Baker	(Personnel)
	H. Javaid	(Marketing)
	D. Rafferty	(Design)
	C. Garland	(Purchasing)

1 Apologies:	An apology was received from G. Johnson (Finance)
2 Minutes of the last meeting:	These were read and approved.
3 Matters arising:	There were no matters arising.
4 Progress reports from worker directors:	
Managing Director	A badge-making machine was available to the group. The only cost involved would be a voluntary contribution from them.
Company Secretary	A request was made that all counterfoils from the share books be returned as soon as possible so that the register of shareholders could be completed.
Distribution	Research into a suitably priced and good quality package was continuing.
Personnel	The training programme for the desk top publisher was now ready to commence. Final details to be agreed with individual worker directors.
Marketing	Results were not yet available from market research. These were in the final stages and would be produced for the next meeting.
Sales/Design	Company documents had been designed and would be produced by the trainees using the desk top publisher. An advertising campaign was being prepared.
Purchasing	A sum of £50 was required to buy in materials before the company could begin to produce the goods.
Any other business:	There was no other business and the meeting concluded at 11.55 a.m.
Date/time of next meeting:	This was arranged for Thursday 8 September at 10.45 a.m.

Signed ....
Chairperson

Who does what?

The chairperson

This is the person who is in charge of the meeting and is referred to as Mr or Madam Chairman. The duties of the chairperson involve:

- opening and closing meetings, including welcoming visiting participants
- checking a quorum is present
- presenting clearly the objectives of the meeting
- keeping order during the meeting
- ensuring topics are discussed in the order given on the agenda and that everyone has an opportunity to present their point of view
- keeping each speaker to the point and preventing them drifting off the subject being discussed
- signing the previous minutes when they are agreed
- counting any votes and giving out the results
- using his or her casting vote (deciding vote) if there is an even number voting for and against a motion.
- closing the meeting with a summary of what has been accomplished and the agreed action which needs to be taken, usually prior to the next meeting.

The secretary

The duties of the secretary involve:

- preparing and sending out the notice and agenda for the meeting
- booking a suitable room, and arranging for refreshments, pens and paper to be available
- reading out the apologies at the meeting of the people who have not been able to attend
- taking notes during the meeting and preparing the minutes after the meeting has ended.

How much can you remember?

1 What are the two main types of meeting?
2 Explain the meaning of a quorum.
3 What is the name given to a small committee formed for a special purpose?
4 Make a list of preparations which have to be made prior to a meeting.
5 Outline the procedures at a meeting.
6 Explain the purpose of an agenda and a set of minutes.
7 What special responsibilities do the chairperson and secretary have?

Activity 9.1 You are the person responsible for organising meetings. The next senior management meeting is to be held three weeks today. Your company has three conference rooms: Room 1 holds 3–10 participants, Room 2 holds 10–25, and Room 3 is a very large room which can hold up to 150 people. Room 1 has already been booked for the full day on the date of your meeting by a group of ten partcipants. Your meeting is to begin at 11.30 a.m. and will last approximately two hours over a working lunch. Rooms and refreshments are booked through Miss M Morgan who is the managing director's secretary. There will be six participants. Details of these together with items for the agenda are given below:

Participants: Managing Director (Chairperson), Financial Director, Sales/Marketing Director, Personnel Manager, Works Manager and Chief Buyer. The Purchasing Officer was invited but has had to send apologies.

Items for agenda: Launch of new product – Marketing Director; costings – Financial Director; maintaining production levels – Works Manager; purchase of raw materials – Chief Buyer; staff training – Personnel Manager; future company policy – Managing Director.

task 1

(a) Prepare a memo to make the booking arrangements.

(b) Prepare the notice.

(c) Prepare the agenda.

(d) The theme of the meeting is to discuss the launch of a new product. Make a list of the preparations that each director will have to make for this meeting.

task 2

The secretary who made notes at the meeting is away ill and the minutes are needed. She wrote out the main points (see below) yesterday so she could type them up today. You have been asked to type them up urgently using the correct format. The secretary has not written down who said what – you will have to sort this out.

Notes for meeting
Product almost ready to trial – packaging bright and attractive but market research shows that orange more popular than brown originally planned. Most of the staff concerned now trained and ready to begin production. Costings completed – agreed chocolate bar would go on sale at 28p. Research shows this is 2p cheaper than similar bars produced by competitors. Costings include a small bonus to offer to production workers to help ensure high production levels maintained. Suppliers contacted and good discounts negotiated. Just one not yet reached agreement. It was confirmed company intended to launch a further two new products within the next five years.

Technology in meetings

Many companies deal with firms located in other parts of the country and abroad. Having face-to-face meetings is effective but can be very time consuming and costly (particularly if two or three members of a company have to attend a meeting and if long-distance travel is required and overnight accommodation). The cost becomes even greater if the meetings are held regularly. Also long journeys result in fatigue and stress for the traveller. Traffic jams, flight delays and late trains can be very frustrating and it is always best to begin a meeting feeling refreshed as meetings are important events, where major decisions are often made. If you are very tired or suffering from jet-lag you will not be at your best.

As UK businesses trade more and more with Europe, more continental travel will become necessary and this can be very expensive. However, with the developments in technology there are now cost-effective alternatives available.

Teleconferencing

Videoconferencing

There are several types of teleconferencing available: audioconferencing, video-conferencing and business television services and systems. These services are provided by British Telecom.

Audioconferencing

This allows individuals and small groups of people at two or more locations to be linked together into one telephone line. A benefit of this system is that no complicated equipment is required.

Videoconferencing

This allows individuals and small groups of people at two or more locations to see and hear each other, face-to-face, through live video and sound links. They can show documents and display a whole range of materials to members of the meeting at the other location(s).

Videoconferencing centres

Videoconferencing centres are specially designed meeting rooms which are located around the UK, generally in city centres with easy access to main roads, rail and airways. Each centre can be linked into as many as six other centres. Each room provides accommodation for up to six participants but there is space to accommodate additional participants if necessary. The rooms can also be used for international meetings as there are videoconferencing centres worldwide. These studios have to be booked prior to the meeting.

Private videoconferencing

This service (previously known as Videostream) allows videoconferencing from a company's own premises. The equipment is built into compact free-standing units which can easily be installed into existing conference and meeting rooms. This latest development allows meetings to be held at short notice and avoids having to book a BT videoconferencing studio. Equipment can be bought or rented, allowing two or more centres to be linked together.

Switched videoconferencing

This allows videoconferencing centres and private videoconferencing rooms to be linked together. Therefore, companies which have their own private room can still communicate with people in a hired videoconferencing studio.

Desk-top videoconferencing

This system can be housed on an office desk top. It comprises mainly a TV monitor, a built-in camera and a keypad. To help highlight discussion points, a document reader can be attached to the system so that graphics and text can be transmitted between locations. At large events, for example press conferences and sales reviews, it is possible using auxiliary cameras and monitors for a large number of people to be present.

Desk-top videoconferencing

This system is not a videophone, which is designed for one-to-one phone calls – it is a videoconferencing unit which provides all the necessary facilities for linking together larger groups. As the unit can be rented, it makes videoconferencing a practical option for smaller firms who may not wish to go to the expense of purchasing a unit.

Business television

This enables a company to broadcast its own live or pre-recorded programmes from a central location of its choosing, to audiences of any size, at any number of other locations. This is an ideal method of communication for one-off special events, like product launches, sales conferences or annual general meetings.

If a business wants its own television network – say for staff training, broadcasting company news to staff or for selling to customers – the equipment for this can be installed. This service offers a two-way sound link to enable question and answer sessions to take place after the live or pre-recorded broadcasts. It can carry several different commentaries at the same time, which is useful for overcoming language barriers.

Benefits of teleconferencing

There are a number of benefits of teleconferencing:

- As participants do not have to travel to the meeting but can stay on their company's premises, meetings are much easier to arrange and at short notice.
- Unexpected situations can be dealt with quickly as discussions can take place and the company can react and make a decision without delay.
- If half-way through a meeting the advice of a specialist is required, that person regardless of which location he or she is stationed at can be brought into the meeting.
- The time saved by not having to travel and stay away from the office can be used more profitably.
- It is a cost-effective alternative to a face-to-face meeting and reduces the stress and fatigue caused by travelling long distances.

How much can you remember?

1 What are the alternatives to travelling to hold face-to-face meetings and what are the benefits?
2 What is meant by videoconferencing?
3 Explain the different types of videoconferencing available.
4 What is business television?

Activity 9.2

As a senior secretary part of your job involves making travel arrangements for the managers of your company. You are based at a branch in Home Town but your company, Porritt & Maradew Ltd, has a branch in Leeds also. A meeting is due to take place two weeks on Thursday at the Leeds branch. Two of the directors, Mr Spinks and Ms Hamilton will travel together to the Leeds office by car for the meeting which is scheduled to begin promptly at 10 a.m. and end by 12 noon. A third director, Mr Cartland, will be in Sheffield the day prior to the meeting and as he is so close he has decided to stay overnight and travel to Leeds by train the next morning.

Mr Spinks and Ms Hamilton will be returning to Home Town immediately after lunch the same afternoon, but Mr Cartland has another meeting in London the next day. His accommodation has been booked but he will require train times to London after the meeting and for his return journey on Friday evening around 7 p.m.

task

(a) Make the necessary travel arrangements for the meeting, assuming Home Town to be your own town:

(i) Find the train times from Sheffield to Leeds, Leeds to London and London to Home Town on the appropriate days at the necessary times.
(ii) Prepare a route map for Mr Spinks and Ms Hamilton for their journey from Home Town to Leeds.
(iii) Send each member of staff a memo confirming the arrangements and enclose individual itineraries.

(b) The next meeting is one month today and is to be held at the Home Town branch. Two managers from Leeds will be attending the meeting. Their own secretaries are arranging the travel but you have been asked to book overnight accommodation in the local area for them. Six staff from Home Town will also be participating in the meeting.

(i) Select a suitable hotel in the local area and write a letter of confirmation.
(ii) The meeting is to be chaired by the personnel manager, Ms R Raynor, in the absence of the managing director. Send her a memo to inform her of the arrangements for the meeting which will be held between 2.30 and 4.30 p.m.
(iii) Send a letter to the Leeds branch, confirming the accommodation and meeting details arranged.

Activity 9.3

Meetings are becoming a regular and costly event for your company. An important meeting is to take place three weeks on Friday and this will involve nine executives travelling to the meeting and staying overnight. Your boss has heard about videoconferencing and has asked you to compare the cost before planning similar meetings in the future.

The meeting will be held in Birmingham. Three executives will be travelling from each of Glasgow, Manchester and France. If a traditional meeting is held the following costs will be incurred:

- Return travel for three people from Glasgow to Birmingham.
- Return travel for three people from Manchester to Birmingham.
- Return travel for three people from France to Birmingham.
- Overnight accommodation at a good hotel in the Birmingham area for one night for nine people.

task

(a) Using the videoconferencing reference guide opposite, calculate the cost/saving if videoconferencing is used as an alternative to a traditional face-to-face meeting.

(b) Present this information in a report to the managing director.

Videoconferencing centres tariffs

	London City (2 rooms)	Birmingham	Bristol	Isle of Man Douglas	Glasgow & Edinburgh	Ipswich	Manchester
Birmingham	£100						
Bristol	£100	£100					
Isle of Man Douglas	£200	£200	£200				
Glasgow & Edinburgh	£200	£200	£200	£200			
Ipswich	£100	£150	£200	£200	£200		
Manchester	£150	£100	£150	£150	£200	£200	
Europe	£415	£440	£440	£540	£540	£440	£490
Rest of the World	£725	£750	£750	£850	£850	£750	£800

This quick reference guide shows you the hourly cost of a videoconference between the locations indicated.

The cost of national calls includes the hire of both rooms, transmission and light refreshments. For international calls the charges for overseas rooms and transmission are raised by the videoconferencing service provider in that country.

A typical international videoconferencing would be charged as follows:

London (UK room and transmission £725 per hour	to +	New York (US room and transmission) $1,150 per hour approx	=	Total charge £1,450 approx

Discounts are available for regular users. To some destinations in the USA lower tariffs apply. Contact BT for details.

All videoconferencing calls are charged in half hour segments and prices exclude VAT.

Multipoint videoconferences

For UK multipoint calls involving three BT Video-conferencing centres the rate is £300 per hour. For each additional room, up to a maximum of 7 locations, add another £100 per hour.

For a multipoint video-conferencing to international centres please contact us.

Activity 9.4

The company you work for is talking of expanding into Europe within the next two years and if its plans are successful there will be job opportunities at the new branch for existing staff. You see this as a great opportunity but as you have not travelled very much you are not sure how you would feel about moving to somewhere in Europe.

You have three weeks' leave due and you have decided to make the most of this and use two weeks to go to Europe for a holiday with three of your friends.

task 1

(a) Collect some brochures from your local travel agent and decide where in Europe you would like to spend your holiday.

(b) Extract information from a variety of sources about the resort of your choice and the surrounding areas. Present this information in an interesting way and display it.

(c) Browse round the room and read the information sheets on the various locations in Europe. Make a firm decision on where you will spend your vacation, make a note of the different places which interested you and explain how you made your final choice.

task 2

(a) Before deciding when you will travel you need to check the expected temperature as you do not like too hot a climate. Use a bar chart to show how the temperature changes during the year. Compare the temperatures to the other places which interested you.

(b) Choose your accommodation and decide on what date and how you will travel.

(c) Complete the necessary application form to book the holiday of your choice.

task 3

You need to ensure you have enough money saved to pay for the holiday and so you must carry out some budget planning.

(a) Prepare a table which gives full details of the cost for each individual on your holiday. This should include your proposed spending money and take account of any surcharges and insurance fees etc.

(b) Your salary is paid monthly. Calculate how much you need to save each month to ensure you have enough money to pay for your holiday and to take with you the proposed amount of spending money.

(c) Find out about local currency and the safest way of taking money abroad. You will also need to check the exchange rate.

Chapter 10 The mail room

By the end of this chapter you should be able to explain:

- the procedure for dealing with incoming mail in business
- the procedure for dealing with outgoing mail in business
- the importance of including a postcode on all external mail
- the equipment available to mail room staff and the benefits of using it.

Personal and business mail compared

At home the mail arrives and it drops through the letter-box in small quantities. Envelopes are opened by the person who the letter is addressed to (addressee) and read. There is no special procedure for dealing with the mail at home – each member of the family opens his or her mail and deals with it as they think fit. There are days when no post arrives at all.

Business post tends to arrive in larger quantities and special procedures are set up to deal with it. If envelopes were opened in a disorganised way, mail could be delayed reaching the addressee and some of it may even go astray. In smaller firms mail is dealt with by general office staff who also carry out a range of other duties. In organisations where large quantities of mail arrive each day a special department takes care of it.

Many office juniors begin their lives in the mail room as it gives them the opportunity to become familiar with the firm and the people who are employed by it.

Incoming mail

Most information which a business receives comes by Royal Mail each day and larger organisations may receive letters by the sackful. Firms like to have their mail early in the morning so that staff can begin work quickly when they arrive. Unfortunately the post does not always arrive until later in the morning, which can be inconvenient particularly if an important letter is expected. Businesses can arrange to collect their own mail early in the morning by renting a private post box from Royal Mail, for which there is a yearly charge.

Even in smaller firms the quantity of mail will fluctuate and some days there will be large quantities. When letters arrive in bulk, it is necessary to organise a system to deal with the mail to ensure that nothing gets lost and that letters reach the correct addressee as quickly as possible.

The mail room staff sometimes begin work early on a rota basis so that they can have the mail ready on the desks of employees when they arrive. The procedures involved in dealing with incoming mail are summarised in the illustration on page 151.

When letters arrive they do not always have the name of the addressee on the envelope – in many instances the envelope just bears the name and address of the firm. It is common, therefore, unless a letter is marked 'Private & Confidential' or 'Personal', for the mail room staff to open all the mail.

Once a letter has been opened it is date stamped and this provides a record of when it arrived. A check is made to see that enclosures are attached and this can be done quickly by glancing at the bottom of the letter to see if it contains the letters 'Enc'. If the enclosure is missing, a pencil note is added to the letter so that the recipient is aware that the enclosure was missing when the letter was opened.

Money, cheques and postal orders are dealt with in a special way. After checking that the amount specified in the letter agrees with the amount actually sent, the relevant details are entered into a book called a remittance book (see illustration right). The money is then sent to the cashier who will arrange to pay it into the firm's bank account.

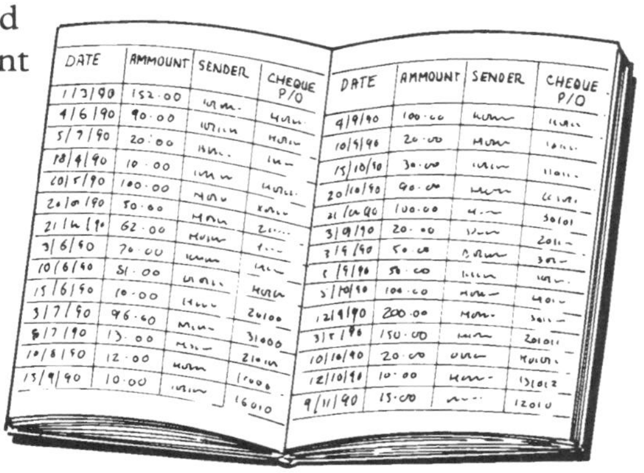

Remittance book

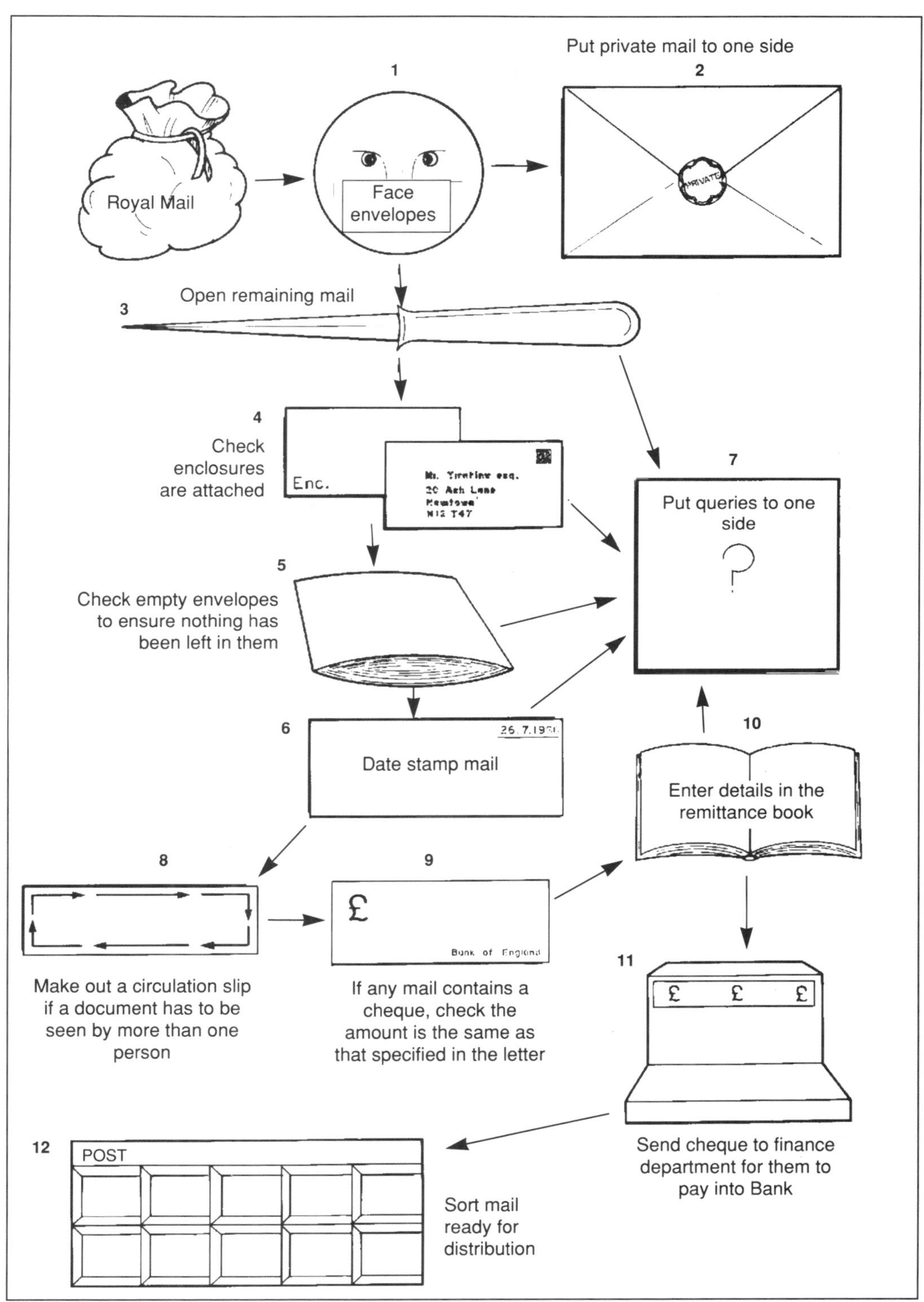
Put private mail to one side
1
2
Royal Mail
Face envelopes
PRIVATE
3
Open remaining mail
4
Check enclosures are attached
Enc.
7
Put queries to one side
5
Check empty envelopes to ensure nothing has been left in them
6
Date stamp mail
10
Enter details in the remittance book
8
9
£
Make out a circulation slip if a document has to be seen by more than one person
If any mail contains a cheque, check the amount is the same as that specified in the letter
11
£ £ £
Send cheque to finance department for them to pay into Bank
12
POST
Sort mail ready for distribution

Procedures for dealing with incoming mail

Outgoing mail

In response to many of the letters an office receives it sends out a large quantity of information, the bulk of which is by Royal Mail. Once the incoming mail has been dealt with, preparations begin to deal with the outgoing mail. Post room staff go round each department at regular intervals throughout the working day to collect letters which are to be posted. Some letters will have already been inserted into envelopes before they reach the mail room. When this is the case, mail room staff will weigh them if necessary, stamp and post them. However, in other firms, the mail room staff are expected to insert the letters into envelopes. Outgoing mail must be organised and prepared for despatch in an organised way and there are procedures which need to be followed (by departmental staff or post room staff) to minimise mistakes:

- Check the letter is dated and signed.
- Check enclosures are attached
- Check the address on the envelope is the same as on the letter (if window envelopes are not being used).
- Place the letter and any enclosures in the envelope.
- Weigh if necessary and stamp/frank the envelope.

It is very easy when dealing with a large quantity of mail to put a letter into the wrong envelope. This can prove most embarrassing for a firm if a letter is sent to the wrong address, and therefore some firms choose to use window envelopes to ensure this does not happen.

The postcode

It is important always to include a postcode on any mail which is being sent as this enables Royal Mail to sort letters much faster using automation. Each part of a code identifies a more and more local area, right down to 15 or so individual addresses. Many buildings, blocks of flats for example, have their own unique postcode. There are 1.6 million postcodes which cover the country's 24 million letter-boxes. The illustration below shows how the postcode works.

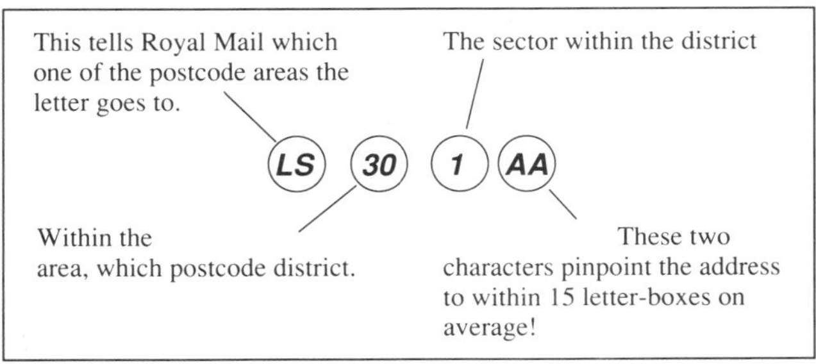

This tells Royal Mail which one of the postcode areas the letter goes to.
The sector within the district
LS
30
1
AA
Within the area, which postcode district.
These two characters pinpoint the address to within 15 letter-boxes on average!

If you are sending mail to an address for which you do not know the postcode, there is a national postcode enquiry line (0345 111222) which will supply you with the postcode of any UK address. All telephone calls are charged at local rates (0345 lines are explained more fully in Chapter 12).

Postage/stamp book

A record of stamps used is kept by some firms in a postage/stamp book (see example below). As stamps are used, more are bought to replace them. The postage/stamp book is kept on an imprest system, which is explained fully in Chapter 14.

Stamps Bought		Date			
£	p				
45	60	17 March 199-	Balance b/f		
			Askews & Sons, Doncaster		25
			Mrs R. Hill, Sheffield		25
			Mr D. Plant, Essex		25
			Millow & Pardow, Northampton		25
			25 circular letters	6	25
			registered packet to Darton & Wold, Shropshire	3	24
				10	49
			Balance to carry forward (£45.60 – £10.49)	35	11
45	60			45	60
35	11	14 March 199-	Balance b/f		

Postage/stamp record book

Franking machine

Sticking stamps on envelopes can be very tedious and very time-consuming, so some firms which send out a lot of mail regularly use a franking machine (see illustration on page 154). This is a machine that prints the impression of a postage stamp on to an envelope or label.

There are two meters on the machine, one which keeps a record of postage used and the other which decreases each time postage is used. It is possible for users to arrange to purchase postage and recredit their machines over the telephone. When a firm recredits its franking machine it can pay automatically through direct debit (see Chapter 13 for explanation of direct debits), which saves time and paperwork. Firms that use franking machines are less likely to run out of postage than those that have to keep going to the post office to buy stamps.

Franking machine

As parcels are too bulky to go through a franking machine, labels are used which, after franking, are stuck on to the parcel. Firms that use franking machines have to obtain a licence, which is free of charge from the Post Office, but the machine itself is purchased or rented from office equipment suppliers.

Franked mail is often referred to as metered mail and it is dealt with slightly differently from post bearing ordinary stamps. Before it is sent to a post office, mail room staff have to face the mail (all addresses facing the same way) and tie it together in bundles. It cannot be put in the post box like ordinary mail – it has to be collected by Royal Mail or taken into a post office and handed over the counter. When it reaches the sorting office it is dealt with more quickly as it bypasses facing and cancelling as mail has already been faced and there is no stamp to cancel.

Metered mail users have the option of including an advertisement or return address on the envelope when the postage is printed and this creates a more professional appearance.

Additional mail room equipment

Besides a franking machine there are other items of equipment which are very useful in a busy mail room.

Electric letter opener

This machine slices a thin strip off the top of an envelope and is useful for organisations that have a large amount of mail to open. However, one disadvantage is that if mail room staff forget to tap the envelope on the desk to ensure the contents fall to the bottom of the envelope before putting it through the machine, it may take a slice of the letter as well as the envelope.

Folding and inserting machine

This equipment does exactly what its name suggests: it folds letters and inserts them into envelopes automatically.

Electronic scales

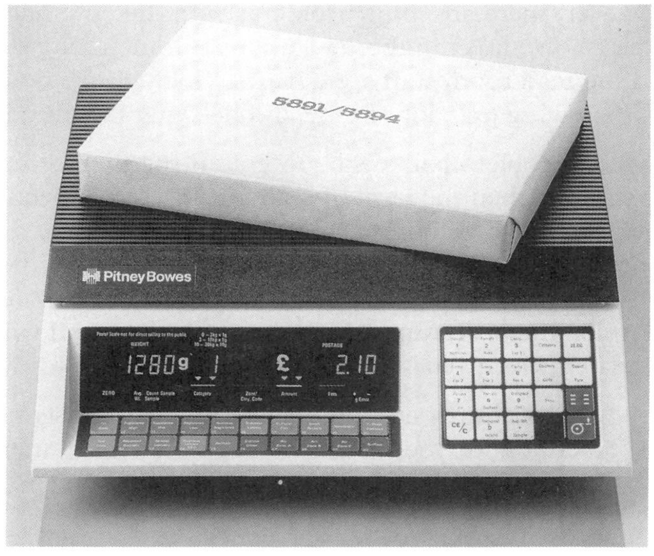

Electronic scales

Modern scales not only show the weight of an item but also the amount of postage required. They are suitable for letters and parcels and when postal rates change they are very easily adjusted.

The latest mail room machines incorporate all the above into one piece of equipment and in addition there is often the facility to seal envelopes.

How much can you remember?

1 Why do larger establishments have a mail room specially to deal with incoming and outgoing mail?
2 Office juniors often begin their duties in the mail room; why do you think this is of benefit?
3 Explain the purpose of a PO Box.
4 Why is it necessary for mail room staff to start work earlier than other office workers?
5 Using a diagram to illustrate your answer, describe a remittance book.
6 What mail is not opened by mail room staff and why?
7 What steps can mail room staff take to avoid a rush at the end of each working day?
8 Why is it important to check that mail is placed in the correct envelope?
9 What are the advantages of using window envelopes?
10 How can a firm keep a record of how much is being spent on postage?
11 What is meant by 'facing' envelopes?
12 What is another name for franked mail?

Activity 10.1

The mail room staff have been congratulated on several occasions for the organised and efficient way in which they deal with the incoming mail. However, there are some problems with the outgoing mail and these need to be resolved. A number of staff are not including a postcode on their mail and the mail room staff are having to look up the codes and add them. This is taking up a lot of time and delaying the outgoing mail.

Another problem being encountered is the time being spent sending out for stamps when the level of mail increases unexpectedly. One evening last week a whole batch of mail missed the 5.30 post and the situation does not appear to be improving.

task 1

Describe the procedure which the mail room staff will follow to deal with these items received:

(i) A letter addressed to the marketing department.
(ii) A letter addressed to the managing director, marked 'personal'.
(iii) A letter with 'Enc' at the bottom but nothing is attached to it.
(iv) A letter containing a cheque for £67.49.

task 2 To help resolve one of the problems being experienced by mail room staff when dealing with outgoing mail, as supervisor of the mail room, send a memo to all section heads and explain to them why it is important that they address letters correctly and that a postcode is included on all outgoing mail.

task 3 Explain how a franking machine could solve the problem regarding postage stamps.

Activity 10.2 As supervisor of a very busy mail room you are becoming very concerned about the increasing quantity of mail being received and sent out. Staff are having to work during the afternoon without a break to ensure that the mail is despatched before they go home. The firm rents a PO Box and mail is being picked up early, but there are so many letters to deal with that staff are not receiving it until 10 a.m. each day. You need more modern equipment or more staff.

task 1 Prepare a report for the office manager making a case for and giving full details of the equipment you need.

task 2 To try to improve the existing service, prepare a checklist for the mail room notice board for:

(a) incoming mail procedures
(b) outgoing mail procedures.

Chapter 11 Postal services

By the end of this chapter you should be able to explain:

- the main factors to be considered before choosing a postal service
- the need for a wide range of postal services to suit businesses and individuals
- the suitability of particular services
- the increasing need for some businesses to send mail abroad.

Royal mail building

Choosing a postal service

Numerous postal services are available and, when you have something to send through the post, you have to find the service that best suits your needs. For example, you wouldn't send a very urgent letter second class ordinary letter post – would you? Some points you need to consider are:

- the size and weight of the letter or packet
- the value of the item being sent – some services offer special security handling and this makes them more expensive than other services
- the speed at which the letter or packet will reach its destination – some services are very fast as speed is their main priority.

Royal Mail services can be classified into four groups, although some services fall into more than one group:

- ordinary
- fast
- secure
- special.

Ordinary postal services

The ordinary services are not intended for anything other than items that do not require special handling and which if lost would not present the sender with serious problems.

For ordinary letters, cards and packets there is a two-tier postal service – first and second class post. First class is the more expensive and the faster of the two. Royal Mail aims to deliver first-class mail on the next working day following collection, and second-class mail by the third working day after collection.

The price of postage is determined by the weight of an item and which service is chosen. There is no upper limit for first-class post but items sent by second-class post must not exceed 750 g.

Proof of Posting

If proof of posting is required, a Certificate of Posting, which is a type of receipt, can be obtained free of charge from the post office (see illustration below). To use this service, take the letter/packet into any post office and ask for a Certificate of Posting. The clerk will copy the name and address of the addressee on to the certificate, stamp it and give it to the sender to keep as proof of posting in exchange for the letter/packet.

Similarly, if proof of delivery is required, an Advice of Delivery can be obtained from the post office. However, this is available only for Recorded and Registered services.

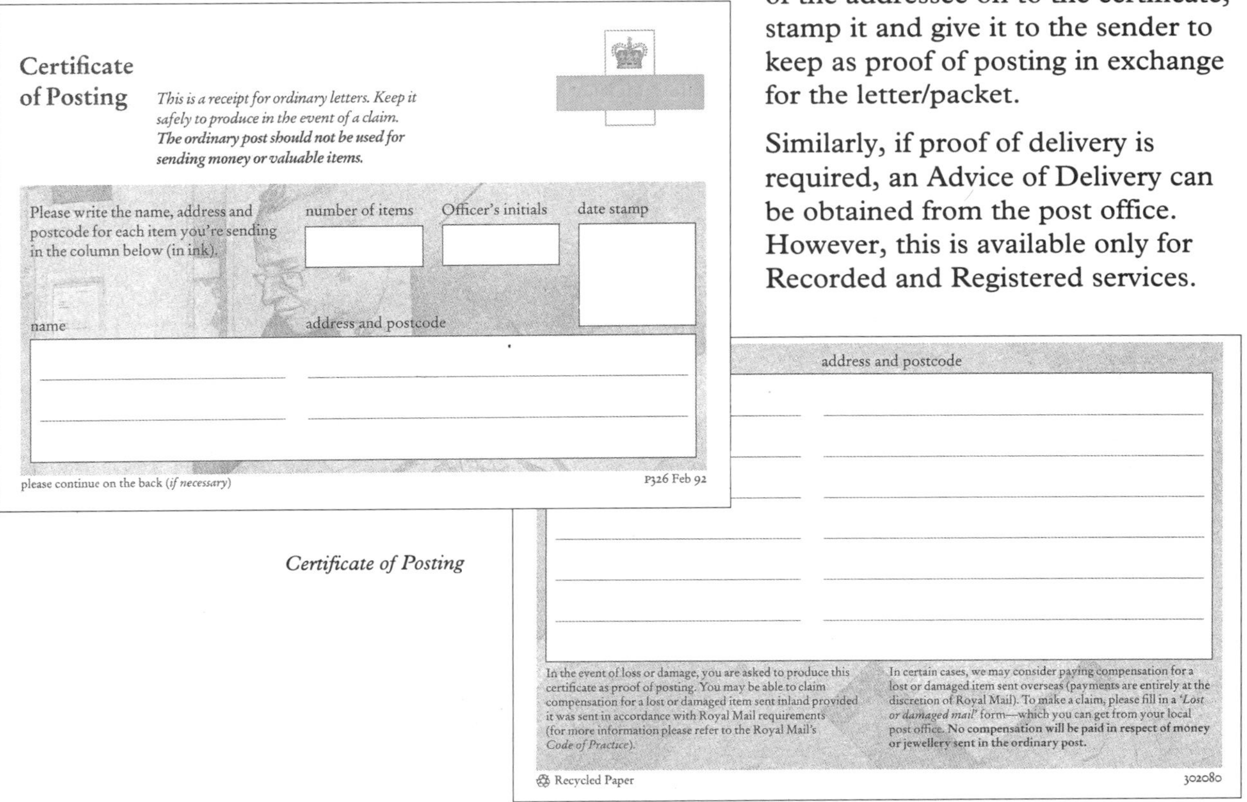

Certificate of Posting

This is a receipt for ordinary letters. Keep it safely to produce in the event of a claim.
The ordinary post should not be used for sending money or valuable items.

Please write the name, address and postcode for each item you're sending in the column below (in ink).

number of items | Officer's initials | date stamp

name | address and postcode

please continue on the back (*if necessary*)

P326 Feb 92

address and postcode

In the event of loss or damage, you are asked to produce this certificate as proof of posting. You may be able to claim compensation for a lost or damaged item sent inland provided it was sent in accordance with Royal Mail requirements (for more information please refer to the Royal Mail's *Code of Practice*).

In certain cases, we may consider paying compensation for a lost or damaged item sent overseas (payments are entirely at the discretion of Royal Mail). To make a claim, please fill in a *'Lost or damaged mail'* form—which you can get from your local post office. **No compensation will be paid in respect of money or jewellery sent in the ordinary post.**

Recycled Paper

302080

Certificate of Posting

Fast postal services

Speed of delivery is often the most important factor in deciding on which postal service to use. There are several services to choose from.

Special Delivery

Special Delivery mail travels first class as it is guaranteed to arrive the next working day after posting by 12.30 p.m. If the item arrives at the destination sorting office too late for the normal delivery, it is taken out by a special messenger. Letters/packets for Special Delivery have to be handed over the counter of a post office with the necessary completed form (see below). A signature is required on delivery. Mail sent using this service is given special priority handling at every stage of its journey over all other ordinary mail, and as it is barcoded it can be tracked throughout the Royal Mail network. This means that the sender can telephone Post Office Customer Care departments to check progress or confirm delivery.

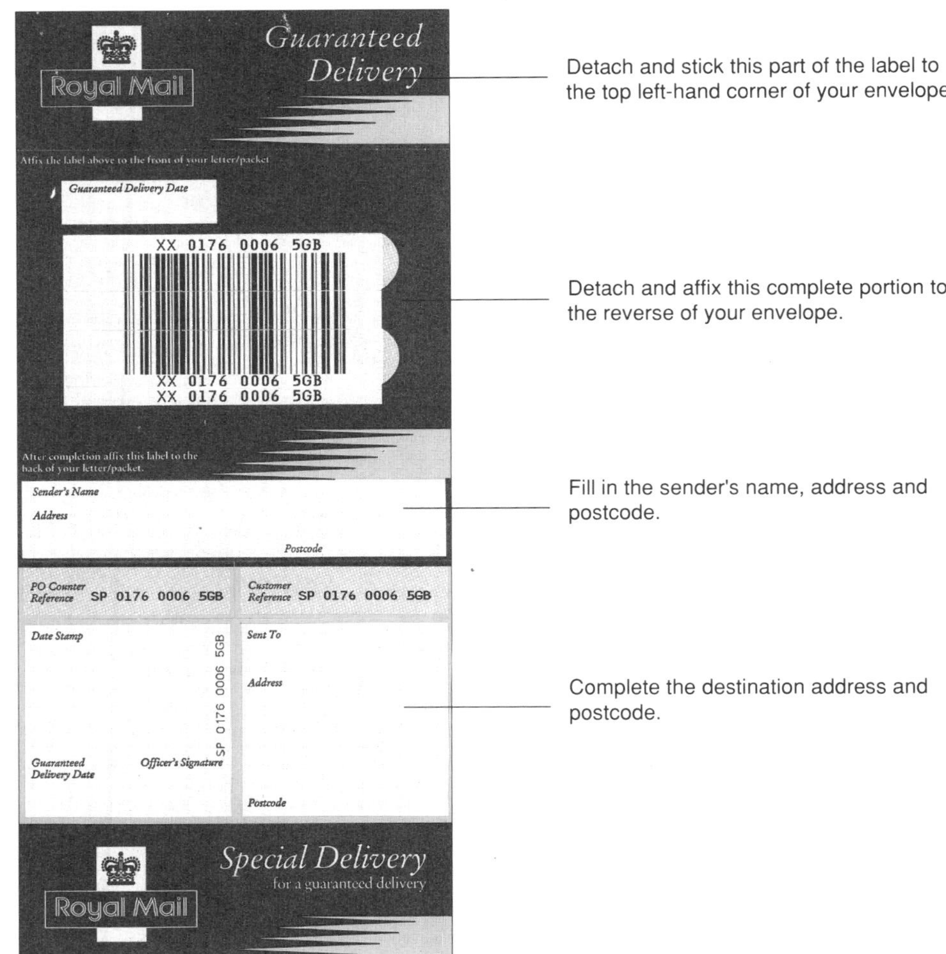

Faxmail

Faxmail is, as the name suggests, a facsimile (fax) electronic mailing service, which has the additional facility of a courier service. (There is more information on faxes on page 182.) Exact copies of documents, both text and drawings, can be sent from one place to another using the telephone network. It's just like sending a photocopy by telephone.

Documents can be taken to any post office offering Intelpost or, for an additional fee, they can be collected. If the recipient does not have a fax machine then the message can be sent to the nearest post office offering this service from which it can either be collected or for a small charge delivered to the addressee. This service is not only used by business people, it is available and used by private individuals. Faxmail is available to destinations worldwide and is not restricted to the UK.

Electronic post

Royal Mail will print out from your computer disk, insert into envelopes and despatch bulk mailings for customers. All the customer needs to do is to provide the message and a computer address list of where the message is to be sent and Royal Mail will do the rest (see illustration below).

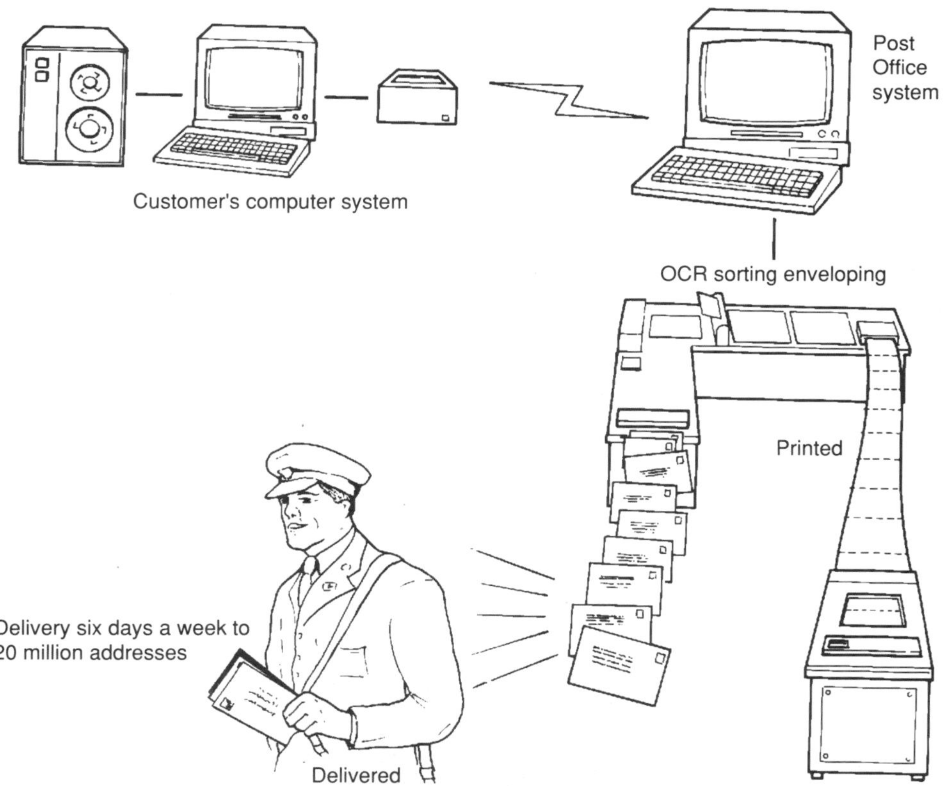

Electronic post

Secure postal services

In some situations, security is the most important factor. When secure services are used, compensation is paid according to the fee paid if there is any loss or damage and, in some cases, delay. Several secure services are available and these are usually quite fast as it is in Royal Mail's interest to deliver important and valuable items as quickly as possible.

Recorded Delivery

Recorded Delivery is an ideal service for sending important papers through the post. It is definitely not for cash and valuables but for documents which, if lost, would cause a great deal of inconvenience to replace. For example, if original examination certificates have to be sent away and they were lost, it would take time to obtain replacements. If they were sent by the Recorded Delivery service, they would be more secure and there would be less chance of them going astray as mail is barcoded, making them easier to trace.

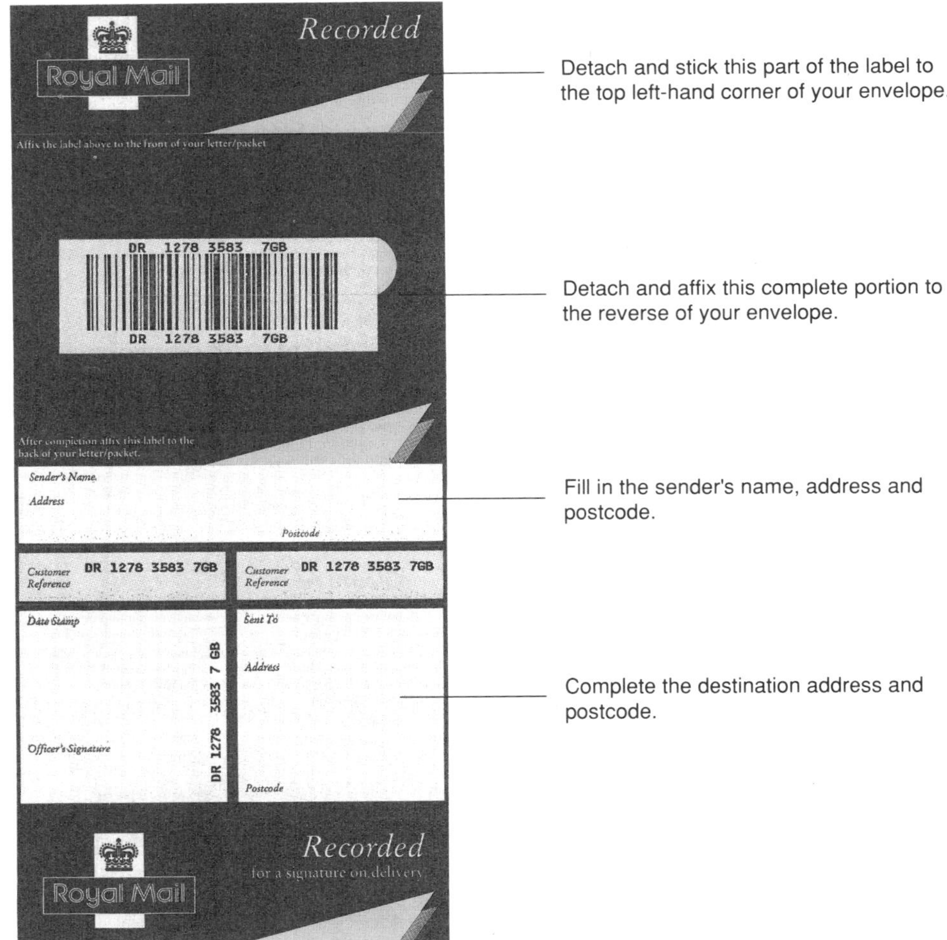

Letters/packets can be taken into any post office and sent Recorded Delivery using either first or second class mail. When posting, the sender is given a certificate which is date stamped and initialled for a receipt. A telephone call to Royal Mail Customer Care the day after delivery is due will confirm receipt.

Registered Post

Registered Post can be used for letters and packets which contain cash and valuables. It is a fast, reliable guaranteed next day delivery service with compensation up to £500. For money or valuables over that amount and up to £2,200 there is a Registered Plus service available which offers even more security.

You can buy special Registered envelopes from a post office, which have first class postage already pre-printed on them. Although any first-class envelope can be registered, if money is being sent in any form then a special pre-printed envelope must be used.

Items sent Registered Post do not travel with the ordinary mail; they receive special security handling at every stage of the journey with priority over ordinary mail. All mail is barcoded to enable tracking throughout its journey.

Consequential Loss

This is insurance cover which is used with Registered Post. Besides compensation being paid for loss or damage, if as a result of there being a delay it can be proved that the sender has suffered from a loss of money, then compensation may be paid accordingly.

Cash On Delivery (COD)

Cash on Delivery is popular with mail order firms. If you send for goods that have been advertised in a magazine enclosing the required amount of money, there is a risk that you may never receive the items, and you will have lost your money. Similarly, if a supplier advertises goods and sends them before receiving payment, the customer might never pay.

With COD, the supplier sends the item and it is delivered by the mail delivery person, who collects the cash before handing the item over. Any item over the value of £50 must be collected by the addressee, at which time payment must be made before the goods are handed over. All mail requiring COD must travel Registered Post. This service is available only for goods up to the value of £500.

The advantages of COD are that the addressee is assured of receiving the goods, while the sender is equally sure of receiving payment. A small fee is charged for this service.

Special postal services

Redirection

When you move house or office you can, for a fee, have your mail redirected for various periods of time. It is a simple procedure: all that is required is the completion of a redirection form which gives details of the old and new address and the individuals living at that address who wish their mail to be redirected.

Similarly firms can have mail diverted from their business address to a private address or vice versa. Another example of diverting business mail is from one branch of an organisation to another branch.

Poste Restante

Poste Restante means 'to be called for' and is suitable for people who travel around the country, as mail can be sent to any named post office for up to a period of three months. The addressee must collect the mail and be able to produce proof of their identity when doing so.

Business Reply service

BUSINESS REPLY SERVICE
Licence No AB1234

The Secretary
EAST MIDLAND REGIONAL EXAMINATIONS BOARD
Robins Wood House
Robins Wood Road
Aspley
Nottingham
NG8 1BR

Business Reply envelope

Firms offer this service to encourage customers to reply to letters. They pay the postage, so no stamp is required on the envelope. Special envelopes, postcards or gummed labels are used and these must be approved by Royal Mail. An example is shown opposite. The Post Office will also issue a licence to use this service. Mail travels first or second class according to the requirements of the business.

Freepost

Freepost is similar to the business reply service, but special envelopes do not have to be printed as the word 'Freepost' can be written as part of the address. A licence is required to use the service and mail usually travels second class. However, if firms have pre-printed envelopes prepared, they can arrange for Freepost mail to travel first class (see example below).

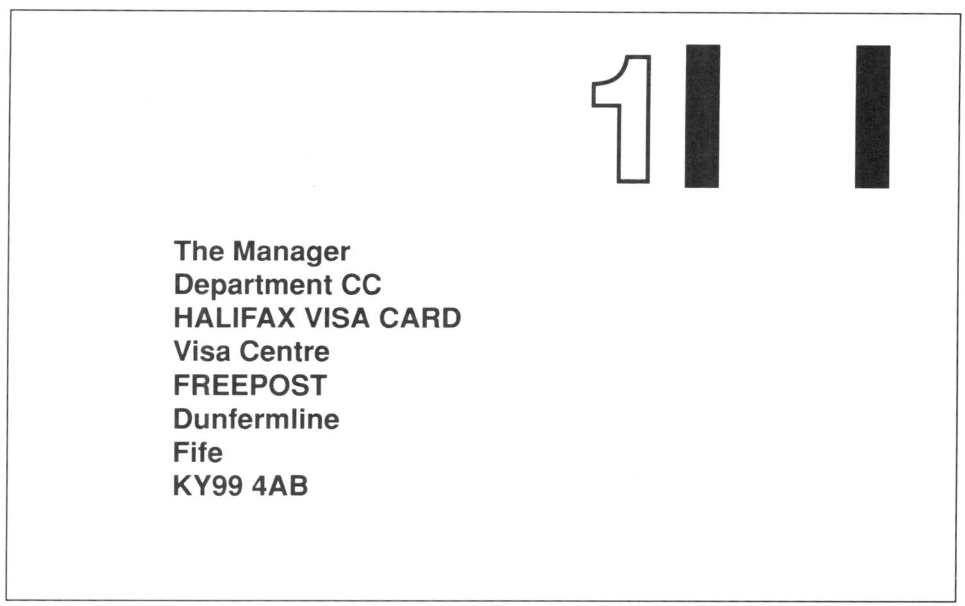

1
The Manager
Department CC
HALIFAX VISA CARD
Visa Centre
FREEPOST
Dunfermline
Fife
KY99 4AB

Collection services

There are a number of collection services available to businesses of all sizes. Where firms post large quantities of mail (that is, 1,000 or more items each day) there is no charge for collection.

Parcel services

Royal Mail no longer deals with parcels. The collection and delivery of all parcels is now the responsibility of Parcelforce, which was established in 1990. To ensure it is able to offer an impressive and efficient national and international parcel service, Parcelforce has invested heavily in new technology and it also has its own fleet of vehicles.

There are many services to choose from and, as with those available from Royal Mail, choice will depend upon the size of the parcel, its value, destination, and speed required.

Datapost

One of Parcelforce's most popular services is Datapost, which guarantees overnight delivery to most businesses within the UK in addition to its international service where express delivery is also guaranteed. However, the delivery time overseas varies according to the destination country. Firms are now able to purchase special Courier Packs for urgent items weighing up to 1 kg. These are tough ready-made packages and customers using them can choose from three next-day guaranteed delivery times: by 10 a.m., by 12 noon or within 24 hours.

Datapost is a very secure parcel service which many businesses use regularly. Not only is it a very fast service, it is also very safe. Confirmation of delivery is available by telephone, together with written proof of delivery, if required. Each customer who uses this service receives a weekly service report which specifies where and when each Courier Pack was delivered. If items are lost or damaged in any way compensation is paid out to the sender.

Compensation Fee

Compensation Fee is for parcels where compensation is paid to the sender if loss or damage occurs. The amount payable depends on the fee paid at the time of posting. No compensation is paid in respect of money sent by this service.

Postage Forward

When using Postage Forward, the sender does not have to pay the postage – the recipient who holds the licence for the service pays it. It is similar to the Business Reply service except it is for parcels. Mail order firms often use the Postage Forward service to save agents having to pay postage when returning goods. Examination boards also use it so that examiners can return marked examination scripts without having to pay out for postage (see example opposite).

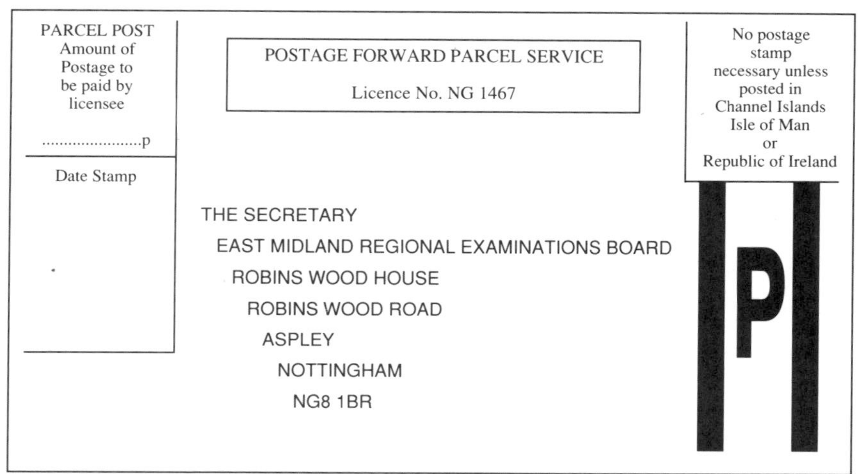
PARCEL POST
Amount of
Postage to
be paid by
licensee
......................p
Date Stamp
POSTAGE FORWARD PARCEL SERVICE
Licence No. NG 1467
No postage
stamp
necessary unless
posted in
Channel Islands
Isle of Man
or
Republic of Ireland
THE SECRETARY
EAST MIDLAND REGIONAL EXAMINATIONS BOARD
ROBINS WOOD HOUSE
ROBINS WOOD ROAD
ASPLEY
NOTTINGHAM
NG8 1BR
P

How much can you remember?

1 Why is it necessary to have such a wide range of postal services?
2 Classify the postal services into four groups.
3 Describe the two-tier ordinary postal service.
4 When might someone ask for a Certificate of Posting?
5 Into which category of postal services would you place Special Delivery, Intelpost and Electronic Post, and why?
6 Which services give most security?
7 Which service would you choose for sending cash through the post?
8 What is the purpose of Consequential Loss insurance?
9 Describe the benefits to both the sender and recipient of using the COD service.
10 Which service would be of benefit when moving location?
11 What is Poste Restante and who will use it?
12 Explain the differences between the Business Reply and Freepost services.
13 Who is responsible for the parcels which have to go through the post?
14 What is the purpose of compensation fee?
15 Which postal service is Postage Forward similar to and why?

Activity 11.1

(a) Choose one suitable item for each of the services mentioned in this chapter, and explain why the item you have chosen should be sent using the service you have matched to it.

(b) Imagine you were actually posting the items listed: select four, one from each category, and obtain and complete the necessary forms where possible.

(c) Explain the step-by-step procedure involved in sending items through the post for each of the items selected in (b).

(d) Identify and present in table form the main features of each postal service mentioned and the approximate cost for each item you have chosen to send.

(e) Suggest reasons why Datapost is so popular with businesses as a way of sending packets and parcels to destinations in the UK and abroad.

Sending mail abroad

Royal Mail plane

With the introduction of the Single Market opening the door to enormous export opportunities for businesses in the UK, there is a growing need to reach the vast pool of potential customers in Europe and beyond. There are numerous international services offered by Royal Mail and Parcelforce to meet individual and business needs.

Firms sending letters overseas can choose between the airmail services, which cost more but are quick, or surface mail (by sea), which is much cheaper but also much slower. Similar choices are available for parcels. However, all letters and postcards to Europe go by airmail, but you can choose to send small packets and printed papers by surface mail to save money. Surface mail to more remote places outside Europe can take up to 12 weeks to arrive.

Where speed is a priority, in addition to Airmail, Swiftair – Express Mail is available. Mail sent using this service arrives even faster than it would by Air Mail and pre-paid Swiftpack envelopes with barcoded certificate of posting labels can be purchased from a post office.

Many of the international services offered for letters, packets and parcels are very similar to the inland ones such as availability of additional insurance cover for valuable items, express delivery, Advice of Delivery and barcoded Certificate of Posting labels with the more secure services. Again, requirements vary depending upon the size, weight and value of the item being sent and how fast it needs to reach its destination.

How much can you remember?

1 When sending mail abroad firms can choose between airmail and surface mail. Outline the main differences.
2 What factors will be taken into consideration before a decision is made as to which service to choose?
3 What are the two main benefits of Swiftair?

Activity 11.2

(a) Discuss in more detail the statement: 'With the introduction of the Single Market opening the door to enormous export opportunities for businesses in the UK, there is a growing need to reach the vast pool of potential customers in Europe and beyond.'

(b) As a firm which is hoping to take advantage of growing export opportunities, find out which services are available that will enable you to reach potential European customers quickly and effectively.

Chapter 12 Telecommunications

By the end of this chapter you should be able to explain:

- the range and features of telecommunication equipment available
- the need for effective communication
- the qualities of a telephonist
- the suitability of particular pieces of equipment
- the way to deal with telephone calls
- the services available from British Telecom and their suitability
- the use of electronic mail.

Making contact with business

The days are gone when all business transactions were carried out between the hours of 9 a.m. and 5 p.m. Many important discussions now take place in the early morning or during the evening. In the case of international dealings, where time zone differences exist, discussions may even occur in the middle of the night.

Many executives are no longer tied to their desks but are constantly on the move, attending various business meetings and functions. Being able to make contact with people in business at any time is very important and there have been many developments in recent years to make this easier. However, the bulk of business dealings are still dealt with during office hours when most staff are present.

Telephone equipment

A large proportion of any firm's business is dealt with by telephone. Modern telephones offer a range of facilities such as last number redial and on-hook dialling which means you don't have to lift the receiver until someone answers. Some telephones have a prompt which stores the number you have dialled if it is engaged and bleeps three minutes later to remind you to try again. The volume of a caller's voice can be adjusted by using a speech volume control and a secrecy button will allow you to speak without the caller hearing what you are saying. A great deal of time can be saved not having to look up frequently used telephone numbers by storing them in memory where they are easily accessible when required.

Switchboard

It would be impractical for larger businesses to have just one telephone, as callers would become frustrated at continually hearing an engaged tone. In addition, if the site covers a large area, callers would be left waiting for long periods of time, while the person they wanted to speak to was found and brought to the telephone.

To solve this problem many firms have their own switchboard. This, in simple terms, is a firm's own private telephone exchange from which calls are made, received and redirected to the appropriate person.

The type of switchboard required will depend upon the size of the firm and the amount of business it carries out on the telephone. Obviously a very large organisation will have requirements different from a smaller one.

The older type of switchboard, PMBX (private manual branch exchange), required an operator to deal with all incoming and outgoing calls. Later models, PABX (private automatic branch exchange), allows users to dial directly out of the system without having to use the firm's operator. The latest systems are even more flexible in that they can be arranged so that all incoming calls are answered from a central point or alternatively so that everyone has access to them.

By taking advantage of new telephone systems, small businesses are now able to enjoy many of the benefits which were previously associated with larger switchboards. Small businesses can start off with a small system and these can be added to if necessary as the business grows and avoids the need to purchase a completely new system.

Mobile telephones

Having a mobile telephone means that you have instant access to a telephone wherever you happen to be. This makes them ideal for people who are constantly on the move, for example sales representatives and busy executives travelling to meetings. They are also useful for the sole trader who is constantly away from the office (or base) but needs the business that the telephone brings. (See illustration right.)

Hands-free telephones

Some phones offer a hands-free operation which allows calls to be made and received without having to lift the receiver. The volume control can be adjusted, thereby giving individuals the freedom to move away from the telephone and yet continue with the conversation. It also enables others in the room to contribute to the conversation.

Car phones

The latest development in this area is a completely voice-activated mobile telephone. This means you can make a call while driving without taking your hands off the wheel or your eyes off the road. Names and numbers which are most frequently used are stored in memory and by speaking out loud the name of the person or company you wish to contact, the number is extracted from the memory and dialled for you. For incoming calls, the telephone is automatically answered after two rings.

Cordless telephones

These are similar to mobile telephones but can be used only within 100 metres of the base unit. They are useful for people moving around factories and for small businesses such as garages, where it is necessary to have a telephone close at hand. The latest models have a two-way intercom facility which enables the user to talk directly to a second person back at the base unit.

Radiopagers

Contact can be kept with the base by using a lightweight paging device which bleeps when the user is wanted. When the bleeping begins, the user goes to the nearest telephone and calls the base. The latest radiopagers have a small screen which displays a message and therefore removes the need to telephone the office. Anyone who has the user's paging number can make contact and leave a message and telephone number on the pager's screen.

Answering machines

These are particularly useful for the small business and can be in the same unit as a fax machine. Calls are answered when no one is in the office and a recorded message can be left for the owner. Many sole traders use these as well as or as an alternative to a mobile telephone. Having an answering machine ensures that you do not miss important calls and it helps to keep your customers informed of where you are. Some models include a time and date facility which lets you know exactly when the messages were recorded.

Public address systems

These are similar to the ones that can be heard on railway stations notifying the public of train arrivals and departures. They are often used in factories to contact staff and direct them to the nearest telephone.

Intercoms

Intercoms are a means of internal communication frequently used between managers and secretaries. Individuals can talk to each other without having to move from their desks.

How much can you remember?

1. What is a switchboard?
2. Explain the difference between a PMBX and a PABX.
3. A business's internal switchboard used to be staffed by fully trained telephone operators who spent their time answering, redirecting and making calls. How has this situation changed and how have small firms benefited from these changes?
4. What are the benefits of having a mobile telephone and what type of people/business would benefit most?
5. How can drivers benefit from new facilities?
6. What is the difference between a cordless and a mobile telephone?
7. What is the purpose of a radiopager?
8. What type of business would benefit most from having an answering machine and why?
9. In which type of establishments might you find a public address system?
10. Who might use an intercom?

Activity 12.1

Schools and colleges are no longer solely educational establishments – they are also businesses, and as such need to make use of new technology for effective communication just like any other business.

task

(a) Consider which, if any, of the equipment mentioned in this chapter would be useful to your school or college.

(b) Explain fully how the equipment chosen in (a) could be used in your educational establishment.

(c) Identify any equipment which you feel would be of little or no use and say why.

Dealing with telephone calls

Businesses spend a great deal of time and money on the telephone and so it is important that, whenever possible, money is saved. The cost of a telephone call will depend on:

- the distance between the caller and the receiver
- the length of time the caller is using the telephone
- the time of day and the day of the week the call is made, as this will determine the rate at which it is charged.

Although the latest telephone systems have reduced the need for a specially trained operator, where the system is arranged such that everyone has access to calls, staff need to be aware of the importance of answering calls in a proper and businesslike manner. The voice on the other end of the telephone may be the first contact a customer has with a firm and much potential business can rest on the impression created.

The person who answers the telephone, whether it is a trained telephonist or another member of staff who has access to calls, has the same responsibilities as the receptionist and therefore requires the same or similar personal qualities.

In a small firm, the telephonist and the receptionist may be the same person. Just as the receptionist is the first person a caller sees when entering the building, the person who answers the telephone may be the first person the caller has spoken to. Both jobs involve dealing with all types of people and therefore both personnel have the opportunity to create a good impression for the firm.

When the telephone rings the correct procedure for answering it in business is to announce the name of the firm, which should be followed by 'good morning', 'good afternoon', and/or 'can I help you?' in a clear and cheerful voice. If it is an internal call it is usual to announce the name of the department followed by your own name (for example, Typing Pool, Diane Evans speaking).

If the person the caller wishes to speak to cannot be found straight away, it is courteous to explain the delay to the caller and not just to leave him or her hanging on. Modern switchboards send calls back to the operator automatically if no one answers the extension within a certain number of rings.

When the person the caller wishes to speak to is not available, it is usual to offer either to telephone them back, pass on a message, or give the caller the opportunity to ring off and telephone later.

If the caller decides to leave a message, the telephonist is expected to write it down and pass it on quickly. A message should be written out neatly and clearly so that the recipient can read it and not misinterpret what it says because of untidy handwriting. Businesses often use special forms for writing down telephone messages (such as the one opposite) as these remind the person taking down the details what questions to ask, for example the caller's name. A well-organised telephonist will ensure that pen and paper/pad of telephone message forms are always near at hand.

There are other rules which an efficient telephonist will put into practice, such as always speaking slowly, clearly and never shouting down the telephone. When unsure of a name or some other item of information, the caller should be asked politely to repeat it and, if there is still some doubt, to spell it.

Sometimes people find it difficult to express themselves on the telephone and explain clearly what it is they want and therefore the telephonist must be a very patient, tactful and courteous individual.

When making a call always say who you are and state clearly who you wish to speak to. Take great care when dialling, careless dialling means you are wasting money on a call which you don't need. At the end of a telephone conversation always say goodbye politely and don't bang the receiver down.

British Telecom services

In our private lives, most of us dial the required number directly and speak to friends and colleagues. Many of the calls we make are local ones. The calls we make which are outside the local area are trunk calls. Subscriber trunk dialling (STD) is when the caller is able to dial directly without the assistance of the British Telecom operator. However, there are still some calls which have to go through the operator.

Freefone calls

Freefone numbers are very useful as callers can ring the number free of charge. Freephone calls have to go through the operator unless they are Linkline numbers which begin with an 0800 number and can be dialled direct. In both instances, the recipient of the call pays any charges incurred. Businesses attract new business in this way as potential customers are more likely to make enquiries when they do not have to pay for the telephone call, particularly if it is a long-distance one.

Numbers which begin with 0345 are an alternative to Freephone or Linkline calls. Callers pay only the local rate for their call regardless of where in the UK it is destined. The firm which receives the calls pays the difference. The reduced charge encourages customers to telephone.

TELEPHONE MESSAGE FORM

URGENT/~~NON-URGENT~~

DATE 4/9/9– TIME 9-05

NAME OF CALLER GILES POTTER

FIRM MEREDITH & ROSCOE

TEL NO. (0404) 652343

MESSAGE FOR Sue Rogerson

MESSAGE

Train delayed, will be arriving 35 minutes late. Apologies but can we delay start of meeting?

TAKEN BY: S. Lawrence

Advice of duration and charge (ADC) calls

ADC calls are useful when someone who is not an employee of a business wishes to make and pay for a telephone call from the office phone, or when an employee wants to make a personal call. A connection is made via the operator, who rings the caller to notify him or her of the duration and cost of the call once it is finished.

Telemessage

A Telemessage is a British Telecom electronic letter. It can be ordered by telephone, telex or fax and it is used by businesses and also by individuals for personal greetings such as weddings, birthdays etc. Telemessages are delivered the next working day with the post and arrive in brightly coloured envelopes.

BT Chargecard

This enables the user to make telephone calls from any telephone (including payphones) with the cost of the call charged to a previously designated account. All calls go through the BT operator and these can be charged to an individual's own bill or his or her company's bill. Users pay only for the calls they make.

How much can you remember?

1 What is the difference between a local and a trunk call?
2 What do the letters STD stand for?
3 What is the difference between Freefone, Linkline and 0345 numbers?
4 When might an ADC call be appropriate and why?
5 What is a Telemessage?
6 Who would use a BT Chargecard and what are the benefits of doing so?

Activity 12.2
task 1

(a) You are about to attend for interview for the post of telephonist, a job for which you feel you have all the right qualities. Make a list of the qualities you possess from which this firm would benefit if it was to employ you as a telephonist.

(b) Outline the correct procedures for making, answering and dealing with telephone calls so that you are able to answer any questions you are asked.

task 2 The last batch of printed telephone message forms was not very satisfactory as important headings such as time of call were omitted. You have been asked to make the necessary changes to the existing design and order a further batch.

(a) Identify the main headings required.

(b) Design a suitable telephone message form using the headings identified.

(c) Write the following spoken message on to your newly designed form:

'This is Mr Pardow speaking from Cribbs & Webster, Accountants. I need some information urgently from your finance department. Please ask Mr Bennett to telephone me no later than 2 p.m. today as the VAT Inspector is due at 4.30 p.m. and I need to clarify one or two matters before he arrives. My telephone number is 596868, extension 12.'

Electronic mail

Fast, reliable and accurate communication is an essential requirement for survival in today's highly competitive business world, particularly with the introduction of the Single Market. The most significant change in communication which has been brought about has been due to the introduction of computers. Telephones and TV sets can now be linked up to computers and access vast amounts of information. Furthermore, companies can communicate not only from town to town or city to city, but also from country to country.

Electronic mail refers to computers communicating with each other. This can be from room to room, building to building, throughout the country or internationally. Communication is made possible by using the telephone network and a modem which converts the signals from a computer into language which can be transmitted down the telephone network.

There are different types of electronic mail services available in the UK. With some systems, text is keyed into a computer and transmitted to another computer somewhere else, while other types of electronic mail (facsimile services) allow an exact copy of an original document to be sent from one place to another.

Fax

The word 'fax' is short for 'facsimile', which means 'an exact copy'. A fax machine is used to send images of documents over the phone lines. You can think of it in terms of taking a photocopy, but instead of the copy coming out in your office it is reproduced on the fax machine linked up to the telephone line you have dialled. It takes only a matter of seconds to send a sheet by fax.

Fax users are given a telephone number, which may be listed in a fax directory. To send a fax, simply place or insert your sheet (usually this cannot be larger than A4) into your fax machine and using the number pad dial the recipient. If the line is free and the recipient's fax machine is connected and switched on, the sheet(s) will be read by your machine, the information will be digitally transferred into a form that is sent down the phone line, transferred back into a form that can be read by the receiving machine and printed out – all in just seconds, anywhere in the world.

Copies are reproduced in black or shades of grey, although some machines can read colour originals quite well. Original may be text, drawings or photographs. Many fax machines can be used as a telephone, and you can use some to take photocopies.

Some fax machines reproduce documents on to thermal paper, which is on rolls. Images on thermal paper will eventually fade away, so any document that is important and/or needs to be kept for some time should be photocopied for your files.

Telex

Telex is an electronic mailing service but it does not send an exact copy of a document. It has the speed of a telephone call but has the advantage of providing a written message for the sender and the recipient. It uses a machine called a teleprinter and messages can be sent worldwide to anyone who has a teleprinter.

Messages can be sent and received when the office is closed provided the power is switched on and there is paper in the machine. The latest machines can store messages and send them automatically to as many people as required. Floppy disks can be used to give extra memory storage together with single and double disk drives. The equipment is similar to that used for word processing, in as much as text is displayed on a VDU and can be edited as required prior to sending. The date and time are automatically inserted on each telex and passwords can be used to restrict access and maintain confidentiality.

BT messaging services

British Telecom's telex and fax bureau services offer facilities to send a telex and/or fax to those firms which do not have their own machine.

There is also an electronic mailing service available which allows letters, memos or messages to be keyed into a computer terminal and then 'posted' electronically to a mail box address via the telephone network to another computer at a different location.

Prestel

Prestel, developed by British Telecom in the UK, was the world's first public viewdata service. Users have access via microcomputers to computer-based information. Prestel is largely aimed at businesses to which it offers a variety of data such as share prices, company credit and market research information.

It is a two-way system, unlike teletext which only gives information. Prestel allows users to respond using the response pages, but this facility is limited.

How much can you remember?

1. What is electronic mail?
2. Electronic mail can be categorised into two types; what are they?
3. Explain the main difference between telex and fax.
4. What is Prestel?

Activity 12.3 SUGGESTED ASSIGNMENT/ESSAY TITLES

1. 'Electronic mail is a far better means of communication than the traditional services.' Discuss this statement in detail.
2. Investigate why a business would choose an electronic mailing system which requires the keying-in of text when there are systems available which do not require this.
3. Prepare a report entitled 'Electronic mail versus traditional post', and examine this topic in detail.

Chapter 13 Banks and building societies

By the end of this chapter you should be able to explain:

- the main services offered by banks and building societies
- the term 'automated banking'
- the clearing house system
- the main types of bank account
- the correct procedure for completing and correcting a cheque
- the benefits of a cheque guarantee card
- the ways of borrowing money
- the implications of paying for goods with 'plastic'
- the differences between Girobank and the high street banks
- the difference between a credit card and a debit card.

Banks

Banks offer a variety of financial services to customers, who range from private individuals to large multi-national companies. Like any other business in the private sector, banks aim to make a profit for their owners (the shareholders). They do this by encouraging people to deposit money with them and in return the bank pays them interest. Lending money to businesses and individuals on which they charge interest, is a major part of a bank's business, but they also offer many other services such as:

- providing and exchanging foreign currency and travellers' cheques
- taking on the role of legal representative when someone dies
- night safe facility
- arranging insurance cover
- safe custody facility for customers' valuables
- financial advice (investment and taxation)
- worldwide electronic payments system (including full payroll system).

Banks now compete with building societies who, under a new law, are allowed to offer a wider range of services and are no longer restricted to just offering mortgages to potential home buyers. Likewise, banks are offering a wider range of services, including mortgage facilities.

Automated banking

Computers are widely used in banks and building societies to keep records of customers and their account details. Information technology allows banks and building societies to respond quickly to customers' needs as it reduces the amount of paperwork, which allows more time for the customers.

Most banks and building societies have a cash dispensing machine or ATM (automated teller machine) as it is sometimes called, often located outside the premises. Each machine is linked to a large computer and this enables customers to draw money out when the banks are closed. The facilities these machines offer vary from bank to bank but generally include such things as being able to obtain a current account balance, order a statement and request an immediate 'mini' printout of recent transactions.

Each user has a PIN (personal identity number) which is keyed into the machine after the card has been inserted. The computer checks that the number keyed in matches the number on the card. If money has been requested, it will also check that there is enough money in the account to pay the amount requested. If everything is in order, cash is paid out and the card returned to the user.

The clearing house system

The clearing house provides a system for sorting cheques very quickly. With the aid of new technology, this is done at a rate of 120,000 cheques per hour. The numbers along the bottom of a cheque are printed in magnetic ink and can be read by a computer (see sample cheque on page 186). Each cheque has three groups of numbers. The first group is the serial number of the cheque and it is repeated on the counterfoil. The second group is the bank's sorting code – each bank and branch of that bank has its own sorting code. The third group is the customer's bank account number. When you open a bank account you are allocated a personal account number and this number is printed on all documentation relating to your account, such as your statements, cheques and paying-in books. It is from this number that you can be identified.

Many banks, such as Barclays, Lloyds, Midland and National Westminster, together with some of the larger building societies, for example Abbey National, Halifax and National & Provincial, are members of the clearing house system.

Clearing refers to collecting payments for cheques that have been paid into the banks and building societies. When the bank on which the cheque is drawn releases the money, the cheque is said to be cleared. This normally takes up to a maximum of three working days. Over seven million cheques are paid into the clearing bank branches every day and they all have to go through clearing.

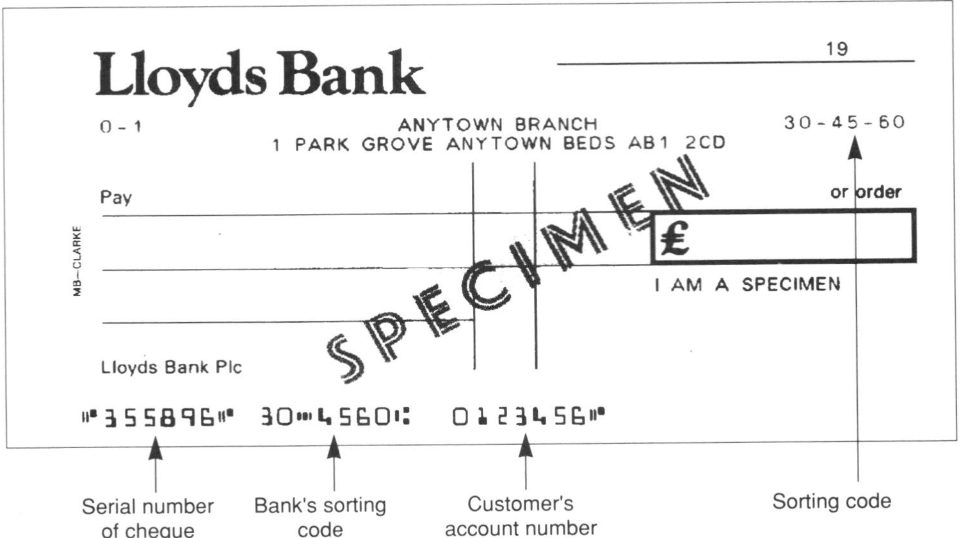

Huge sums of money pass between the banks as a result of the clearing house system, and at the close of every working day each bank will owe money to other banks or be owed money by them. The Bank of England keeps the accounts for all the British banks and makes the necessary adjustments each day according to the day's transactions.

How much can you remember?

1 What is an ATM and where will you find one?
2 What do you understand by 'the clearing system'?
3 What role does the Bank of England play in relation to the banks?

Activity 13.1

SUGGESTED ASSIGNMENT/ESSAY TITLES

1 Customers, banks and building societies will benefit now that banks and building societies can compete for business. Discuss.
2 Discuss the following statement in detail: 'Information technology allows banks and building societies to respond quickly to customers' needs as it reduces the amount of paperwork and therefore more time can be given to the customers.'

Activity 13.2

(a) Choose one bank and one building society and using no more than two sides of A4 paper for each establishment, investigate and summarise the services they offer.

(b) Based on your research, write a brief report comparing the two financial institutions and say which one you would choose to take care of your financial affairs and why. In addition to the services offered you may wish to consider the environment and how helpful the staff are to customers.

(c) In what way(s) could these financial institutions help you if you owned or were planning to buy a small business?

Bank accounts

Although much of the remainder of this chapter talks about banks and bank accounts, some of the services and facilities mentioned are also now available from building societies.

Opening a bank account

The procedure for opening a bank account will vary slightly depending upon the bank you choose and the type of account you wish to open. However, there are some similarities – for example, you will have to complete and sign an application form giving details about yourself. In addition you will be expected to produce positive proof of identity, for example your birth certificate or passport. This ensures you are who you say you are and therefore helps to combat fraud.

Most people today have a bank account, of which there are two main types: current (cheque book) account and deposit (savings) account.

Deposit accounts

Several types of deposit account are available, offering varying rates of interest, which depends on:

- the amount invested
- the period of time the money remains in the bank
- the length of notice required for intention to withdraw
- the state of the economy (prevailing base rate).

Deposit accounts are often referred to as interest bearing accounts and there is a variety of them which target different groups of people within the community. People and businesses have different types of commitments and they all want something which will suit their individual needs. For example, a young child with a few pounds will be looking for something different from a prosperous business person with a large sum of money to invest.

Current accounts

Current accounts are used for paying bills and day-to-day expenses and many banks now offer interest on current accounts remaining in credit. The most popular methods for paying bills, apart from writing a cheque, are standing order and direct debit.

A standing order is used when a specified amount of money is paid to the same person or firm at regular intervals for an agreed period of time. The bank pays out the money until the end of the agreed period of time or until the account holder cancels or changes the instruction.

Direct debits are very similar to standing orders except that the amount and the intervals between which payments are made can be changed by the person/firm receiving the money (payee). However, the payee is obliged to inform the account holder before the revised amount is claimed.

Most firms offering the facility of spreading payments over a period of time prefer customers to pay using direct debit rather than standing order. When a standing order is being used, if the payment changes, the recipient has to write to the account holder and instruct them to go into or write to their bank and make arrangements to change the amount. The recipient then has to wait until the account holder has done this. With a direct debit, the recipient changes the amount of the payment and writes to the account holder to inform him or her of the new payment, and this makes it much quicker.

Money is easily withdrawn from a current account using either a cash dispensing machine or a cheque made out to 'self' or 'cash'. Money is paid in using a paying-in slip, sometimes referred to as a Bank Giro Credit Slip (see example opposite). Current account holders will be issued with a personalised paying-in book shortly after they open a current account.

Cheques

There are three parties to a cheque:

- the payee (the person to whom the cheque is made out)
- the drawer (the account holder who makes the cheque out)
- the drawee (the bank on which the cheque is drawn).

Cheques are usually personalised – that is, the name(s) of the account holder(s) is printed on each cheque. All cheques must be written in pen and any changes signed. Cheques which are post-dated (dated in advance) are not accepted by a bank for payment, neither are stale cheques (those which are older than six months).

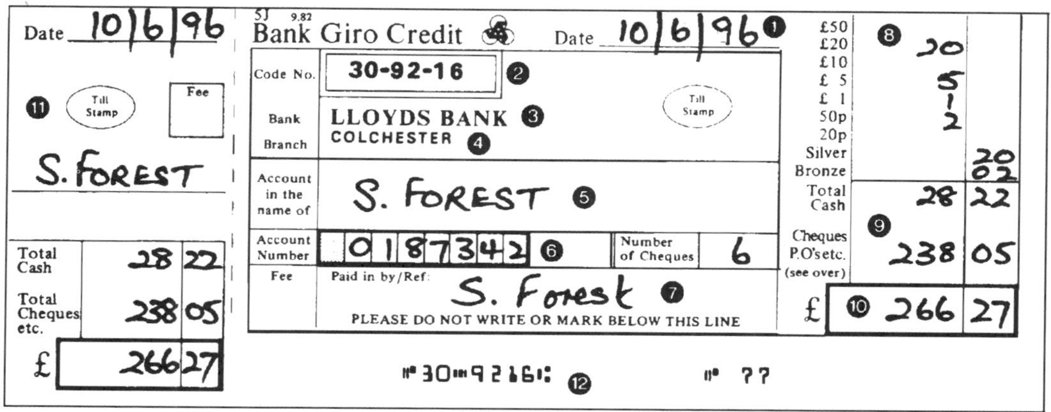
Date 10/6/96
11 Till Stamp
Fee
S. FOREST

Total Cash	28	22
Total Cheques etc.	238	05
£	266	27

5J 9.82
Bank Giro Credit
Date 10/6/96 1

Code No. 30-92-16 2
Bank LLOYDS BANK 3
Branch COLCHESTER 4
Till Stamp
Account in the name of S. FOREST 5
Account Number 0187342 6 Number of Cheques 6
Fee Paid in by/Ref: S. Forest 7
PLEASE DO NOT WRITE OR MARK BELOW THIS LINE

8		
£50		
£20	20	
£10		
£ 5	5	
£ 1	1	
50p	2	
20p		
Silver		20
Bronze		02
Total Cash	28	22
Cheques P.O's etc. (see over) 9	238	05
£ 10	266	27

⑈30⑉92161⑆ 12 ⑈ 77

Bank Giro Credit slip

1. Date.
2. Sorting code number of the account holding branch.
3. Name of account holding bank.
4. Name of account holding branch.
5. Account holder's name.
6. Account number.
7. Signature of person paying the money in.
8. Breakdown of cash paid in.
9. Total of cheques paid in, details of which are listed on back.
10. Total of the credit to the account (cash and cheques).
11. Counterfoil (your record of what you've paid in).
12. Magnetic ink symbols to enable automatic processing by the computer.

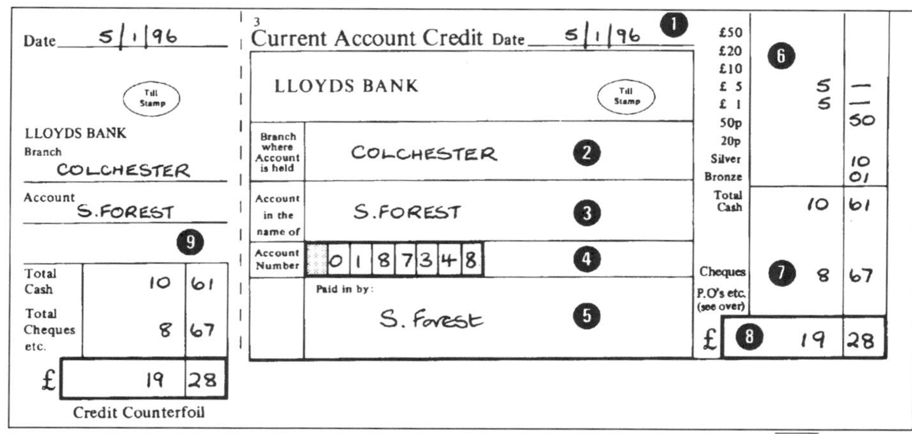
Date 5/1/96
Till Stamp
LLOYDS BANK
Branch COLCHESTER
Account S.FOREST
9

Total Cash	10	61
Total Cheques etc.	8	67
£	19	28

Credit Counterfoil

3
Current Account Credit Date 5/1/96 1
LLOYDS BANK
Till Stamp
Branch where Account is held COLCHESTER 2
Account in the name of S.FOREST 3
Account Number 0187348 4
Paid in by: S. Forest 5

6		
£50		
£20		
£10		
£ 5	5	—
£ 1	5	—
50p		50
20p		
Silver		10
Bronze		01
Total Cash	10	61
Cheques P.O's etc. (see over) 7	8	67
£ 8	19	28

Current Account Credit slip

1. Date.
2. Name of account holding branch.
3. Account holder's name.
4. Account number.
5. Signature of person paying the money in.
6. Breakdown of cash paid in.
7. Amount of cheques paid in.
8. Total of the credit to the account (cash and cheques).
9. Counterfoil (your record of what you've paid in).

Most cheques are crossed for extra security – they have two parallel lines running down the middle. This ensures that cheques are paid into a bank account and not exchanged for cash. Crossed cheques are much safer than open cheques (those without the lines down the middle), which do not have to go through a bank account. The Cheques Act 1992 specifies that all cheques containing the crossings 'A/C Payee' or 'A/C Payee only' are no longer transferrable. In other words, prior to this Act the payee could sign a crossed cheque on the back and pass it on to someone else. The person who it had been passed on to would then pay it into his or her account. New legislation prevents this – any cheque with the above crossings has to be paid into the payee's account and it cannot be transferred to anyone else.

Completing a cheque and correcting mistakes

There are five basic steps in completing a cheque. These are illustrated below.

Lloyds Bank
9th March 1994
8-22 COLCHESTER BRANCH 30-92-16
27 HIGH STREET COLCHESTER ESSEX CO1 1DU
Pay United Stores or order
Seven Pounds 49 £7—49
S FOREST
S. Forest
Lloyds Bank Plc
536125 30-92-16 0187348

1. Write the date in the top right-hand corner.
2. Add the name of the payee on the top line of the cheque where indicated where it states 'Pay'.
3. Write the amount you wish to pay in words.
4. Inside the box write the amount in figures and make sure it agrees with the amount in words.
5. Sign the cheque in the bottom right-hand corner.

If any mistakes are made then each correction must be signed. This shows that the account holder has made the changes and not someone else.

Cheque guarantee cards

Anyone over the age of 18 who has a current account can apply for a cheque guarantee card. It is a promise by the bank to pay the sum specified on the cheque up to a limit of £50, or in some instances £100. Providing cheque guarantee conditions are fulfilled, payment cannot be stopped when a cheque card has been used, thus the payee can be sure that the cheque will clear.

Cheques sometimes 'bounce', that is they are dishonoured. There are a number of reasons why a cheque might not be honoured:

- inadequate or uncleared funds in the account
- incorrect date
- amount in figures and words are different
- cheque is not signed
- cheque is not made out in ink
- alterations have been made but not signed by the account holder
- cheque has been countermanded
- cheque has been mutilated.

Bank statements

With so much money going into and coming out of the bank, the account holder may find it difficult to keep a record of the balance. A bank statement solves this problem. It is sent at regular intervals, typically at the end of each month although large organisations may receive them more regularly. It gives details of all money paid to the account (credits) and all payments made (debits) since the previous statement was issued. It also shows the balance at the date of the statement.

How much can you remember?

1. What is the main difference between a deposit account and a current account?
2. How is money paid into and drawn out of a current account?
3. What are the three parties to a cheque?
4. What information does a bank statement contain and how often is it usually issued?
5. Explain what the terms 'debit' and 'credit' mean on a bank statement.
6. Suggest why a cheque may be dishonoured.
7. List the benefits of owning a cheque guarantee card.
8. Outline the differences between a standing order and a direct debit.
9. Prepare a list of instructions for the correct completion of a cheque.

Activity 13.3 (a) Investigate the different types of account offered by local banks.

(b) Using information researched in (a), choose the most appropriate account for each individual detailed and explain the reasons for your choice:

(i) A small baby has just received £500 from his grand-parents. A condition of the gift is that it is not touched until the child is 18 years old.
(ii) A young married couple are living in rented accommodation while they save up enough for a deposit on a house. They have regular bills to pay but they try to save at least 50 per cent of their income each month towards the deposit.
(iii) A retired couple have £20,000 to invest and they want to use the interest to help with everyday expenses and holidays. They do not envisage needing the capital urgently in the near future.
(iv) A business person has £5,000 but needs to be able to draw on the money quickly if and when required.

Borrowing money

There is a wide range of borrowing facilities which meet the needs of both personal and business customers.

Overdraft

An overdraft is a popular way of borrowing money in the short term. This is when the bank allows the account holder to withdraw more money than is in the account, up to a specified limit. This can be very useful to small businesses in helping to avoid cash flow problems. In other words, a firm does not necessarily have to wait to be paid by a debtor (person who owes them money) before an urgent bill can be paid if there are insufficient funds in the account to cover it. An overdraft covers the gap between payments being made by a firm and money being received.

An overdraft can be a cheap and flexible way of borrowing money provided the account holder does not go over the agreed maximum. Interest is charged on a daily basis and this makes it an attractive option for some firms.

Personal loan

This type of loan is designed more for personal customers than businesses and is used for purchasing a large item such as a car. When a bank lends money it may require some security to ensure that it will still receive its money if the customer finds he or she cannot pay. The most common form of security for this type of loan is a property. Loans are taken out over an agreed period of time and have fixed rates of interest which are specified at the start of the loan period. The customer makes repayments each month until the specified period of time expires and the debt is paid in full.

Banks also offer home improvement loans to personal customers to help them improve their property, for example to install central heating or fit a new kitchen. These loans are often available over a longer period of time than personal loans.

Loan account

Many businesses have loan accounts, which they use to help them purchase large items such as a piece of machinery or a van for delivering goods etc. These are similar to home improvement loans which are offered to personal customers.

Paying for goods with 'plastic'

The most well-known credit cards are Barclaycard (Visa) and Access (Mastercard). Credit cards enable the holder, who must be aged 18 years or over, to buy goods without paying cash. When a purchase is made, the card holder presents the card and signs a voucher which authorises the transaction.

Once a month, the holder receives a statement and has the choice of paying for the goods in full and incurring no interest or paying a minimum specified payment towards the total cost of the goods. The remaining balance incurs interest and a new statement is issued the following month. All account holders have a credit limit which varies depending on individual financial circumstances. In addition to paying for goods, cards can be used to obtain cash from the bank.

Electronic banking

The UK clearing banks are continuing to develop Electronic Funds Transfer at Point of Sale (EFTPOS) in retail establishments around the country. EFTPOS is currently in use in the form of a combined cheque/ Visa card more commonly referred to as Switch. Switch is like an electronic cheque and wherever you see a 'Switch' sign you can use it to pay for goods.

This system is similar to the credit card system in that no cash changes hands between the retailer and the customer, but the difference is that payment is taken from the customer's bank account in full within three working days. It's the same as paying by cheque using a guarantee card, except that you use only the card, no cheque is necessary. Therefore, Switch is a debit card not a credit card. One advantage of Switch is that, unlike a cheque and cheque guarantee card, when you use it, you are not restricted to the £50 limit and it costs less than using a cheque. Therefore, if you pay bank charges it is cheaper.

When you want to make a purchase by Switch:

- You hand your card to the sales assistant.
- It is passed through a card reader from which a receipt is produced (see Tesco's sales voucher below).
- You sign the receipt.
- The amount payable is debited from your current account within three working days.

As it is a combined card you can use it to withdraw cash from the dispensing machine and to guarantee a cheque where the Switch system is not available. Most of the banks offer their own version of Switch.

SALES VOUCHER
Please keep this copy for your records

RECYCLED PAPER

TESCO

Card Number: 4936 600639 81942222
Pre-valid Date:
Expiry Date: 05/94
Card Type: SWITCH
Branch Number: 2418
S
Date: 16/04/94 Time: 17:43
Merchant Number: 01818671
Authorisation Code: 94202185
Register: 015 Operator: 1086 Sale No. 0940

PLEASE DEBIT MY SWITCH ACCOUNT WITH THE TOTAL AMOUNT. GOODS AS PER THE ATTACHED RECEIPT.

CASHBACK £50.00
TOTAL £64.45

CARDHOLDER COPY

Transaction confirmed – Cardholder's Signature

PLEASE WRITE FIRMLY

Printed on envision Recycled Carbonless Paper from Stora Feldmuehle by Ritchie (UK) Ltd.

Example of a debit card voucher

Banking by telephone

A facility offered by some banks which when set up gives account holders access to information from their accounts via the telephone. This service can be used to pay bills, check the balance, obtain details of the last few recorded transactions, or order a statement, cheque or paying-in book. As it is a computerised service it is available 24 hours a day, seven days a week, so account holders who have access to this service can take advantage of cheap rate calls.

Girobank

In 1988, the government announced its intention to privatise Girobank and invited bids from potential buyers. In 1990, the Alliance & Leicester Building Society purchased the company and the bank is now a subsidiary of that organisation.

Girobank has more branches than all of the other banks put together because it uses the post offices around the country for counter facilities. Although post office staff do not have access to Girobank customers' personal banking information, customers can use post offices to deposit money into their account or to draw it out.

Girobank offers the same type of services as the high street banks, but it is open longer hours than many other financial institutions.

Customers are offered similar facilities to customers of the high street banks – a cheque book, cheque card, combined cheque/Visa card, debit card, monthly statement, bill paying facilities – and no bank charges are made while the account remains in credit.

Girobank building

High street post office

Credit transfer

This allows a customer to pay another Girobank account holder by transferring money directly into the payee's account. This is possible because all of its customers' account details are stored on the same computerised system. People who do not have a Girobank account can use the Transcash service to pay money into the account of someone who is a Girobank account holder. This transaction can be carried out at any post office over the counter.

Credit

A number of services previously provided by banks are now provided by the Alliance & Leicester to Girobank customers. These include personal loans and mortgages.

Automated banking

Girobank is a member of Link, a network of cash dispensing machines. The Link network service is a system shared by a large number of financial institutions including the Halifax Building Society. Cardholders have access to ATMs which are located throughout the country at post offices, banks, building societies, airports and shopping centres.

Currency

Customers can order travellers' cheques and foreign currency from Girobank by post or telephone.

Girobank through Link has reciprocal arrangements with ATM networks in other countries such as USA, Japan, Spain and Portugal. This enables customers to use ATMs around the world to withdraw cash in local currency straight from their account.

How much can you remember?

1. What method would you recommend for short-term borrowing, and why?
2. Explain how a personal loan works.
3. What method would a business use for larger amounts and longer-term borrowing?
4. What are the benefits and drawbacks of using a credit card?
5. To what does EFTPOS refer?
6. How does Switch differ from a credit card?
7. Briefly explain the background to Girobank plc.
8. Identify and explain the similarities and differences between Girobank and the high street banks.
9. What is the Link network system to which Girobank belongs?
10. Do you think the change of ownership of Girobank will change it in any way, and if so how?

Activity 13.4
task 1

(a) ABC Company Limited has an agreed overdraft limit with the bank to help avoid any cash flow problems. Unfortunately this month the business spent £230 over the agreed limit because one of its largest customers did not pay on time. The bank manager was not pleased and wrote to ABC Company Limited to say so. Had its customer paid on time the amount owing of £1,590.53 the firm would have remained well in credit and not had to use the overdraft at all. Using the figures on page 198 calculate:

(i) The balance at the end of the month.
(ii) The agreed overdraft limit.
(iii) What the balance would have been at the end of the month had the customer paid on time.

	£
Balance at 1st of Month	1,646.96
Payment made to supplier	361.69
Payment made to supplier	1,021.54
Credit received from customer	149.67
Payment made to supplier	937.21
Credit received from customer	326.78
Payment made to supplier	532.97

(b) The problem with the bank manager has now been sorted out and ABC Company Limited has asked to increase its overdraft limit so that it can purchase a second-hand van. The price of the van is £6,500 but the company needs only to borrow 75 per cent of this amount. The bank manager has advised ABC Company Limited to take out a loan for this item and not to use its overdraft.

(i) Why has the bank manager advised the company against using its overdraft to buy a van?
(ii) Why is a loan more suitable for this purpose?
(iii) Find out the monthly repayments for a period of three years on the loan required by ABC Company Limited. Calculate the total amount of interest payable.

task 2

A confused customer in the bank is unsure whether she wants to apply for a debit card or a credit card. Explain the difference to her.

Chapter 14 Petty cash

By the end of this chapter you should be able to explain:

- the need for petty cash
- the way an imprest system works
- the procedure for dealing with petty cash
- the documents involved in recording petty cash transactions.

Why petty cash?

As the name suggests, petty cash refers to a small amount of money. In any business, there is a necessity to keep some cash available for purchasing small items such as tea, coffee, stamps, fares and small items of stationery. It would be impractical to pay for such things by cheque, and so a small amount of cash is kept in a lockable box for such occasions.

Documentation for petty cash

Money cannot be given out to anybody for just anything and so records are kept. The details recorded will include the amount paid out, the person who received the money and what it was used for. There are two documents involved in a petty cash system for recording expenditure and these are the petty cash voucher (see below) and the petty cash record sheet (see page 200).

Petty Cash Voucher No. 0104

Folio: 32

Date: 12 June 199-

For what required	VAT amount		Amount incl VAT	
Postage for registered packet			3	45

Signature: C. May   Passed by: R Bmitey

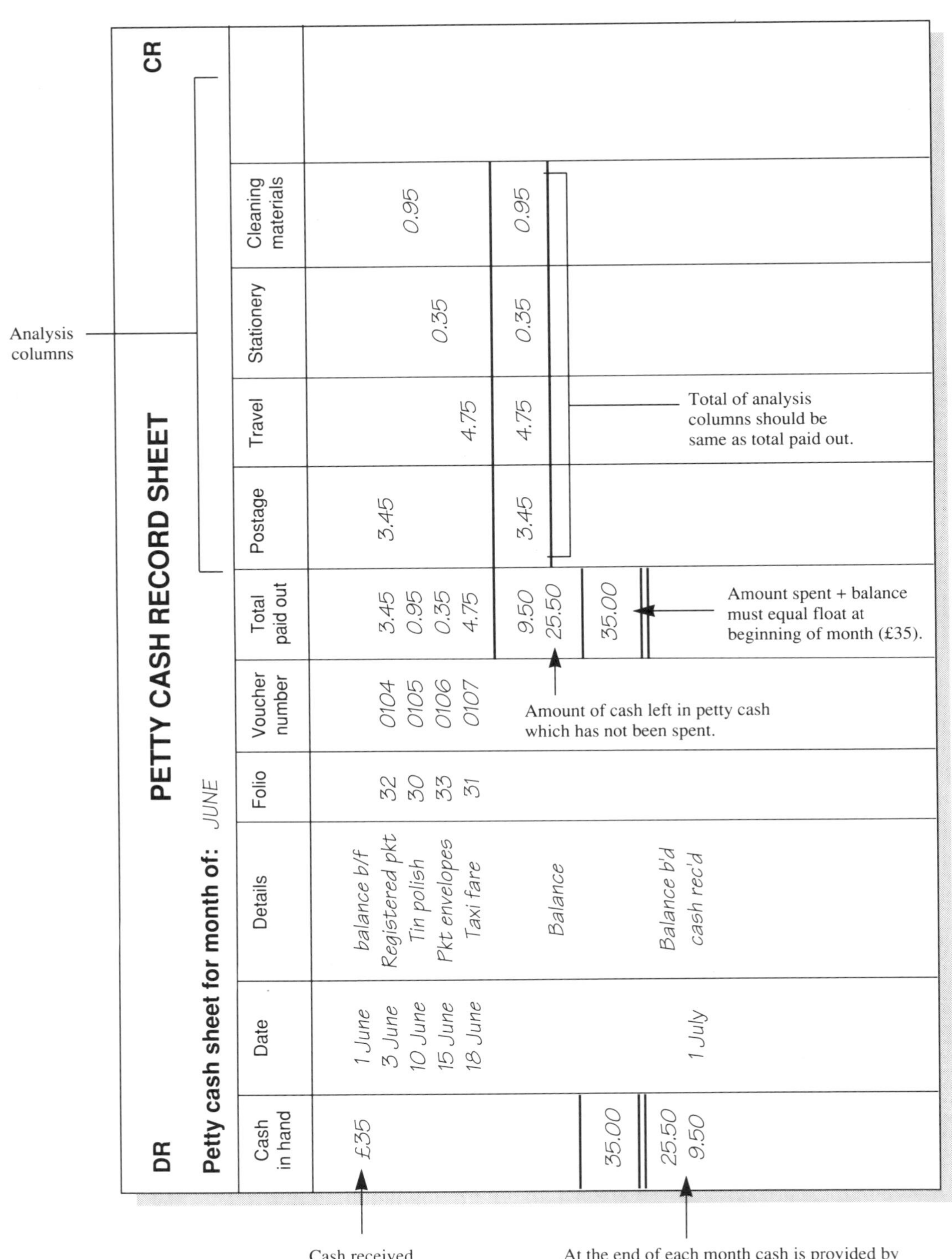

DR **PETTY CASH RECORD SHEET** CR

Petty cash sheet for month of: JUNE

Cash in hand	Date	Details	Folio	Voucher number	Total paid out	Postage	Travel	Stationery	Cleaning materials	
£35	1 June	balance b/f								
	3 June	Registered pkt	32	0104	3.45	3.45				
	10 June	Tin polish	30	0105	0.95				0.95	
	15 June	Pkt envelopes	33	0106	0.35			0.35		
	18 June	Taxi fare	31	0107	4.75		4.75			
					9.50	3.45	4.75	0.35	0.95	
		Balance			25.50					
35.00					35.00					
25.50	1 July	Balance b'd								
9.50		cash rec'd								

Analysis columns
Total of analysis columns should be same as total paid out.
Amount spent + balance must equal float at beginning of month (£35).
Amount of cash left in petty cash which has not been spent.
Cash received from cashier.
At the end of each month cash is provided by Finance Dept to replace what has been spent.

When a request is made for cash, a petty cash voucher is completed. This records the amount paid out and gives details of how the money is to be used. The voucher must have two signatures: from the person receiving the money and from someone who is in a position to authorise the request for payment. The amount of VAT is always shown separately and receipts obtained whenever possible as VAT-registered firms can reclaim VAT on some items.

At regular intervals the details from the petty cash vouchers are transferred to a petty cash record sheet. Every total is entered twice: once in the total paid column and once in the appropriate analysis column (see opposite). Analysis columns are used to categorise the money spent regularly in specific areas, for example travel or postal expenses. This information is eventually recorded in the appropriate section of the firm's ledger from where checks can be made to establish how much money has been spent and in what areas. Firms include this information in their financial records and use it when estimating future budgets.

The imprest system

Petty cash is usually organised using an imprest system. Imprest is another word meaning 'float' and an imprest system is when each week/month begins with the same set amount of money. All expenditure is recorded and money spent is replaced at the end of each imprest cycle. In other words, if the petty cash system is carried out using a monthly cycle, at the beginning of each new month, the petty cash vouchers which record what has been spent are exchanged for cash.

To simplify imprest even further, it might be helpful to consider the procedures involved in this system:

1 A request is made for a small amount of money.
2 A petty cash voucher is completed and signed twice.
3 The petty cashier gives out the cash in exchange for the completed voucher.
4 A purchase is made according to the details on the voucher and where possible a receipt obtained.
5 At the end of the week/month, the petty cashier will:
(a) add up the cash in the box
(b) add the vouchers up to calculate the total money spent. The remaining cash in the box, plus the total money spent should add up to the starting float (imprest).
6 The details are transferred from the petty cash vouchers on to the petty cash record sheet for that period of time.
7 The vouchers are taken to the finance department and exchanged for cash in readiness to begin the new imprest period.
8 The new week/month begins with no vouchers and the same amount of cash as the previous week/month.

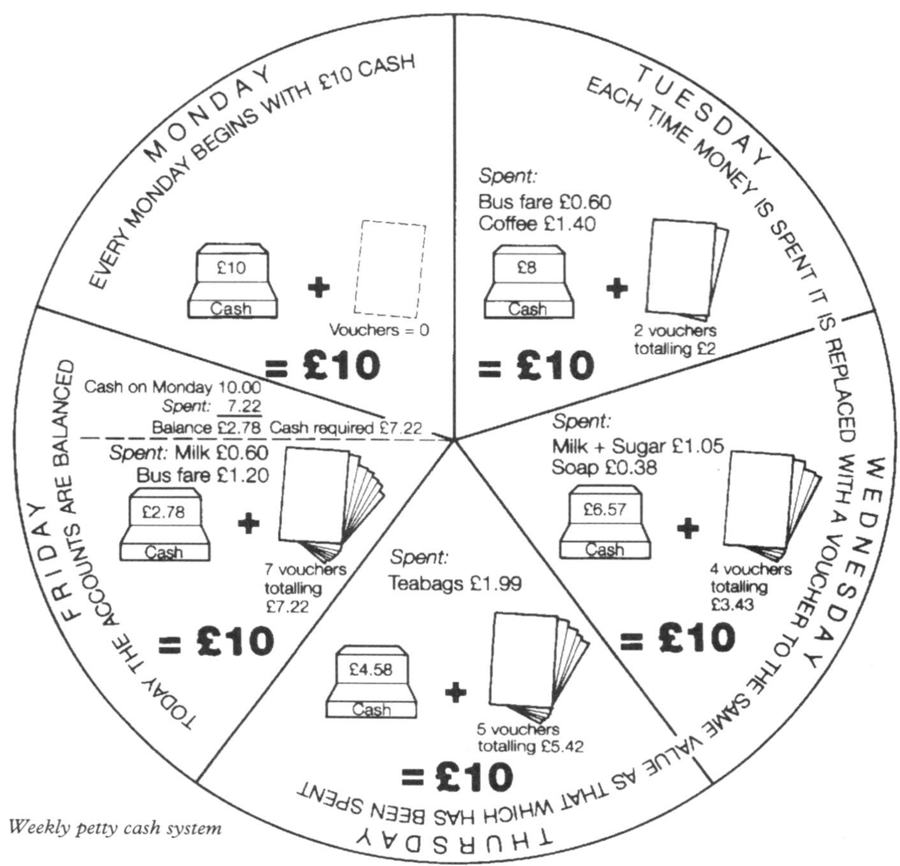

Weekly petty cash system

Looking after the petty cash

As the finance/accounts department looks after all matters relating to money, it is often a member of that department who is responsible for the petty cash. However, not always – sometimes it is more convenient for the receptionist to take charge or, where money is often needed for postage, the mail room supervisor.

The person in charge of petty cash has several important responsibilities, to ensure that:

- The petty cash box is kept locked away in a safe place at all times.
- Anyone requesting money, completes a petty cash voucher.
- No money is paid out without it being signed for and authorised.
- Vouchers are kept detailing all expenditure.
- Details are transferred carefully from vouchers to record sheets so that when they are entered in the firm's ledger the details are accurate.

How much can you remember?

1 To what does 'petty cash' refer?
2 What is petty cash used to buy?
3 Where is petty cash kept?
4 Who is responsible for looking after the petty cash?
5 Petty cash is kept using the imprest system. Use a diagram (different from the one opposite) to explain what this means.
6 What are the two documents used to record petty cash transactions?

Activity 14.1

(You will need petty cash vouchers and a petty cash record sheet for this activity.)

task

(a) Make a list of at least 20 items which may be purchased using petty cash.

(b) (i) Choose ten items from your list and complete petty cash vouchers totalling no more than £35.00.
(ii) Transfer details on to a petty cash record sheet and balance the figures using an imprest of £50.00.

(c) Describe the qualifications and personal qualities which the person who looks after the petty cash will possess.

(d) Explain the necessity for:
(i) Using analysis columns to categorise expenditure.
(ii) Recording VAT separately on vouchers and record sheets.

Chapter 15 Wages

By the end of this chapter you should be able to explain:

- the methods used to establish how much an employee has earned
- the difference between gross and net pay
- statutory and voluntary deductions from pay
- the PAYE system
- why we pay taxes
- the benefits for employers and employees of using credit transfer for payment of wages and salaries
- the purpose of a P45 and a P60
- computerised payroll.

What is a wage?

Employees receive a wage or salary from their employer at the end of each week or month in exchange for their working skills. A wage is paid on a weekly basis and a salary is paid monthly. Large firms may have clocking in and out systems for some employees so that thay can monitor the hours each employee works.

Methods of payment

Clocking in and out

Piece work

Receiving weekly wage

Some workers are paid piece rate, which means the amount of pay they earn depends on the number of items they produce. This type of payment is most commonly used in factories which have an assembly line where production can be measured. The more work you do, the more you get paid.

Another method of payment is time rate where employees are paid for each hour worked. Employers specify the minimum number of hours per week which they expect employees to work and any additional time is classed as overtime.

Some employees, such as teachers, do not receive any additional payment for extra hours worked as it is considered to be part of their job. However, many employees are paid overtime and this is normally paid at time and a half or double time.

Time and a half means that the earner receives the normal hourly rate and half as much again. In other words, someone who is paid £3.00 per hour would receive £4.50 per hour when working overtime at time and a half. Similarly, if overtime is paid at double time they will receive double the normal hourly rate.

Sales representatives are often paid on a commission basis, which means that they receive a percentage of the total amount sold – for example, if representatives are paid commission at 5 per cent and they sell goods to the value of £2,500, they will receive £125 commission. Sometimes they receive a low basic wage plus commission; other selling posts are paid commission on sales only.

Some process workers are paid a bonus, that is, a sum of money in addition to their wages. Bonuses might be paid if employees finish an important job on time, or a Christmas bonus might be given as a reward for hard work during the year.

Gross and net pay

If an employee earns £6,000 per annum (per year) the monthly pay would be £500 (£6,000 divided by 12) – this amount is called the gross pay. However, most workers have some deductions taken from their pay – some are statutory (compulsory by law) while others are voluntary, and these can only be deducted with the permission of the employee. Examples of voluntary deductions are subscriptions to sports and social clubs, charities and company pension schemes. The amount of money left after all deductions have been made is called the net pay.

Statutory deductions

These are deductions which all workers have to pay depending upon the amount they earn. They include income tax and National Insurance. Statutory contributions are deducted directly from an employee's pay by the employer.

National Insurance

National Insurance is paid by both employers and employees. The employee's contribution – the amount deducted from an employee's pay – depends on the amount earned. Where an individual's earnings are less than the earnings limit for National Insurance, no deduction is made. All school leavers are issued with a personal National Insurance number and this remains the same throughout their life. National Insurance contributions are used to provide a range of benefits, such as unemployment pay and statutory sickness and maternity pay.

PAYE

PAYE (pay as you earn) allows workers to spread the payment of Income Tax over the tax year (6 April – 5 April) instead of having to pay a lump sum. When Income Tax is deducted from an employee's pay it is sent to the Inland Revenue (the government department that deals with the collection of taxes).

Everyone is allowed to earn a certain amount of money before being taxed (freepay). The amount of tax you pay depends on your tax allowance, which is calculated according to your personal circumstances, how much you earn and the rate of tax, fixed by the government.

Every employee is assigned a code by the Inland Revenue that indicates the amount the individual may earn before paying tax. The Inland Revenue also issues special tax tables to help employers calculate the correct amount of tax to be deducted from employees' wages. The Department of Social Security (DSS) issues similar tables for the calculation of National Insurance.

Pay advice

Employers have a legal obligation to provide each employee with an itemised payslip every time he or she is paid. This shows how much has been earned (gross pay), what deductions have been made, and how much the employee receives (net pay).

Why do we pay taxes?

We pay taxes so that the government can use the money it raises to help towards the payment of benefits and to help provide public services for the whole community (see Chapter 1). It could not do this if we did not contribute as it does not have any money of its own. Most public revenue is raised by taxation in one form or another, for example VAT or income tax. The pie charts below show public sector income and expenditure for 1994–95.

Where it comes from	£ billion
Income tax	64.4
National Insurance contributions	42.8
Corporation tax	17.6
Value added tax	43.1
Excise duties	27.1
Other receipts	57.4
Borrowing	37.9

Where it goes	£ billion
Social security	83.0
Health	31.7
Defence	23.5
Local government	71.7
Other spending	57.5
Debt interest	22.8

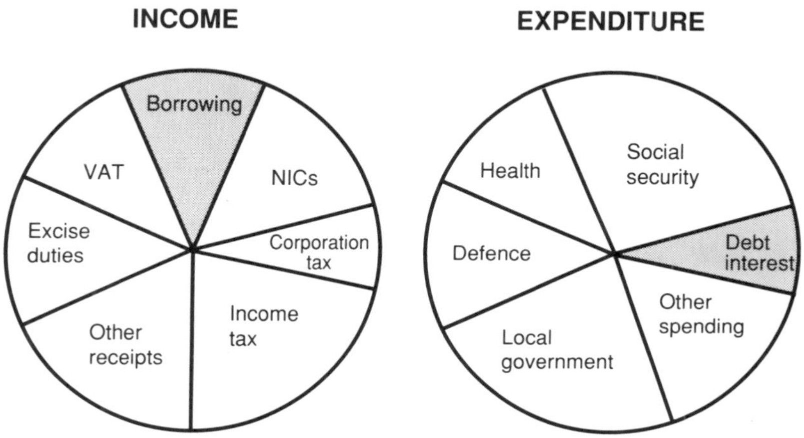

Who pays income tax?

When you start earning money you become part of the taxation system. Everyone under the age of 65 is given a personal allowance. This means that they are allowed to earn the amount of money specified each tax year before starting to pay income tax. At the point where your earnings rise above the personal allowance allocated to you, you must pay tax on the difference. For example:

	£
Earnings during year	5,684.00
Personal allowance	3,256.00
Taxable income	2,428.00

(Difference between your earnings and your personal allowance)

At the end of every tax year, each employee receives a P60 (example on page 208), which gives details of how much has been earned and how much tax was deducted during the previous year. This should always be retained and kept safe by employees so it can be referred to in the event of any future query from the Tax Office.

P60 Certificate of pay, tax deducted and National Insurance contributions **Do not destroy**

Employee's National Insurance number	Enter here "M" if male "F" if female

Employee's surname *in CAPITAL LETTERS* | First two forenames

National Insurance contributions in this employment

Contribution Table letter	Total of Employee's and Employer's contributions payable 1a	Employee's contributions payable 1b	Employee's contributions at Contracted-out rate included in column 1b 1c
	£	£	£
	£	£	£
	£	£	£
	£	£	£

Tax District and reference | Year to 5 April 19

Employer's full name and address

Employee's works/payroll number etc.

Employee's private address

SPECIMEN

Amount of Statutory Sick Pay included in the "Pay" section of the "This employment" box below £

Total for year		Previous employment		This employment	
Pay	Tax deducted	Pay	Tax deducted	Pay	Tax deducted or refunded *"R" indicates refund*
£	£	£	£	£	£

I/We certify that the particulars given above include the total amount of pay for income tax purposes (including overtime, bonus, commission, etc.) paid to you by me/us in the year ended 5 April last, and the total tax and National Insurance contributions deducted by me/us (less any refunds) in that year.

To the employee. Keep this certificate. It will help you to check any Notice of Assessment which the Tax Office may send you in due course. You can also use it to check that your employer is deducting the right type of National Insurance contributions for you and using your correct National Insurance number. If he is not, you should tell him. You cannot get a duplicate form P60.

P60

Final tax code	Employee's Widows and Orphans / life insurance contributions in this employment	Week 53 payment indicator
	£	

Payment of wages

More and more employees are choosing to have their wages/salaries paid directly into their bank account by credit transfer. Paying employees by credit transfer is less time-consuming and much safer than dealing with cash.

A list of employees, their bank and bank account number, together with the amount of money they are to be paid, is forwarded to the firm's bank with one payment for the total amount. The bank credits the appropriate amounts to the individual bank accounts on the day specified by the employer.

Although the employees' wage/salary is paid directly into the bank, the employer still has a legal obligation to provide an itemised pay slip. This is handed to each employee on the day on which the money is paid into the bank.

Changing jobs

To avoid any difficulties when you change jobs your previous employer is expected to complete a P45 (see page 210). This is a certificate which gives details of your tax code number, your total pay to date and total tax paid to date.

There are three parts to this form, the first is sent to the Tax Office so they know you have changed jobs and the remaining sections are given to you to take to your new employer. One part is kept by your new employer and the other is sent to your new employer's tax office as different tax offices deal with different employers. Your new employer is then able to deduct the correct amount of tax from your pay and the new Tax Office has a record of you when this amount is forwarded to them.

Computerised payroll

Payroll is the term used to describe the record of employees' wages or salaries and deductions. Computers are widely used in business today for payroll purposes. Full details of pay and deductions are printed out on to individual pay slips. When pay is increased because of a pay rise, overtime or tax code change or reduced because of absence or tax code change, the necessary alterations can be done quickly using a computer with a payroll program. If the same calculations were carried out manually it would take much longer.

How much can you remember?

1. What do you understand to be the difference between a wage and a salary?
2. Explain four methods by which workers are paid.
3. What is the difference between gross and net pay?
4. How do statutory deductions differ from voluntary ones?
5. Give at least two examples of each type of deduction to support your explanation in (4) above.
6. Explain how the PAYE system works.
7. On what dates does the tax year begin and end?
8. Who receives a P60 and when?
9. What happens to the taxation monies which we pay?
10. What is the most common arrangement by which workers are paid?
11. How do employers inform employees of deductions made from pay?
12. When you change jobs how does your new employer know how much tax to deduct and how much you have already paid?

P45 — **Details of EMPLOYEE LEAVING** — PART 1

1. PAYE reference	District number	Reference number	
2. National Insurance number			
3. Surname (*Use BLOCK letters*)			Mr. Mrs. Miss
First two forenames (*Use BLOCK letters*)			
4. Date of leaving *(in figures)*	Day	Month	Year 19
5. Code at date of leaving *If Week 1 or Month 1 basis applies, please also write "X" in the box marked "Week 1 or Month 1"*	Code		Week 1 or Month 1

6. Last entries on Deductions Working Sheet *If Week 1 or Month 1 basis applies, complete item 7 instead*	Week or Month number	Week	Month
	Total pay to date	£	p
	Total tax to date	£	p
7. Week 1 or Month 1 basis applies	Total pay in this employment	£	p
	Total tax in this employment	£	p
8. Works Number		9. Branch, Contract Department, etc.	

10. Employee's private address ....

....

.... Postcode ....

11. I certify that the details entered at items 1 to 9 above are correct.

Employer

Address

Date

Postcode

INSTRUCTIONS TO EMPLOYER

- Complete this form according to the "Employee leaving" instructions on the P8 (BLUE CARD).
- Detach Part 1 and send it to your Tax Office **IMMEDIATELY.**
- Hand Parts 2 and 3 (unseparated) to your employee **WHEN HE LEAVES.**
- IF THE EMPLOYEE HAS DIED, please write "D" in this box and send ALL THREE PARTS of this form (unseparated) to your Tax Office **IMMEDIATELY.**

For Tax Office use		
For Centre 1 use		
Amended	M/E	P

P45 HPB 1439 9/84

Activity 15.1

Test your numeracy skills:

task

(a) Calculate the total deductions and net pay of each employee detailed below.

	Gross Pay	*Tax*	*NI*	*Voluntary*	*Total deducts*	*Net pay*
	£	£	£	£		
	135.64	23.12	7.68	2.00		
	220.71	37.69	12.90	15.24		
	154.50	26.28	9.08	0.10		
	365.39	60.09	21.40	23.68		
	1,548.75	261.00	96.71	65.63		
TOTAL						

(b) Complete the table by totalling all columns.

(c) Calculate the gross pay of the four employees below. The hourly rate is £3.52 and they all have one hour for lunch (which is not paid time). The basic week is 40 hours and overtime is paid at time and a half except for Saturday morning when it is paid at double time:

	Monday	*Tuesday*	*Wednesday*	*Thursday*	*Friday*	*Saturday*
1	7.30–4.30	8.00–6.30	7.30–5.45	7.30–5.30	7.30–6.15	8.30–12.00
2	8.00–5.00	8.00–5.00	8.00–5.30	8.00–5.30	8.00–5.00	
3	8.30–5.30	8.30–5.30	8.30–5.30	8.00–5.30	8.30–6.00	8.00–10.15
4	8.15–5.15	8.30–6.00	8.00–7.00	8.00–5.30	8.00–5.30	9.00–12.00

Activity 15.2

Examine the situations below and decide:

(a) Which method of payment would be most suitable for each one, and why.

(b) Whether it is likely that they will receive their pay in the form of a wage or a salary, and why.

(c) Who will be paid overtime if they have to work additional hours and who won't, and why.

Details:

(i) An employee who works in a factory on the assembly line.
(ii) A cleaner in a factory.
(iii) A clerical worker in a factory office.
(iv) A director of a company.
(v) A cash and carry till operator.

(v) A cash and carry till operator.
(vi) Someone who addresses envelopes at home.
(vii) A babysitter.
(viii) A kitchen sales representative.
(ix) An accountant.
(x) A Tupperware party demonstrator.
(xi) A teacher.
(xii) A car mechanic.

Activity 15.3

(a) In business a special payroll program would be used to calculate pay, but for the purposes of this activity, you may use a spreadsheet program.

Enter the information below and insert suitable names alongside each set of details:

PAYROLL FOR WEEK NO 15

NAME	HOURS WORKED	HOURLY RATE	GROSS PAY	TAX	NI	TOTAL DEDUCTS	NET PAY
	44	3.42		21.50	8.85		
	35	2.55		12.75	5.25		
	46	3.24		21.29	8.76		
	35	4.21		21.05	8.67		
	25	3.45		12.32	5.07		
	40	5.85		33.57	13.76		
	43	3.45		21.19	8.73		

(b) Calculate, using appropriate formulae, for each individual:

(i) Gross pay.
(ii) Total deductions.
(iii) Net pay.
(iv) The total amount to be sent to the firm's bank.
(v) The total amount to be sent to the Tax Office.
(vi) The total amount to be sent to the National Insurance Office in respect of employees' National Insurance.

(c) All employees are paid by credit transfer, explain what this means and the advantages it has for both employee and employer.

(d) The firm is considering offering its employees a 4.5 per cent increase. Make the necessary calculations on your spreadsheet and find out what this increase will actually cost the company in terms of employees' gross pay.

Chapter 16 Purchase and sale of goods

By the end of this chapter you should be able to explain:

- the difference between personal and business buying transactions
- the documents involved in a buying/selling transaction
- the discounts available to businesses
- the correct procedure for deducting discounts and adding VAT
- the roles of the purchasing, sales and production teams in a buying/selling transaction
- the use of computerised documentation
- the ways businesses pay for goods.

Personal and business transactions

Personal shopping:

When you shop for a jumper or some other item, you:

- take funds with you to pay for the item
- travel to the place where you intend to shop
- have a good look around
- compare prices
- select an item and assess its suitability
- pay for it, after which you take the item home
- take it back and exchange it or ask for a refund if you are not happy with it.

Business shopping:

In business it is not very practical and sometimes it is impossible to follow the same procedures as those identified for personal shopping:

- You select most items by mail order or from a company that will deliver goods, as staff do not have the time to visit suppliers personally; often goods and raw materials are not available locally.
- Instead of looking round several stores you look at several suppliers' catalogues.
- You compare price-lists
- You select an item from the catalogue, but at this stage you are unable to accurately assess its suitability at the time of purchase.
- You order the item and wait for it to be delivered.
- If it is unsuitable you send it back and ask for an exchange or refund.

There are other differences in addition to those identified above, one of which is that unlike personal shoppers, many firms buy goods in large quantities. This is referred to as buying in bulk. By doing so, better and bigger discounts can be negotiated.

Types of discount

There are two types of discount: trade and cash. A trade discount is one which is given to business people so that they can resell goods at a higher price to the consumer and make a profit. Trade discounts are also given for bulk buying.

Firms need to have money coming in constantly so that they can pay their bills. A cash discount is not given for paying cash, as its name would suggest, it is simply an extra discount to encourage firms to pay promptly. If it states on a bill '2.5%, 7 days', it means that the buyer will be entitled to a further 2.5 per cent discount if payment is made within seven days.

Unlike most personal buying, business transactions are not dealt with in cash because such large sums of money are involved. Most bills are paid by cheque or credit transfer.

Due to the complexities of business buying and selling transactions, there is a flow of documents, which when completed form the buying/selling transaction (see illustration on page 216). Although procedures vary from organisation to organisation, the documents contain basically the same information. Trading takes place between buyer and seller and the purchasing, sales and production departments are the ones mainly involved in the transaction.

The purchasing department

The purchasing department has a great deal more to do than just ordering goods. Finding a suitable supplier and negotiating the best deal for the firm can be quite a task in itself. The type and amount of discount firms offer can be quite varied and the purchasing department while looking for a good price will also want the best value for money, and this is not necessarily the cheapest.

A firm may offer the most competitive prices around but if the customer's delivery dates cannot be met then it will not be the best choice. When deciding which supplier to use the purchasing department will consider:

- Does the supplier stock the type of good(s) the firm requires?
- How much will the goods cost?
- What discounts are available and how much will be deducted?

- Can the supplier meet the required deadline?
- Does the supplier have a good reputation – in other words, if a delivery date is stated, will the firm keep its promise?
- Will the goods be of a good quality?
- Does the supplier offer a good after sales service?

Once a suitable supplier has been found an order will be placed. (An example of an order is given on page 217.)

The sales department

The sales department, which was dealt with in more detail in Chapter 2, will want to convince its customers that its firm is the best choice. There are a number of ways it can do this:

- It will offer the best discounts possible.
- It will ensure that it liaises effectively with the production department to ensure customer deadlines are met. (This department has also been dealt with in Chapter 2.)
- Its prices will be competitive with those of similar firms.
- It will deal with customer complaints/returns promptly.
- It will do everything it can to ensure that the customer is satisfied and therefore encouraged to place further orders.

Computerised documentation

Many firms now use computers to print out documents which are needed in the buying/selling transaction. Special programs are available which allow the operator to key-in the variables and these are printed out in the correct place on to preprinted sets of documents. One advantage of having a computerised system is that the program will calculate discounts and add VAT. This saves the manual task of working out the net amount due from the customer.

When calculations are carried out manually and discounts and VAT are being worked out, all discounts should be deducted from the gross amount prior to VAT being added. Obviously a cash discount is offered to encourage payment quickly but there is no guarantee a customer will take advantage of this. However, for VAT purposes, it is assumed that the customer will accept this offer and therefore it is deducted prior to VAT being added (see the sample invoice on page 219).

BUYER **SELLER**

Enquiry

When an item is needed, several enquiries are sent out to various suppliers. An enquiry asks about prices, delivery and discounts.

Quotation

A supplier sends a quotation in reply to an enquiry. This answers all the buyer's questions.

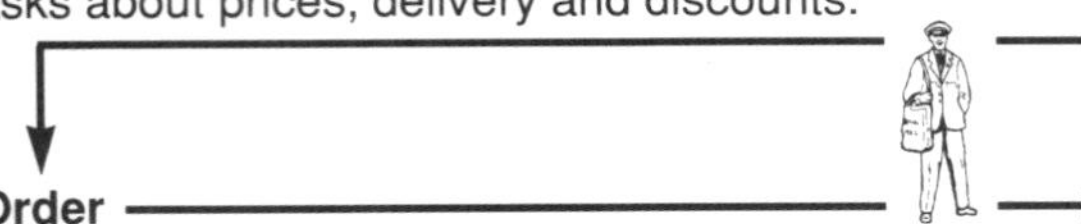

Order

When all the quotations have been received, the buyer selects the one that offers the best value for money and sends an order.

Advice note

On receipt of an order, the seller prepares to deliver the goods. An advice note is sent to notify the buyer of the delivery date.

Delivery note

The goods are dispatched on the pre-arranged date. If the supplier's own transport is used, a delivery note is sent with the goods. This is signed by the buyer on receipt of the goods. One copy goes back to the supplier with the van driver.

Consignment note

If the supplier's own transport is not being used,a consignment note is sent with the goods, instead of a delivery note.

Invoice

Once the goods have been delivered and accepted, an invoice (bill) is sent. When this is calculated by the supplier, all discounts are deducted before VAT is added.

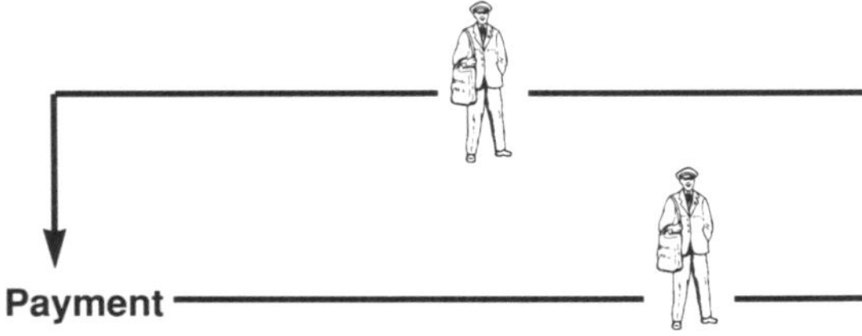

Payment

When the accounts department has checked that the invoice is correct, payment is made.

Credit note

If any of the goods were found to be damaged or missing, or if the buyer was overcharged for any reason, a credit note is sent to rectify the matter.

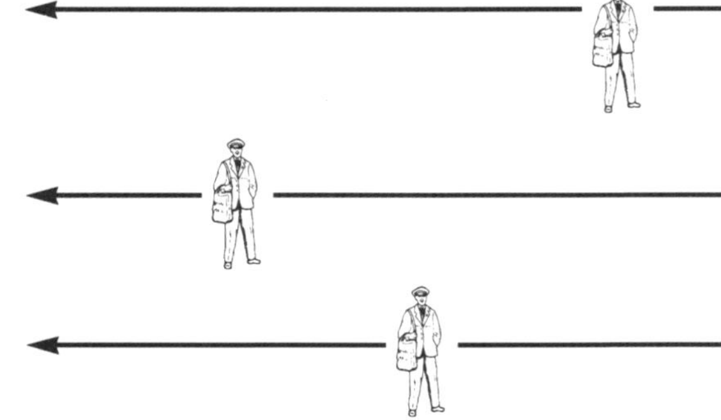

Debit note

If the buyer is undercharged, a supplementary invoice is sent (debit note) to rectify the error.

Statement

A statement is sent to the buyer each month, giving details of all purchases, payments, (credits/debits) and the amount owed to the supplier at the date of statement.

Documents involved in a buying/selling transaction

UP-TO-DATE STYLES
10 Styles Road, Styletown, Datish.

Telephone: 3745 293151
VAT Reg No: 672 9876 54

PURCHASE ORDER

To: Fashion Highlights Limited
(Wholesalers) 3 Fashion Road
Highlight Town, Fashionbridge

Order No: 00314
Date: 30 August 199-

Delivery required by: 14 Sept 199-

Quantity	Details	Price
10	Ladies dresses Cat XJ2314E Size 12 Black - @ 27-99 ea.	279-90
15 Prs	Black Girls Shoes Cat EF6123F Size 4. @ £15-00 per pair.	225-00
24 Packs	Ladies Fashion Tights - one size FY3210G. @£1-50 per pack.	36-00
	Trade Discount 12$^1/_2$%	

Signed: B. Iolet
Purchasing officer

Paying for goods

Most business payments are made by cheque as it is not practical to use cash. There are several types of arrangement which exist between buyers and sellers in business.

New customers may be sent a pro-forma invoice which requests payment in advance. Alternatively they may be asked for cash with order (CWO) or to pay cash on delivery (COD). This is a precaution taken by suppliers to ensure they receive payment for the goods sent. Customers will not be allowed to buy on credit until their creditworthiness has been checked out.

More established customers will be expected to pay on receipt of the invoice or within the time limit agreed and specified on the invoice. To encourage them to pay promptly, a cash discount may be offered in addition to the agreed trade discount.

A trade credit agreement is not uncommon between a supplier and an established customer. This is where goods are purchased and the customer settles the bill at the end of the month.

Fashion Highlights Limited
3 Fashion Road • Highlight Town • Fashionbride
Telephone: 3990 276865 Vat Reg No: 729 9898 89

INVOICE

To: UP-TO-DATE Styles
10 Styles Road
Styletown, Datish

Invoice No: 002345
Date: 15 Sept 199-

Your order no: 00314	Date of order: 30 Aug 199-	Delivery date: 12 Sept 199-

Quantity ordered	Quantity delivered	Description	Unit price	Total amount
10	10	Ladies Dresses - Black Size 12. XJ2314E	27.99	279.90
15 Prs	15 Prs	Girls Shoes - Black - Size 4. GF6123F	15.00	225.00
24 Packs	24 Packs	Ladies Fashion Tights - one size. FY3210G	1.50	36.00
			Total amount	540.90
			($12\frac{1}{2}$% trade discount) Amount less discounts	473.29
			VAT at current rate	82.83
E&OE			Total amount due	556.12

Calculating the invoice

1 Total up cost of all items purchased.
2 Deduct trade discount agreed.
3 Calculate the VAT on the total amount less the discount.
4 Add VAT to total amount less discount.

errors and omissions excepted

How much can you remember?

1. What are the main differences between the buying procedure in business and that of a private individual?
2. List the documents involved in a buying/selling transaction and give a brief explanation of the purpose of each one.
3. Why do firms buy in bulk?
4. Explain the difference between a trade and cash discount.
5. Are discounts deducted before or after VAT has been added?
6. What is the current rate of VAT?
7. What is the purpose of a pro-forma invoice?
8. What is a trade credit agreement?
9. Which departments have key roles to play in the buying/selling transaction?

Activity 16.1

(a) From the details given below, calculate how much each customer owes to the supplier, remember to add VAT at the current rate and assume the offer of a cash discount will be taken up:

Customer	*Goods purchased*	*Trade discount*	*Cash discount*	
1	4,367.87	12.5%	5%	7days
			2.5%	30 days
2	341.56	10%	2.5%	7 days
3	1,472.83	10%	2.5%	7 days
4	120.81	10%	2.5%	7 days
5	2,506.02	12.5%	5%	7 days
			2.5%	30 days
6	294.85	10%	2.5%	7 days

(b) Explain why two of the customers above have been offered:
(i) a larger trade discount
(ii) a choice of cash discount.

(c) Why will new customers not be offered a trade credit agreement?

Activity 16.2

Business has not been too good at the moment and as owner of Up-to-date Styles you are becoming a little worried. Several customers have come into the shop for items of clothing for their younger children but your present stock caters for age seven upwards and so you have been unable to supply them. You have decided to extend your range on a trial basis and cater for smaller children.

Your regular supplier, Fashion Highlights Limited, in response to previous telephone enquiries has agreed to give you a ten per cent trade discount on orders up to £250.00 and 12.5 per cent discount on anything over £250.00. As an existing customer you will also have the opportunity to take advantage of a 2.5 per cent cash discount if you pay within 14 days. However, nothing has yet been put in writing and you have been requested to send in a written enquiry to which they will respond.

task

(a) Using DTP or any other method available to you prepare the necessary documentation required for a full buying/selling transaction between the above two firms.

Details of buyer and seller:

Buyer:

Name of firm:	Up-to-date Styles
Type of firm:	Small Clothing Shop
Address:	10 Styles Road, Styletown, Datish.
Tel:	(3745) 293151
VAT Reg no:	672 9876 54

Seller:

Name of firm:	Fashion Highlights Limited
Type of firm:	Clothing Manufacturer. Sells by mail order direct to public and to small clothing shops.
Address:	3 Fashion Road, Highlight Town, Fashionbridge.
Tel:	(3990) 276865
VAT Reg no:	729 9898 89

(b) Using any mail order catalogue as the supplier's catalogue, decide which stock you wish to order initially and complete the documentation which will be necessary for both buyer and seller for the full transaction, including the enquiry.

(c) Prepare a circular letter to send out to regular customers notifying them of your new range.

Chapter 17 Stock control

By the end of this chapter you should be able to explain:

- the reason stock control affects all firms
- the importance of effective stock control
- the need to stocktake
- the calculation of the value of stock in hand
- the reasons why the written records do not always agree with the amount of stock actually being held
- the documentation used to record stock
- the need for stock levels to be established
- the procedure for storing and caring for stock
- the duties of a stock controller
- the computerisation of stock control.

Stock

All firms keep a stock of some items. For example,

- Manufacturing industries stock raw materials which are used to make products. They also stock finished goods ready to supply to customers when orders are received.
- Retailers stock extra supplies of the goods on display.
- All firms have an office of some sort and keep stocks of stationery (office consumables).

Although this chapter deals mainly with the issue of office materials, many of the points raised also relate to other types of stock as the main principles of stock control are the same for any product.

Purchasing, storing and issuing of stock are very important as they can cost or save a firm money. As stock is part of a firm's assets it is shown on its balance sheet.

What is stock control?

Stock control involves taking responsibility for stock on the premises and maintaining accurate stock records. In other words, looking after the goods in stock and ensuring that items which are low in quantity are re-ordered in plenty of time.

Similarly, checks are kept on how quickly items are being used, so that too much is not ordered at one time, to avoid stockpiling. Apart from wasting valuable space by storing unwanted or slow-moving items, over-ordering ties up a firm's capital unnecessarily.

Perishable goods, such as food, cannot be kept for long periods; similarly, some materials, such as paper, discolour if kept for too long. Keeping a record of how much stock is actually on the premises, who is using it, how often and how much money is being spent on it all form part of stock control.

Stocktaking

At some point, it is necessary to check that the records and the amount of stock on the premises agree. This involves physically counting the items in stock and this activity, known as stocktaking, is usually carried out once or twice a year.

When a stocktake is in progress, nothing must be issued or added otherwise the final figures will not be accurate. As this can be most inconvenient, staff will normally be notified in advance and the stocktake will take place during one of the quieter times or outside normal working hours.

Where there is a large stock of items, stock controllers carry out random checks at various times throughout the year. To make this method more effective, staff are not warned prior to a random check. This method encourages staff responsible for stock control to do their job thoroughly, as they never know when they will be checked. It also discourages pilfering. This type of stocktaking is called perpetual inventory.

Value of stock in hand

At certain times, firms need to know how much money they have tied up in stock and the most accurate time to determine this is straight after a stocktake. The value of stock is calculated by multiplying the unit cost of each item by the number of items in stock.

Discrepancies

Sometimes the written records and what is actually in stock do not tally. There can be several reasons for this:

- Items may have been taken out of stock and written records not completed.
- Some items may have been damaged and had to be scrapped.
- Some items may have been pilfered.

Once discrepancies have been identified, stock records must be amended immediately, preferably using a different coloured pen so that the alterations can be seen clearly. The new and correct balance must be shown as this will affect the stock value. To keep deterioration of stock to a minimum, a system of 'first-in, first-out' (FIFO) is adopted. This means that the stock which was bought first (the oldest) is used first.

Written documentation

The two main documents used internally for stock control are the stock requisition card, which is used to request stock, and a stock record card which shows how much stock is being held, and details of what has been used and who by.

Stock requisition card

STATIONERY REQUISITION **No:** 624

From: TYPING POOL **To:** STORES

Quantity	Item(s)
20 reams	A4 letterhead

Signature: R. Hepworth Date: 17 September 199-

This is a request for an item or items from the stores, by an employee or department within the firm. It gives details of the items and quantity required, the date and the name and department of the person making the request. The details on the stock requisition are transferred to a stock record card. Stock which is stored in readiness for purchase by customers of a firm will be issued against an order, not an internal requisition.

Stock record card

For each item kept in stock, there will be a stock record card. This gives an up-to-date balance, details of any stock on order, past receipts, plus details from the stock requisition. It is from the information on the stock record card that goods are ordered.

STOCK RECORD CARD

Item: A4 LETTERHEAD (REAMS) Max. level: 200 Re-order level: 75

Supplier: PAPER SUPPLIES Min. level: 50

Receipts			Issues			
Date	Quantity	Invoice No	Quantity	Req. No.	Department	Stock balance
1/9/199-					Balance b/f	50
1/9	150	E7650				200
4/9			10	601	Admin	190
10/9			2	605	Purchasing	188
10/9			4	613	Sales	184
13/9			5	619	Personnel	179
17/9			20	624	Typing Pool	159

Details of deliveries into stock.

Details of internal issues.

When re-order level is reached, new stock is ordered.

Stock levels

Whether you work in a small office or a large factory, the principle of handling stock is much the same and includes the following:

- ❍ Establishing the maximum amount of stock needed at any one time.
- ❍ Establishing the minimum amount of stock below which it must not fall.
- ❍ Maintaining stock at appropriate levels at all times.

Before a decision can be reached on the maximum amount of stock required at any one time, a stock controller will take into account how often an item is used and in what quantities.

Similarly, when a minimum level is being determined, allowance must be made for any unexpected delays by suppliers. If, for example, an employment agency uses 20 reams of typing paper per week and it takes two weeks for delivery from the time of the order, the minimum level would be set at 40 reams. However, this assumes that there will be no unexpected delays and that the paper will arrive as promised within two weeks.

To ensure a firm is not left without materials, a re-order level is established and this is slightly above the minimum level – say, 60 reams. This will leave the firm with three weeks' supply – that is, two weeks allowing for promised delivery and a further week's supply to cushion any hold-up period by the supplier.

Storing stock

Stock needs to be handled carefully and stored away safely. Firms spend a great deal of money buying and storing stock and damaged materials means money wasted. Good security is essential to prevent unauthorised personnel accessing stock.

With so many items in stock, containers, cupboards etc. should be carefully labelled. In the case of stationery, where all the stock may be stored in one large lockable cupboard, it is necessary to display a list of items available in a prominent place, so that staff are aware of what is in stock. Items which are required regularly should be placed within easy reach with the heaviest on the lower shelves to avoid accidents. Any flammable liquids for office machinery etc. need to be stored in a fire-resistant and cool place, perhaps a metal cupboard.

Duties of a stock controller

A stock controller has a variety of duties to carry out. If accurate records are not kept then a firm will not be aware of exactly how much stock is being used, how often it is used, how much is being wasted and which items are no longer required.

Maintaining appropriate stock levels is extremely important. Too little stock can be as damaging to a firm as too much. If materials are not readily available, a job might be held up and this could result in a lost order.

Looking after and issuing stock in a manufacturing concern is often a full-time job but in an office this will not be the case. Therefore, one way of avoiding constant disruption to the person who looks after the office consumables, is to set times when stock is issued.

When materials arrive which are to be placed in stock the following checks should be made:

- The quantity on the delivery note is noted and the number of parcels is checked to ensure the two agree.
- A note is made of any discrepancies, after which the person receiving the goods signs for them. If the delivery person cannot wait until the

goods are checked, then the delivery note is signed 'received but not checked'.

- Any discrepancies are reported to the supplier immediately and confirmed in writing.

Computerised systems

Many firms have computerised stock control systems. The advantage of this is that as stock is used levels are adjusted automatically and stock valuations can be printed out at the touch of a button.

When re-order levels are reached a signal is given by the computer and some machines are programmed to print out an order ready for posting. Computerised systems are most suitable for establishments where large stocks are kept.

Many large department stores and supermarkets are now using computerised tills, called point of sale (POS) terminals which are linked to a main computer. Each item on the shelves is labelled with a bar code. A bar code is a series of thick and thin lines which are numbered, and these are read at the checkout point by the computer. A bar code can be read using a light pen or a scanner. With the POS terminals being connected to a computer, the stock records are updated each time an item is sold. From the information it receives, a computerised till prints out an itemised sales receipt.

Advantages of POS

The advantages of POS are:

- Stock records are updated automatically each time an item is sold.
- Stock is re-ordered automatically.
- The customer gets through the checkout quicker than before, so there is less likelihood of large queues forming.
- Fewer mistakes are made as there is no keying-in. A light pen is passed over the bar code or the item is passed across a scanner.
- As it is quicker, fewer staff will be needed.
- Each customer receives an itemised receipt.
- It can provide information for management on which goods are selling well and which ones are not.

How much can you remember?

1. Why does stock control affect all firms?
2. Why is it important to take good care of stock?
3. What is meant by 'stockpiling'?
4. What are the advantages and drawbacks of stockpiling and holding very small amounts of stock?
5. Why is it necessary to maintain accurate stock records?
6. What documentation is used to maintain stock records?
7. Why is stocktaking necessary when detailed written records are kept?
8. Why do some larger establishments carry out random stock checks?
9. What is an inventory?
10. Where will you find details of maximum, minimum and re-order stock levels and why are these necessary?
11. What are the duties of a stock controller?
12. What is meant by 'POS' and what are its benefits?

Activity 17.1

task 1

(a) Using an up-to-date supplier's catalogue, choose 30 items of stationery which are commonly used in an office and find out how much they cost.

(b) Estimate the maximum level of each item for a small office and calculate what the stock value would be if that amount was ordered initially.

(c) Prepare a list suitable for display of all stock held.

task 2

(a) Choose six different items from someone else's list and make out appropriate requisitions. Get them to do the same with your list.

(b) Exchange requisitions and prepare stock record cards for the six items requested from your list.

(c) Update your stock record cards using the requisitions you have been given.

Activity 17.2
task

(a) Arrange with a local supermarket or other type of store to investigate its stock control system and the use of bar codes where appropriate.

(b) Find out what happens for items with bar codes when prices go up or down.

Index